The Sailing Lifestyle

Other Books about the Sea and Water
by John Rousmaniere

A Glossary of Modern Sailing Terms

No Excuse to Lose (with Dennis Conner)

The Enduring Great Lakes (editor)

Fastnet, Force 10

The Luxury Yachts (with Maldwin Drummond)

America's Cup Book, 1851-1983

The Annapolis Book of Seamanship

The Student and Instructor Workbook
for The Annapolis Book of Seamanship

The Dolphin Book Club Sailor's Log

The Golden Pastime: A New History of Yachting

The Sailing Lifestyle

Almost everything you need to know
before going afloat

JOHN ROUSMANIERE

British edition adapted by
Dick Hewitt

Illustrations by Mark Smith

NAUTICAL

First published in Great Britain 1986 by
NAUTICAL BOOKS
an imprint of Conway Maritime Press Ltd
24 Bride Lane, Fleet Street
London EC4Y 8DR

ISBN 0 85177 397 4

British edition adapted by Commander R L Hewitt LVO RN
Illustrated by Mark Smith and Brad Dellenbaugh

Printed in Great Britain by
The Bath Press

Acknowledgements

The idea for this book was suggested by my editor, Fred Hills, who, after the *The Annapolis Book of Seamanship* was finally in his hands, with his typically economical acuity simply asked for a book that would tell people how to cool a bottle of wine in a boat. The rest has fit more or less comfortably around that goal (which I trust is satisfactorily met in Chapter 13), but only due to the generous help of many friends and acquaintances, some of whom are acknowledged in the text but several of whom deserve special attention here.

Since my attempts at gracious eating in a boat have usually been limited to pouring a bit of wine into the canned stew, I felt sadly deficient when it came to recommending stylish cooking routines. So I asked some highly experienced sea chefs to tell me what they knew about galleys, cooking, and the good life below. The following people, whose cumulative galley experience must total close to three centuries, kindly waded through my long questionnaire and provided enough information to fill a book, much less to be the basis for Chapters 12, 13, and 14: Linda and Steve Dashew, Mimi and Dan Dyer, Dorothy Greenlee, Adra Kober, Harvey Loomis, Faith McCurdy, daughter Sheila McCurdy, Carol Nicklaus, Betty Noyes, Susie Page, Bill and Jane Robinson, Diana Russell, Pat and Spencer Smith, Brooke and Eric Swenson, and Marcia Wiley.

Chapter 15 never would have been written without the cooperation of my father and mother, Jim and Jessie Rousmaniere, who introduced me to sailing as a child, and my sons, Will and Dana, who introduced me to sailing as a father.

A shorter version of Chapter 2 was published in the May 1984 issue of *Sail*, an early draft of Chapter 18 first saw light as an address I presented to the United States Naval Academy's Safety at Sea Seminar, in January 1984, and part of Chapter 9 (on the limits of electronic navigation instruments) was written for *Sailor* magazine.

I am especially pleased to thank both Peter Johnson, of Nautical Books, for making the book available to British readers and Dick Hewitt for his sensitive and skillful job of anglicizing some portions of the text. While making all the necessary changes in regulations, buoyage, and terminology, Dick has succeeded in retaining the spirit of the original and in adding much information of particular interest to British sailors.

John Rousmaniere
Stamford, Connecticut

For C. T., a Harbour Master

Contents

Part II: Welcome Aboard

Part III: Cooking and Gracious Living Afloat

Part IV: When Sailing Gets Difficult

Foreword

This book is for anybody who is fascinated by the sailing life and yet is a bit intimidated by it. That is lots of people, not all of them beginners. They include the seasoned skipper who has fallen into bad habits and stopped enjoying the pastime, the person who has not been in a boat for years and who needs to relearn some skills before heading off on a cruise, and the new sailor eager to get out there and do it correctly *now* without first spending a lifetime acquiring the necessary rules of thumb and helpful tricks of the trade.

I wish that a book like this had been available when I first got seriously interested in sailing, some twenty-five years ago. It would have saved me considerable time and frustration. Typical of many sailors, I think, is my sister-in-law Katherine Perls Rousmaniere. Like many people, Katherine has come to sailing in her thirties and has quickly fallen in love with it. While she does not think of herself as very athletic or technically-minded, she is intrigued by and eager to learn more about the complicated relationships between boat, water, and wind. Though she likes steering and sail trimming, what she enjoys most is relaxing in nature.

But Katherine has her reservations about sailing. When I asked her to describe them, she laughed and said:

> Sunburn, that is what worries me most. And of course whether the boat will sink. It does not help much when people explain why it will not tip over. Before I first went cruising I worried whether I would be able to take a shower in the boat, and I learned quickly enough that I would not—at least in *that* boat, which was fairly small. I do not like being *cold*, either, so I always try to prepare as well as I can for it. At first I did not know what kinds of clothes to take so I would be both warm and functioning.

This book addresses those and many other, often unspoken, concerns about the 'people side' of seafaring for pleasure and especially about that most delightful side of sailing, cruising. After more than twenty years of going out in just about every kind of boat—after racing, cruising, and day-sailing in all sorts of places in weather ranging from the idyllic to the appalling—I have finally realized that I most enjoy what just about every other sailor most enjoys: a two- or three-day weekend cruise in a boat large enough to hold me and three or four friends but also small enough so that I and one other good sailor can handle her safely in tough conditions. In my experience, that means a boat whose length lies somewhere between 30 and 40 feet (9 and 12 metres). Since that size range also seems to be most popular among the many sailors I know, almost everything in these pages deals directly with them. However, that is not to say that somebody heading off on an ocean race in a 50-footer or for a round-the-world voyage in a 25-footer, or out for just a couple of hours on a day-sailer will not find something of interest here.

Where my big sailing manual, *The Annapolis Book of Seamanship,* focuses on the technology of the boat and the thousands of special techniques used by masterful seamen to sail her, here we are dealing with the human factor. We will see how to dress right for warmth and dryness, how to eat simply but well, how to cruise graciously and enjoyably, and how to get along with shipmates. Along the way, we will also look at essential skills for safe and enjoyable sailing in both normal and wild conditions and summarize the fundamentals of coastal navigation, collision avoidance, sail trimming, and steering. As when writing *Annapolis,* I have tried to make the prose as lively and non-technical as possible for the sake of readers who are new to this pastime's dense theory and special terminology. A glossary in the back of the book includes the most important terms, and I have also included the fascinating etymologies of thirty key terms.

Because flexible routines are all-important on a boat, I have included plenty of lists and succinct guidelines to take you step by step through all the important ones. I have tried to cover most of the challenges you can expect to face—whether buying foul-weather gear, tacking and gybing, lighting the stove, anchoring, cooking a fish stew, piloting, rigging a flying trapeze for your kids, or treating seasickness. The epilogue in *The Annapolis Book of Seamanship* applies to below-deck comfort just as much as to on-deck safety:

> Throughout this book we have suggested a truth
> that some might think ironical: to enjoy sailing, the
> most individualistic of all sports, you must try to
> standardize your techniques and your equipment
> and do every job the same way, time after time.

... With repetition come good habits, with good habits comes good seamanship, with good seamanship comes security, and with security comes enjoyment. And after all, that is what we are looking for in the first place.

Have fun.

John Rousmaniere

Foreword to British edition

It has been a privilege to adapt, where necessary, John Rousmaniere's book for British readers. Some of the work has involved replacing American terms by their British equivalents, and of course amending the American spelling. But there have been several places where more important revisions have been needed. For example, the American buoyage system is different from that used in Europe, the US Coast Guard exerts much greater power than HM Coastguard in all matters concerned with pleasure boating, the conventional terms used in chartwork are different, and American yachtsmen obviously thrive on a diet which would not be very acceptable on this side of the Atlantic—so various recipes proposed by the author's panel of sea cooks have been omitted.

Since the term 'helmsperson' has little attraction, 'helmsman' has been substituted, on the understanding that it applies equally to the growing number of helmswomen. There are however one or two terms of American origin which have been retained—because they are apt and there seem to be no English equivalents. One is 'rode', for whatever connects the anchor to the vessel, be it chain cable, a nylon warp, or a combination of the two. Another is 'dock' (together with 'docking', 'undock' and 'undocking'). These are terms which have in the past been associated with large ships, but with a growing number of yachts occupying marina berths they are words which are useful in our marine vocabulary. Like 'rode', they seem to deserve encouragement.

In other matters I hope that the author will bear with me in my interpretation of American procedures for British readers.

Dick Hewitt

PART I

What to Wear and Where to Put It

———

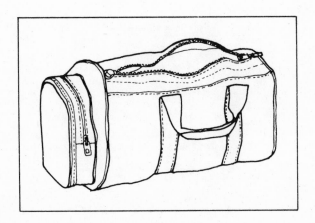

CHAPTER 1

Dry, Warm, and Ventilated: Sailing Clothes and Shoes

―――

It seems simple enough: sailing clothes should keep you dry, warm, and functioning. Actually, those three words say pretty much the same thing. A dry, warm body is a comfortable, strong, and alert body. Common sense tells us that much, and medical science reinforces common sense with some information about how the body sustains its vital functions when it gets cold.

This is what happens. When its temperature is lowered even one or two degrees, the body must work harder to keep blood circulating in the vital organs in the trunk unless it can find a way to decrease its work in less critical parts elsewhere. In the interest of greater efficiency, then, it automatically begins to slow blood circulation in the extremities—the hands, feet, and head. If the body temperature is allowed to drop into the hypothermic ranges of the low 90s and high 80s, blood flow all but stops in the arms, legs, and head. The bad news about this remarkable feat of self-preservation is that when the blood flow slows in your fingers, toes, and brain, your movements become awkward and your thinking becomes lethargic. In other words, the more uncomfortable you get, the more inefficiently you behave. On a sailing boat, whose own welfare depends on her crew's, this can lead to problems, emergencies, and even disaster, as we will see in Chapter 18.

All this happens when you get cold, and the quickest way to get cold is to get wet. Later on, in Chapter 2, we will look carefully at waterproof foul-weather gear—how it works to keep you dry and what you should look for when you buy it. Here we are concerned with the non-waterproof clothes that you wear alone on fine days and underneath foul-weather gear on wet days.

Unfortunately, the problem of staying dry is not as simple as it sounds. Dampness (leading to cold and loss of agility and strength) comes from two directions: from the outside in, from rain and spray; and from the inside out, from perspiration and condensation. To stop the first source of moisture we can seal off our bodies with waterproof fabrics, but to minimize the second kind we must allow our bodies to be ventilated. Absolute waterproofness and breathability are contradictions in clothing; to achieve the best of one we must sacrifice some part of the other. That is the paradox of sailing clothing, whether simple shorts and T-shirts for hot, steamy summer day or heavy foul-weather gear for a cold gale. Every clothing choice must balance those two factors against each other in selecting from a wide variety of fabrics, fit, detailing, and style.

Which Fabrics Work Best When

Most of the time on a boat, you are going to risk getting at least a little wet. How can you best prepare for it? The answer is complicated, but it begins with fabrics. Each of the natural and synthetic fabrics used in the clothes you wear, alone or under foul-weather gear, offers its own trade-offs between comfort and resistance to wet and cold. The best way to exploit their advantages and minimize their disadvantages is to layer relatively light garments made of one or the other so there are several thin, insulating buffers between the body and the cold, cruel climate outside. We will have much more to say about layering in Chapter 3; here is a survey of the fabrics you may be using in the garments you will be piling on and peeling off.

Natural fabrics
Cotton, when dry, is wonderfully soft against the skin and quite windproof, and it quickly ventilates perspiration without picking up odour. It is the most popular fabric for T-shirts and shorts and long-sleeved shirts, jeans, and corduroys. No comfort matches the feel of a soft cotton 'chamois' shirt or rugby jersey against sun-baked skin as a hot, dry afternoon fades into a warm evening. Yet cotton absorbs moisture quickly, and when wet adheres to the body and so does not provide an insulating baffle of warm air. Wet cotton also dries slowly (even if the water is fresh), mildews, and bunches up in a soggy, uncomfortable wad.

Tough fabrics,
double seaming, and
a loose fit are all the
hallmarks of good
sailing clothing. High
collars on shirts and
jackets are especially
desirable for keeping
out sun, wind and
spray.

Wool warms well whether dry or wet because its long, scaly fibres trap dead air, which provides considerable insulation. For years, wool has been the material of choice for cold-weather garments like heavy sweaters, long underwear (often with an inner, nonscratchy cotton layer against the skin), and hats called watch caps. It also has a role on warm and cool days in socks and light shirts and sweaters. But wool does not block the wind very effectively, is relatively heavy and scratchy, and absorbs moisture like a sponge.

Work hard to keep your cotton and wool clothes from getting wet, especially with salt water, whose crystals will continue to absorb moisture well after the original dousing has evaporated. While staying dry is no easy trick, getting the moisture out of wet natural-fabric clothes can be even more difficult since, even in sunny weather, on-deck and below-deck humidity generally hovers around 90 per cent. Fog or clouds can block off all solar drying power for days. To dry clothes when you are cruising, first shake or wring them out hard (on deck, please) to cast off all attached moisture; then hang them over an improvised clothes line near the warm galley stove. At a pinch, wear your wet underwear or other light clothes to bed in a sleeping bag; your body heat will bake the moisture out within a few hours. Just in case the sun does appear, take along a dozen clothes pegs so you can hang damp clothes on the lifelines. If you sail in salt water, shake out dried crystals and give your dried clothes an occasional fresh-water rinsing.

Synthetic Fabrics

Modern synthetics—polyester, nylon, acrylic, and polypropylene— wear well, hold their press, are non-absorbent, and dry quickly. Small amounts of synthetics are often blended with wool to provide strength and with cotton to improve drying and insulation, but manufacturers have begun to use them on their own in a wide variety of practical clothing for active wear. In outer shells, synthetics provide excellent water repellency or, when coated with a waterproofing such as vinyl and polyurethane, even water resistance. In a sailor's clothing, synthetics are most important in warm, quick-drying garments used in place of wool in damp, cool weather.

Fibre pile (or fur fabric) is a synthetic version of wool, usually made in polyester or polypropylene. Unlike wool, it dries very quickly and does not smell too bad when wet. Fibre pile has a fairly hard, spray-repellent outer surface and, on the inside, thousands of long, soft fibres that trap dead air and provide a thick buffer of insulation around the body even when they are wet. Fibre pile is commonly used in outer clothing—jackets, pullover trousers, and cold-weather boot and glove liners. Like wool, fibre pile is not very wind-resistant.

Fleece (or polyester bunting) is a variation on fibre pile, and more expensive. Unlike pile it has short, trim, soft fibres on both sides; as a result, it provides less insulation than fibre pile, so it may be the best material for very warm climates, where pile may be stifling. Fleece is used in top and bottom pullovers, socks, gloves, collars, and hand-warming pockets in foul-weather gear.

Polypropylene underwear, developed originally for cross-country skiers, has gradually replaced wool and wool-blend long underwear. The polypropylene insulates just as well as wool when dry and perhaps even better when wet. More important, its absorbency allows it to wick perspiration from the body. Sweat passes from the skin through the underwear to outer garments, leaving the skin dry (and warm) under a thin, insulating buffer (but also leaving the underwear somewhat smelly after a couple of days). Polypropylene long underwear is available in light, medium, and heavy

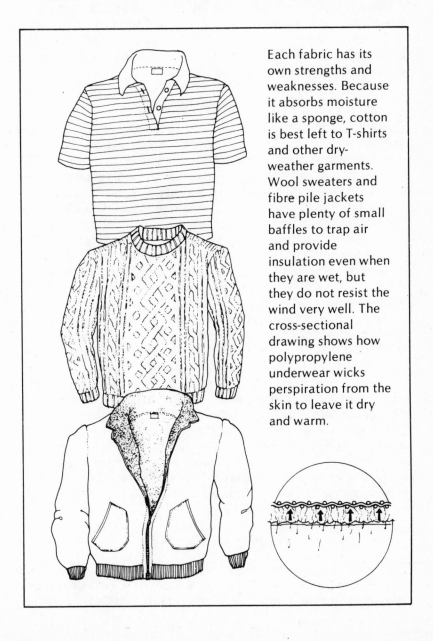

Each fabric has its own strengths and weaknesses. Because it absorbs moisture like a sponge, cotton is best left to T-shirts and other dry-weather garments. Wool sweaters and fibre pile jackets have plenty of small baffles to trap air and provide insulation even when they are wet, but they do not resist the wind very well. The cross-sectional drawing shows how polypropylene underwear wicks perspiration from the skin to leave it dry and warm.

weights for uses ranging from extremely active to relatively inactive, and for bodies whose sensitivity to cold ranges from low to high. In hot, sticky weather, polypropylene long johns serve surprisingly well as outer garments or as your only clothing under foul-weather gear.

Modern technology points to even more striking developments in thermal insulation with materials such as Flectalon, which is constructed from very thin polymer film onto which a thin coating of aluminium is deposited. The sheet is divided into thin filaments and is simultaneously bulked to produce a matrix which has resilience and outstanding insulating properties.

How Clothes Should Fit

'A sailor has a peculiar cut to his clothes and a way of wearing them that a green hand can never get'. So wrote Richard Henry Dana 150 years ago in his classic account of seafaring, *Two Years Before The Mast*. According to Dana, the pants should be 'tight round the hips, and thence hanging long and loose around the feet'—the traditional bell-bottom trousers that leave the legs free for all the movements required during a normal day afloat. Most activity on a boat is abrupt and quick, so you will have little time to hitch up your trousers to keep your crotch and seat from ripping when you stand up abruptly. The seat, knees, and ankles should be roomy, the waist and crotch fairly tight. Suffice it to say that skin-tight designer jeans may well blow apart the first day they go to sea.

Higher up, the shirt should be roomy around the chest, neck, elbows, and wrists to allow abrupt movement. On long-sleeved wrists, elastic wristlets are more forgiving than buttons (which can snag on fittings and lines, anyway).

When trying on clothes, remember that all or part of your body will be exposed to intense sunlight for perhaps the first time in months, and that sunburn is one of the most debilitating of all out-door illnesses. Make sure, then, that your trouser legs and shirt sleeves are sufficiently long to cover you down to, and even over, your tan lines when you are sitting with your arms and legs extended to perform ship's chores. The back of the neck is particularly vulnerable to vicious burns, so wear a shirt with a collar that can be turned up.

Functional Details

Practicality is a function of detailing as well as overall design and materials. Seams should be double-stitched and smooth on the inside next to your skin. Buttons and pockets, which are particularly vulnerable to ripping, should be sewn on strongly. Collars should be roomy so they can be buttoned up in cold weather without choking, and wool shirts should have a nylon or fleece (bunting) neck liner to eliminate scratchiness.

Certain small added features can make your days aboard more pleasant or meet your special needs. For example, while you should choose clothes for active wear, anticipate that you will be sitting down and inactive at least 75 per cent of the time that you are on board. Perhaps your rear end will be cushioned by a small pillow, but do not count on it. The rough, nonslip surface on many decks will quickly wear through most unreinforced trouser seats. For that reason, consider buying at least one pair of fairly heavy trousers with double layers of fabric on the seat. At least, take along a pair made of heavy cotton with large back pockets.

Seasoned sailors take seriously details that other people might consider trivial. Many seamen are careful to buy sailing shirts and trousers with deep, wide, button-down pockets for knives, sunglasses, fittings, handkerchiefs, and the other small objects that always seem necessary at short notice. Others insist on having belt loops on which to hang knife lanyards. Since sailors are a prejudiced lot, it is not surprising that a whole different school of thought considers pockets to be dangerous protrusions just waiting to be snagged by fittings. Myself, I like to have a short pocket, at least two trouser pockets, and belt loops. You may not. Either way, decide if you want these accessories before you make your purchase.

The Style of Sailing Clothes

The style of sailing clothes has hovered somewhere between teenage brightness and military practicality. On the one hand, an easily identified Establishment sailing look has hung on in the more exclusive yacht clubs and marinas for many years. For men, it consists of a blue jacket or sweater worn with blue trousers. For women, a blue or white skirt is *de rigueur,* although (blue) trousers are universally accepted as more practical wear afloat. On the other hand, self-consciously non-Establishment types have swung toward a much more informal look that includes faded long or cutoff jeans, corduroys, army surplus khakis, white undershirts, and T-shirts. This dichotomy in apparel, which has been around ever since I took up sailing thirty years ago, may be due to an exaggerated sense of social distinction borrowed from shore life. Perhaps more important than status identification is the fact that the relatively small sailing community has not been given much choice by clothing manufacturers more interested in larger markets.

But all sorts of boating traditions are changing. For example, two generations ago most boats were painted either white or black and were named after women, ideals, or constellations. Now boats are orange with red stripes and their names are inspired by rock songs. Likewise with clothing. Both extremes—the Establishment and the semihippie—have swung toward a common style of handsome, colourful, and functional clothing that began to appear in the mid-seventies with the booming interest in the outdoors and fitness. Men and women who care about looking good can now buy colourful clothes that are appropriate both on and off the water— outfits that can be taken aboard a boat without fear of being thought too flashy by your conservative skipper-host or -hostess.

However, there is one trend that you should steer away from: if you want to impress your hosts with your eagerness to learn seamanship, *do not* come aboard wearing a shirt that advertises 'A shipwreck can spoil your whole day,' 'Sailors do it in the sheets,' or some other suggestive or ironic news. For people who spend so much time, energy, and money presumably enjoying themselves, sailors can be extremely serious—even pompous—characters. Though they may kid each other about their sport in the privacy of their own cabins, like all members of a beleaguered minority they will skin alive any outsider who dares to belittle their cherished values. The most sacred of those values is that going out on a boat, even for a two-hour sail on a calm August afternoon, is altogether too serious a matter for crude jokes.

Shore Clothes
Bathing suits and other skimpy, informal clothes may be all right on board, but when you go ashore to a town or a village, be prepared to dress up a little to meet local standards. In many sailing areas, strangers who appear in stores and government offices barefoot or in swimsuits or shorts are treated rather coolly. A man should at least change into a pair of clean, pressed shorts and a shirt with a collar, and a woman probably should wear a sun dress or long trousers and a shirt over a bikini top. At night, slightly smarter attire is usually required—perhaps even a blue reefer over a light shirt with a collar for men, and long cotton trousers or a skirt and a blouse for women. Ties and dresses are required after sunset at some yacht clubs and waterfront restaurants.

Shoes for Sailing

In the old and not so good days, seamen often went barefoot, but only because suitable footwear did not exist. Today's average 30-foot cruising boat has more toe-stubbing deck fittings than the typical 150-foot square-rigger, and besides, few of us sail enough to toughen up our feet to the point where they can take the beating handed out by the sea. Sailing barefoot may seem salty, but unless you have run an occasional barefooted marathon, always wear shoes on deck. An exception to this rule is when sailing a small boat like a Laser or a sailboard—and even then shoes are a good idea if your feet are soft or if you must clamber across rocks or rough sand to get to and from the water.

In the last twenty years the shoe industry has developed a whole line of so-called deck shoes or boat shoes for the sailing market. While the uppers on these shoes look much like those on normal shore sneakers or moccasins, the soles are very different. That is because in a boat, unlike ashore, you must be able to keep your footing when the surface under you is tilting, rolling, and wet. One way to improve a sailor's footing is to make the deck itself less slippery. Wooden decks, particularly those with grainy teak, have a wonderful sole-grabbing surface, but since wooden decks are expensive, heavy, and difficult to maintain, boatbuilders usually cover the fibreglass deck with a nonskid coating. But even the best surface can turn into a skating rink in bad conditions. That is why the nonskid rubber sole found on modern deck shoes and sea boots is so helpful. It is broken into thousands of tiny horizontal slits that stay closed when no weight is put on the shoe but open up when weight is applied. As they open, they do two things. First, the sole's surface area is greatly enlarged, and second, the slits work like squeegees to grip the deck. Most shoes and boots sold for boat use have this kind of nonskid sole. To identify it in the store, pull back hard on the toe and look for the opened slits.

Deck shoes come in a variety of styles, of which the slip-on moccasin is widely considered the most fashionable as well as the most practical. With treated leather uppers, tongues, and thongs, with rubber soles, and with brass rust-resistant eyelets, a Top-Sider moccasin (a trademark of the Sperry Company) or one of its competitors should have a long life in the harsh saline atmosphere of the oceans. Unlike some other styles, the moccasin can be pulled on without untying the lace and can be worn barefoot with some comfort, though cotton, wool, or polypropylene socks provide insulation in cool weather and soak up perspiration, which may eat into the shoe's seams. The major drawback of moccasins is that they provide little foot support. They do not allow the use of arch supports—something that probably bothers more older sailors than younger ones—and when well broken-in are so flexible that they may fall off. Some brands of moccasin may bleed when wet, and thongs may be skinny, brittle, and hard to replace when broken.

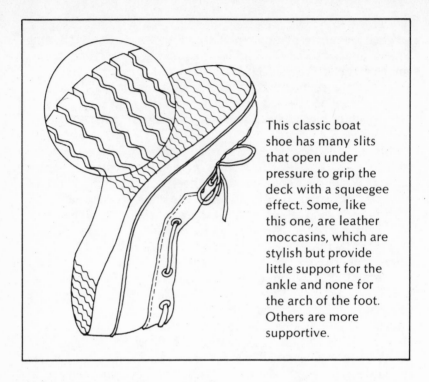

This classic boat shoe has many slits that open under pressure to grip the deck with a squeegee effect. Some, like this one, are leather moccasins, which are stylish but provide little support for the ankle and none for the arch of the foot. Others are more supportive.

Even soft thongs will become untied under the slightest abrasion, so be sure to tie a double knot.

Besides the moccasin, deck shoes come in other styles, most of which have good arch supports. Some sneakers have nylon uppers that dry out extremely rapidly, even after a soaking in salt water (unfortunately, they pick up foot odours just as quickly). Whatever style of shoe you buy, be sure to check for double- or triple-stitching and for reinforcements at stress points, like the heel and toe. Regular washing with fresh water and the application of a suitable polish help to preserve the stitching and the leather.

Of course, there is no law requiring sailors to wear specialized deck shoes. Slit-soled running or basketball shoes, or even work boots, may grip a wooden or nonskid deck as well as a real deck shoe. However, any footwear taken aboard must have white soles, since black soles will leave indelible marks all over the deck.

Experienced sailors wear their deck shoes only when on board, since all those neat little slits pick up the gravel, tar, and dirt even more efficiently than they grip decks. If you must wear your boating shoes ashore, inspect and scrub off the soles on the jetty before you climb aboard. Many owners leave a damp mop on deck as a not-so-subtle hint for their guests.

Now that we have inspected the normal clothes you will wear aboard, let us take a look at the most expensive item in any non-boatowner's nautical inventory—the slick, functional, and (presumably) waterproof outer garments called foul-weather gear.

CHAPTER 2

How to Buy
and Use
Foul-Weather
Gear

If the key to comfortable, safe sailing is staying warm, then the key to staying warm is staying dry. It is a significant fact that heat can be lost 240 times faster through wet clothing than through dry. The primary means of keeping dampness out is to wear the waterproof outer clothing that, more than any other object (except, perhaps, the lighthouse) symbolizes the sailor's life. It is usually called foul-weather gear. Sometimes going by other names (including oilskins, oilies, and wet gear), it is the sailor's armour against the damp slings and arrows of his outrageous environment. When worn over several light layers of insulating clothing, foul-weather gear is also the outer skin of a dry, warm cocoon that can sustain the sailor through just about any storm.

Today, most foul-weather gear is made by putting a waterproof —that is, leakproof—coating on one side of a water-repellent—or spray-proof—nylon shell. In the old days, when clothes were painted with linseed oil to make 'oilskins,' the end result was little better than a seaman's chances of being asked to dine with his captain, and until the 1960s most foul-weather gear was not much better than that improvised, leaky stuff. But as with dry-weather clothing, foul-weather gear fabrics, detailing, and even style have improved by leaps and bounds. We are now presented with a bewildering variety of materials, details, and styles that make a purchase of foul-weather gear much more difficult than it used to be. If you know a bit about what is available, and if you are rigorously honest about your own needs, you should end up with the best gear for you.

Waterproof **and** Breathable:
What They Mean and Do not Mean

Before charging off to look at gear, let us reflect upon the meaning of two adjectives that appear so frequently in the literature of foul-weather gear that they may mislead many people into expecting miracles. These words are *waterproof* and *breathable*.

Waterproof means 'keeping out water completely.' Water-repellent, on the other hand, means 'repelling water but not thoroughly waterproof.' (There is also *water-resistant:* 'repelling water for a short time').

Now, just because a bolt of treated fabric is waterproof—that is, will not leak if a hose is turned on it—nobody should expect a garment stitched together from that fabric to be equally effective at keeping out moisture. 'Making a high-quality garment is not very hard,' says one of the most prominent manufacturers of foul-weather gear, 'but making a high-quality garment that's waterproof *is* hard.' Good suits are available (later on in this chapter we will find out how to pick one), but even gear assembled carefully, with double-stitched and taped-over seams, may let in water around its edges, through cuffs and collars. The best way to block off your neck is to plug the hole. You can make your own stopper out of a length of fleece or a small bath towel, cutting a slit near one end through which to stick the other end to form a bulky necktie. Or you can buy a neck cloth from a foul-weather gear manufacturer who, far from trying to cover up some defect in his product, is simply being honest about its natural limits.

Breathable is the other word that bears examination, although in scientific terms it is more helpful to think about materials that are air permeable or non-air permeable. With average activity the human body loses about 1¼ pints (¾ litre) of liquid through the skin every 24 hours, so in bad weather it needs a covering which will keep out rain and spray, and yet dispose of unwanted condensation on the inside. A waterproofing that is air permeable allows the sweat-laden air to escape, but also allows a serious loss of heat. What is needed—and what has been produced for example by one British firm, Peter Storm—is a proofing that is non-air permeable and yet which will permit water vapour to pass from inside to outside.

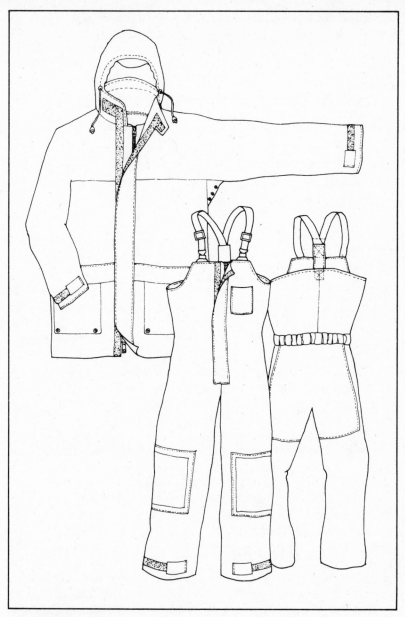

A good two-piece foul-weather suit has many of the details shown
here: tight-fitting hood, high collar, top- and bottom-opening zip
for the jacket, Velcro flaps over the zip and Velcro closures at
cuffs and trouser legs, pocket and armpit drain and vent holes,
chest-high trousers, adjustable braces, several pockets, elastic
trouser waist, reinforced knees and seat.

Different materials rely on different techniques, and later on we will see how the marine clothing industry has attempted to deal with the paradoxical relationship between waterproofness and breathability. For the present it is enough to say that when you go shopping, do not expect any gear to be both completely dry and air conditioned in very wet weather, whatever the claims of the sales literature.

The Seven Types of Foul-Weather Gear

Manufacturers provide seven types and combinations of foul-weather gear, each of which meets a relatively broad need.

The Jacket

The foul-weather jacket to protect the upper body comes in three styles.

Thigh-length, the most popular, covers the upper body from wrist to wrist and from the neck to several inches below the waist, thereby protecting the whole torso. It may be insulated with quilting or fibre pile for cold weather. Some jackets have a lining which provides warmth and also nominal buoyancy, but not to the standard required of a proper lifejacket.

The waist-length bomber-style jacket, usually seen in water-repellent windbreakers but also available in waterproof materials, offers no protection below the belt line but is easier to move around in than the thigh-length models.

The pullover smock, which extends to the knees, is worn in warm weather and water to protect most of the body without the need for confining foul-weather trousers.

Most foul-weather jackets are sold with zip or press-stud fronts. Water may creep through the zip or between the studs (even when they are covered with a Velcro flap), but most sailors are willing to accept that minor loss of waterproofing in exchange for the assurance that they can easily put the jacket on in a bouncy boat. Hoods (either retractable or removable) are standard accessories on good jackets. So, too, are at least one deep pocket with a waterproof flap and drain, elastic wristlets or Velcro straps to seal off cuffs, a high collar to keep wind and spray off the lower half of the head, and a liner to separate the wearer from any condensation that accumulates inside the jacket shell. Other options include a built-in safety harness, whose lifeline is clipped to the boat in heavy weather when there is a chance of falling overboard.

A thigh-length or smock jacket may be all the foul-weather gear you will need if the worst weather you can expect is a warm, light afternoon shower, or if the cockpit or cabin always protects your legs from spray. In fact, the jacket need not even be waterproofed if the weather is consistently warm and the wind is light; a nylon, water-repellent windbreaker might do quite nicely. But if you anticipate cool, damp weather, pay the extra price for a good jacket.

The Trousers
Foul-weather trousers are either waist-high and held up with a drawstring, or chest-high with braces. Foul-weather trousers may not be necessary on day-sailers with cockpits, but you will need them if it is raining and if you must sit on the deck when spray is flying; a surprising amount of water can creep from the rail up your back and down inside to your rear end. The higher the spray, the higher the trousers should be. Good trousers have a pocket for a knife or handkerchief, anklets or Velcro straps to seal off the ankle cuffs, reinforced knees and seat, a liner, and strong elastic braces securely attached.

The Two-Piece Suit
The most common foul-weather gear on boats sailing in moderately rough (and worse) weather is a two-piece combination consisting of the thigh-length jacket and chest-high trousers. The suit offers excellent protection as well as the most versatility. The large overlap between thigh and armpits provides a double seal, and water must work hard to make its way up inside the jacket and down the trousers. Since each piece individually covers more than half the body, the wearer has good protection when taking either the jacket or trousers off on a hot day to improve ventilation.

The One-Piece suit
This is a one-piece version of the combination jacket and trouser suit, offering more protection (since there is no opening near the waist) at a sacrifice of some flexibility (since the jacket and trousers cannot be separated). Moving around the boat in a one-piece suit is easier than in a two-piece combination. Accessories available include pockets, liners, reinforcements, and cuff closures.

The Dry Suit
If staying absolutely dry is a must—say when sailing dinghies or sailboards in cool or cold water—the dry suit may be the answer. Most dry suits are one-piece jump suits made of light fabric with waterproof seals at the cuffs and collar. At least one brand has a separate top and bottom connected with a rubber seal at the waist. The wearer climbs in and out of the suit somewhat awkwardly

through a back access hole, which is a disadvantage for people, like cruising sailors, who must put the suit on and pull it off frequently.

The Survival Suit

A kind of super dry suit which may have built in buoyancy, the specialized survival suit offers all-body protection for fishermen and navy personnel exposed to arctic conditions. While heavy and awkward, survival suits have saved the lives of many mariners who have gone overboard or abandoned ship into life rafts in freezing weather. A yacht heading off on a long cruise in cold water might consider carrying a survival suit for everybody on board. However a survival suit is an expensive extra at about £200 a piece.

The Wet Suit

While as the name suggests it does not keep the wearer dry, the wet suit does provide warmth by trapping a layer of water between the skin and its flexible rubberized surface. The body heats the water, which provides a thin barrier of insulation. Difficult to put on and take off, wet suits are usually worn by boardsailors and dinghy racers sailing in cool water. They come in a variety of styles—top, bottom, full length, and short.

Waterproofing Materials

The effectiveness and cost of foul-weather gear are determined by the materials and the amount and kind of detailing built into it. The most simple and least expensive type of wet gear is made of water-repellent (not waterproof) nylon. Though not suited for extended use in even moderate spray or rain, nylon trousers and jackets are lightweight, wind-resistant, and breathable, and may well provide all the protection you need.

However, most people who get serious about sailing eventually buy a top and trouser suit of waterproof gear made of a nylon or cotton outer shell coated with one of three types of waterproofings. Each coating has its own advantages and disadvantages. In the chandlery you can determine which waterproofing is used on a suit by rubbing the shell between your thumb and fingers, reaching under the nylon liner if there is one. If the shell has a shiny exterior and textured fabric interior, it could be waterproofed on the outside with PVC or polyurethane. If the shell exterior is textured and the interior smooth, the coating is on the inside and could be neoprene, polyurethane, PVC or PTFE (although the last is not now in common use for sailing clothing in the United Kingdom).

PVC Coating

Polyvinyl chloride (PVC) is a rather heavy, glossy outside coating applied in one layer or, on the more expensive suits, two layers. It is the oldest form of waterproofing and, because it is the type applied to the most familiar gear, it is the most readily recognized.

PVC has two major advantages over the other waterproofings: relatively low cost and welded seams. The seams in a PVC garment can be heated and stuck together in a welded joint that can be as waterproof as the fabric itself. (Since the other coatings are not heat-sealable, their seams must be sealed with tape). In the better PVC gear, the seams are first sewn and then welded over. PVC tears can be easily repaired using kits provided by manufacturers. When PVC loses its integrity and begins to leak—an inevitable fate of all foul-weather gear—it frankly announces its demise by cracking on the outside. Inside coatings, on the other hand, fall apart out of sight, and the first a wearer finds out about their failure is a vague sense of dampness.

However, PVC has two disadvantages, one stylistic and the other functional. The first is that with its crisp surface and protruding seams, it looks more like the uniform for storm troopers than like normal clothing. Some manufacturers seem to be trying to turn this detriment into a benefit by making gear with stripes and unusual colours like green and white (an unsafe combination, since it cannot be seen in whitecapped waves). The other disadvantage is that while a well-made PVC suit is satisfactorily waterproof against rain and spray, it can be stifling. It may get even wetter inside than outside. The first problem, its plastic appearance, seems not to bother the thousands of people who like PVC's waterproofness, but the second, its heavy feel, is less easy to live with for many sailors in warm climates.

In 1986 prices, a PVC two-piece suit can cost anywhere between about £40 (for the simple kind) to about £100 (for a more sophisticated offshore brand).

Neoprene Coating

While PVC and polyurethane are the only exterior waterproofings, there are different types of interior coatings. Probably the most nearly waterproof (and also the most expensive) is neoprene, used on several well-regarded suits made by a pair of British companies, Henri-Lloyd and Musto. Like most sailing gear made in Britain, this is tough, heavy stuff. Sailors in temperate and semi-tropical areas may find it, like PVC gear, hot and confining.

At the top of the neoprene lines are £200 suits (1986 prices) for serious offshore work in extreme conditions—like sailing around

Cape Horn in the Whitbread Round-the-World Race. This gear is so pricey partly because neoprene costs much more than PVC and partly because its thorough detailing includes heavy seam taping, built-in safety harness, strips of tape which reflect the beam of a torch to facilitate recovery should you fall overboard at night, neat waterproof cuffs that function like gaiters, and flaps and baffles over every conceivable watercatcher.

Urethane Coatings

That leaves the crowd of materials known by the catchall title *urethane* that are used today by many companies. In this group are urethane (polyurethane) which is applied to the nylon fabric as a liquid, and a urethane-derived film, which is glued to the shell. Though a couple of urethanes (such as Cyclone by Carrington Fabrics) are claimed to be breathable, most are simply lightweight, waterproof, and good-looking, with a fabric-like textured appearance and feel. For example, urethane coated fabric is used for the Transatlantic range of sailing clothing produced by Edward Macbean & Co of Glasgow, and polyurethane proofed nylon is featured in the Channel and Adventure ranges of garments from Henri-Lloyd.

Like any inside coating, urethane can leak along seams, especially at the rear end, the crotch, and other flexible places. All seams should be double-stitched and thoroughly taped on the inside; some manufacturers use a different colour tape to facilitate inspection. Outside seat and knee patches should be heavier than the shell and securely sewn onto it.

Jacket and Trouser Liners

Waterproofing keeps outside water off your clothes and body, and breathable fabrics allow muggy air from your body to escape before it makes you damp and cold. For different reasons, both systems have proved to be less than perfect. But there is another stay-dry tactic: using a liner in the gear to isolate condensation on the inside of the outer garment. At first, liners were sewn only into jackets, but manufacturers began to put them in trousers, too, since annoying condensation can develop at the rear end and crotch. Besides helping to keep inner clothes and the skin dry, a liner has three other advantages: it protects your skin from the clammy inside of the shell; it protects the shell's seams from chafe from your clothes; and its slippery surface facilitates pulling the suit on. The liner should be sewn in throughout the garment except at the bottom, where an opening or drain will allow water to pour out if the wearer is doused by a wave or falls overboard.

Styling: Almost Like Real Clothes

If you remember the shapeless yellow bags that used to fill the clothing racks at chandleries, a glance at a 1986 display will tell you that something has happened to foul-weather gear design. Many fascinating and appealing developments have been inspired by the skiwear industry (graduates of which, not coincidentally, now run several marine clothing companies). Alongside traditional suits with the sharp-edged functional look of an army field jacket, hang jackets and trousers with sexy colours (some in two-tone schemes), tapered arms and waists, hidden drain holes, and slash pockets. On the more practical side are high, waterproof collars, retractable and zip-up hoods, firm cuff elastics, and warm collars and pockets lined with fur-fabric or fleece.

It is a wonderful development, for if people look good in protective clothing they are bound to wear it more often. But there is one stylistic trend that is not progressive: the use of cool colours like white and blue. They are almost invisible in the spray of breaking waves. Pray that you never fall overboard in a suit that is not orange, yellow, or red. A few manufacturers have attempted to deal with this safety issue by adding red hoods to blue suits—which is fine so long as the unlucky swimmer has the hood on. Others sew strips of reflective tape on hoods and shoulders, which certainly will help during a night search. But the best choice is highly visible, if slightly unfashionable, hot-hued gear.

What You Should Expect to Spend

Of course, all those fancy new materials, accessories, and styles cost money, but you need not spend a fortune to stay dry. In 1986 the top-of-the-line British neoprene suits, with built-in safety harnesses and other good things, weigh in at over £200; if you sail an awful lot, say daily for six or more months a year, that is an excellent investment. However, most of us will be perfectly happy in a suit costing much less. At the bottom of the list in price and detailing is the simple, unlined, £40 PVC suit, which may be fine in mild rain and protected water but is not sufficient in rougher weather. For about £100 you can buy a good all-round, partially lined PVC or urethane suit. For £200 or so, you can get a deluxe, fully lined, thoroughly detailed urethane outfit that should keep you dry in just about all conditions.

Budgeting the difference between a 'better' £100 suit and a 'deluxe' £200 outfit over a five-year suit life gives you an extra cost of £20 a year. You may not need the £200 suit. But if you plan to do a lot of sailing, please remember how uncomfortable you were—and how poorly you sailed—the last time you were cold and wet. A boatowner should be able to justify that marginal added expense quite easily, since good foul-weather protection might make the difference between loving or hating a £50,000 plus yacht.

How Foul-Weather Gear Should Fit

When trying on foul-weather gear in the chandlery, wear exactly the same clothes and boots you will have on when the going is wet. As with all sailing and other outdoors clothing, the fit should be on the baggy side with the important exception that the crotch should conform to your own so that you can spring into action without having to hitch up the legs. Give the gear a good tryout. Throw yourself down on your knees and grind away furiously on an imaginary winch handle. Leap up and reach high for a broken lower batten and low for the mooring buoy. Quickly pull the suit off and on. For a man, an important consideration may be the relative ease of opening the zip one-handed while meeting a call of nature in rough weather, with the other hand providing secure anchorage, either to a grabrail in the head or to a lifeline along the leeward rail. If your jacket zip opens from the bottom, you will not need to remove the top during this exercise. As you go through these gymnastics, check if there is sufficient material in the back and elasticity in the braces to allow the gear to move smoothly with your body.

A Checklist for Buying Foul-Weather Gear

Before making your final selection, get it clear in your mind exactly how you will use the gear that you are shopping for. This will help you purchase no more or less than you need. I cannot tell you what your requirements are, but I can tell you mine as I listed them before making my own recent purchase. They may well be representative of other people who sail in temperate waters in a variety of climates.

Use. The suit should be versatile. I usually sail on thirty-foot-plus cruising boats and ocean racers, generally in relatively warm, easy conditions but sometimes in cold, rough stuff. I can be found anywhere between the helm, in light spray, and the bow, hip-deep in water while wrestling with a recalcitrant jib. Since I usually wear only boots, chest-high trousers, and a T-shirt in warm spray, a one-piece suit is not appropriate.

Accessibility. I will often be hastily putting the gear on and removing it in a crowded, damp, on-edge cabin rather than on a stable deck. The jacket and trousers should pull on easily, so I will want a smooth liner, plus zip, press studs, and Velcro sealers that open and close with one hand (no buttons, please).

Colour. Orange, red, and yellow are the *only* sensible choices.

Detailing. There should be at least one waterproof pocket each in the jacket and trousers for my knife and paper towels (to wipe my glasses). Since the boats I generally sail in are equipped with good safety harnesses, I will not need a built-in harness. Pulled up, the hood should not be too loose or restrict my hearing and peripheral vision. Since I use a hood very rarely—they tend to funnel warm air up from my body to fog up my glasses—it should be removable or thoroughly retractable into the collar. The cuffs should be closed off outside with Velcro straps and inside with elastic liner wristlets. (The elastic should not be so tight that it cuts off circulation).

Construction. I remember these past failings when inspecting gear in the chandlery: braces lose their spring and their attachments pull out of the trousers; unreinforced knees wear out; a cleat or rough, nonskid surface tears off a thin, poorly sewn seat patch; seams, cuff elastics, and zips leak; a stiff jacket collar does not mould to my neck and water drips in.

Phobias. I hate getting wet even in warm weather: damp feet and the sadistic drip-drip-drip of a leaky neck stimulate dark humours. Better no clothes at all than stiff, bulky ones. A tight collar makes me gag. Claustrophobia sets in when I get hot and cannot ventilate by opening the cuffs and neck or quickly peeling off the jacket.

Cost. No more than £200.

All that left me with a simple shopping list: a traditional two-piece suit consisting of a zip-up jacket and chest-high trousers, strongly built of medium-weight, flexible materials and with a modicum of functional detailing. Add a pair of shin-high seaboots and I am ready for sea.

Accessories: Seaboots, Hats, and Gloves

Since heat pours off the extremities, anybody going out in cool weather and water should have a pair of seaboots, a hat, and perhaps a pair of gloves.

Seaboots

Many sailors—me among them—can almost tolerate being wet anywhere but in their feet, and pull boots on long before they would even think of donning their foul-weather trousers and jacket. Of course, seaboots should have nonskid soles. Most boots are shin- or calf-high, but some, used by people who regularly sail in very rough or cold weather, are almost knee-high. The shorter ones are less bulky and, in warm weather, less stifling, but they also offer little protection against water surging high up inside your foul-weather trousers and then pouring down onto your socks as you wrestle with a jib on a foredeck plunging into steep waves. Knee-high boots are laceless and so are fairly loose on your foot, providing an insulating air barrier (and a sloppy fit). Most low models have laces so that they can be tightened to fit snugly for small-boat and dinghy racing.

The legs of foul-weather trousers are worn outside the boots and should be kept tight around them to cut off water flow up the leg. If the trousers do not have cuff closures, you can make your own by leaving a heavy rubber band or a loop of elastic shock cord over the boot top and pulling it up over the cuff whenever you put the trousers and boot on. The 1986 retail price of a pair of good seaboots is about £30.

Hats

Sailors are an individualistic lot, and one place where that is most obvious is in the choice of headgear. Some wear old-fashioned PVC sou'westers, whose long front and back brims protect the face and neck—at some sacrifice to good vision. Others like hoods, which keep the hair and ears dry but make it difficult when steering. (Hoods also funnel warm body heat, which fogs up eyeglasses.) A few sailors, myself among them, try to get by with wool watch caps, which continue to insulate long after they are soggy. No hat is perfect, as you can discover through endless experimentation. Fortunately, no hat costs much more than about £10 either, so experimentation will not break your budget.

Gloves

Most sailing gloves are no more than water-resistant, with leather palms and coated fabric backs. Some have thermal liners which are removable and quick drying. Such gloves cost upwards of £20 a pair.

How to Take Care of Foul-Weather Gear

With a little bit of care, a urethane suit may enjoy a lifetime of four or five years of moderate to heavy use, thirty to fifty days a year. PVC and neoprene suits should stay waterproof even longer. Maintaining gear is quite simple. After a saltwater wetting, hose it down (inside and out) to eliminate all those crystals that, when dry, will only absorb more moisture. Wash off accumulated dirt according to the manufacturer's instructions, using soap flakes. To keep dark nylon liners and shells from bleeding onto lighter-coloured fabrics, thoroughly dry the gear before hanging it in a crowded locker.

If we are to believe the astonishing stories that manufacturers tell, consumers apparently understand the word *waterproof* to have talismanic value. Every year warranty claims come in from people who think that suits should resist all leaking even after being ripped, dry-cleaned, or doused with harsh chemicals, such as acetone. Read labels carefully, not only before buying your gear but also before cleaning; some fabrics require special care. The manufacturer can fix rips and leaky seams, which you can locate by tying up the cuffs and filling the garment with water. PVC is the easiest material to patch up; PVC repair kits are often sold in chandleries.

Like your foul-weather suit, seaboots, hats, and gloves should be rinsed out occasionally with fresh water and then thoroughly dried. Most boot rips and holes can be repaired temporarily with heavy tape or more permanently with tyre-patching material or even silicone sealer.

All right, now you know something about the variety of inner and outer clothes that sailors can wear. What should *you*, sailor, take aboard, and where should you put it?

CHAPTER 3

What Clothes

to

Take Aboard

When choosing clothes to carry with you, either to take aboard a cruising boat or to leave in the car while you are boardsailing or day-sailing in a small boat, think about the needs and functions they must satisfy. In particular, try to anticipate the range of temperature and dampness, and plan accordingly. In this chapter, we will survey different types of containers for carrying clothes aboard, then go on to look at some questions you should ask yourself when packing. We will discuss 'layering'—a way of dressing for cool, wet weather. Finally, we will end with some sample packing lists for different types of sailing.

The Ubiquitous, Essential Seabag

Pack your gear in a flexible container that (1) can be folded up and stuck out of the way once you have put your clothes in a locker (boats are not equipped with stowages for suitcases) and (2) provides quick access to all your clothes if, as sometimes happens, there are no lockers on board and you must live out of your bag. As in so many other aspects of sailing, you will need some specialized equipment here, since for a variety of reasons normal shoreside luggage just will not work. A hard-sided suitcase meets the second requirement—easy access—but not the first—collapsibility. A camp

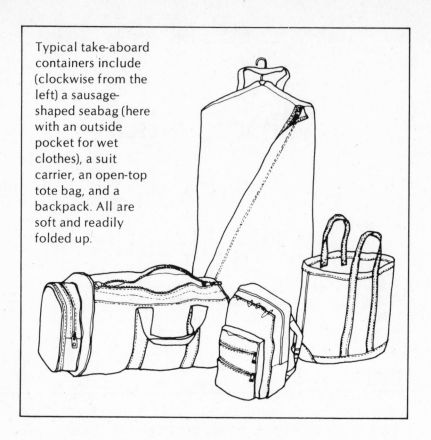

Typical take-aboard containers include (clockwise from the left) a sausage-shaped seabag (here with an outside pocket for wet clothes), a suit carrier, an open-top tote bag, and a backpack. All are soft and readily folded up.

or army duffle bag with a drawstring or snap opening at one end meets the first but not the second. An open-ended canvas tote bag satisfied both needs, but because it cannot be closed your stuff may spill out when the boat heels.

The only container that meets both requirements is the mariner's old standby, the sausage-shaped seabag. Modern versions may be square or rectangular, but regardless of their shape all seabags have a long opening secured by buttons, snaps, or a zip that provides quick access to the contents. A seabag's non-rigid construction permits it to be folded up out of the way.

With the rediscovery of simple, traditional outdoors gear, seabags are now available in synthetic fabrics from a variety of stores and mail-order firms. When selecting one, do not skimp on size; you will always want to be able to take a lot of clothes. Look for a large, waterproof, recessed container for wet clothes and some inside pockets for valuables. For best security, the handles, which take a big load, should be extensions of heavy straps that extend all the way around the bag. The zip should be heavy plastic or coated steel. Seabags designed for offshore use may have a Velcro flap over the zip to forestall leaks.

A single medium-sized seabag, 9 by 26 inches, should suffice for all the sailing clothes you need for a short cruise in warm weather. Take two for longer cruises or cool or wet weather, when you will have bulky sweaters or pile clothing and plenty of underwear, socks, shorts, and shirts. Being a bit of a fanatic about both warmth and efficient gear stowage, I have accumulated several seabags and duffles that I pack to within an inch of explosion with plenty of back-up clothes. A medium-sized sausage bag is big enough for an afternoon day-sail or a warm-weather weekend cruise. For longer or cooler trips, I use a big PVC-coated 15-by-19-inch bag. On cruises, each of my sons carries his own colour-coded, medium-sized seabag and an open-ended canvas tote bag, 13 by 21 inches, for snacks, books, games, the cassette player, tapes, and other odds and ends that he will need in a hurry.

Stowing Shore and Foul-Weather Gear
Since seabags and duffles are not rigid enough to keep nice clothes wrinkle-free, carry jackets, ties, pressed trousers, skirts, and shirts in a flexible suit-carrier, which you can hang in the ship's main hanging locker. If you are worried about leaks or moisture (which will cause natural fabrics to mildew and some synthetics to run), stick the carrier's hanger hook through the bottom of a large plastic garbage bag and pull the bag down around the clothes. Leather shore shoes, if stowed in the bottom of a locker, are too easily forgotten and left to mildew; wrap them in a heavy bin liner with the throat tightly sealed.

Foul-weather gear should not be carried around with the other clothes in the seabag, both because it takes up too much room and because it may be carrying salt crystals, those breeders of dampness and mildew. Instead, roll the jacket and trousers up tightly and stick each in a seaboot, then tie the two boots together with a two-foot length of light line (I use my knife lanyard) and drape the bundle over a free shoulder as you walk to the boat so that both hands are left free for other luggage. On board, unpack and hang up the gear in a designated hanging locker. Because foul-weather gear is prone to dampness, this locker should not be (but unfortunately often is) the same one as is reserved for shore clothes.

What Clothes Do You Need?

The first answer to this question always is, 'More than you think'. But exactly what kind of 'more' you take along depends on the

weather (which you can only guess at) and your own physical capa-
bilities (which you probably know fairly well). So as you sit in your
bedroom contemplating the open seabag lying there ready to be
filled, ask yourself the following questions.

'How wet will I get?' Always assuming that there will be
spray, carry along a windbreaker, a water-repellent jacket, or,
better still, a waterproof foul-weather jacket. Take at least one
extra set of dry socks for each day you will be afloat. If there is
any chance of getting wet, take foul-weather trousers, seaboots, and a full set of back-up dry clothing.

'How cold will I get?' Remember that the water temperature
is almost always lower than the air temperature. Air that is
sweltering on shore may be barely tolerable out at sea.
Remember, too, the wind-chill factor. Each knot of apparent
wind (the wind felt on the moving boat) lowers the temperature a sailor on board feels by about one degree. Therefore,
when the air temperature is 80 degrees and the true wind (the
wind felt on a stationary object) is 12 knots, the felt temperature is 68 degrees when the boat is standing still, and even
lower when she is sailing into the wind. Since sailing boats are
rarely standing still, the apparent wind (the wind created
jointly by the true wind and the boat's speed) can considerably
affect the temperature felt by people on board. When a boat
sails into or across the wind (on a close-hauled or reaching
course), the apparent wind is greater than the true wind by a
little less than her own speed. But when she is sailing with the
wind (on a run), the apparent wind is less. For example, on an
80-degree day with a 12-knot true wind, a boat sailing close-
hauled into the wind at a speed of 5 knots has an apparent
wind of just under 17 knots, and her crew feels a temperature
of just 63 degrees. On the same day, a boat running with the
12-knot true wind at 5 knots has an apparent wind of only 7
knots, and the temperature felt on board is 73 degrees, ten
degrees warmer than the close-hauled temperature.

Obviously, then, the air temperature you feel on deck
varies enormously when you are sailing. While packing, try to
anticipate those fluctuations. In an air temperature of 63
degrees, most people would feel chilly without a medium-
weight sweater or pullover.

'How much sun will there be?' No matter how warm the
air temperature is, if there is a good chance of burning—
especially hazy—sunlight, take at least one long cotton shirt,

and a pair of long trousers to protect your arms and legs. Also pack some sort of head protection, such as a sun hat or a peaked cap. The glare on your eyes may be intolerable without sunglasses. For years I clipped Polaroids onto my prescription glasses; recently I bought and have been very happy with a pair of prescription photosensitive glasses that automatically darken in the sun. However, they do not absorb glare off the water as well as Polaroids do.

'How long will I be out there?' Add up the number of days and nights and take a pair of socks and a pair of underwear for each day, plus one dry-weather outfit (depending on the temperature, shorts and T-shirt or long trousers and long-sleeved shirt) for every two days. For every day of warm, dry sailing there are likely to be at least two days of damp or cool weather. Be conservative; fill every nook and cranny in your seabag.

'How much privacy will there be?' Except on large boats, cruising in mixed company is not an activity for prudes. Many ocean-racing boats as long as fifty feet have only one big cabin and a tiny head, where you can barely sit down much less comfortably change your clothes. Even if everybody observes a few common-sense customs aimed at allowing some privacy when dressing or washing, you will inevitably learn more than you ever wanted to know about your shipmates' personal habits and private anatomies. For both your and your friends' comfort, then, think carefully about how revealing or skimpy your swimswuit and pyjamas should be. The guiding word is *appropriate.*

Layering for Warmth and Dryness

For a long time sailors dressed for cool, damp weather quite simply: they pulled thick trousers and a heavy woollen sweater over their normal clothes, climbed into their foul-weather gear, and headed out to sea aware that their gear would be about 75 percent successful, at best. They knew that water would inevitably leak in from the outside through cuffs and collars, that their perspiration would soak their underwear, and that once wet, they would stay wet until salt sores began to appear. And they knew that there was no alternative.

Since the late 1970s a whole new approach to outdoors clothing, borrowed from such land activities as cross-country skiing and mountain climbing, has led sailors to expect better performance in wet- and cold-weather clothes. Instead of pulling on a couple of heavy natural-fibre layers under the shells, sailors now wear several relatively light ones, made mostly from synthetics. This practice, called layering, provides a number of thin, insulating barriers that can either be increased as the weather gets colder or the wearer becomes inactive, or be decreased as his body warms up.

The classic layering garment is cotton fishnet underwear, which, on first viewing, looks irrelevant, but whose honeycomb structure provides hundreds of insulating air pockets between the skin and the next layer out. Woollen shirts and sweaters are woven more tightly than fishnet, but not so tightly that all the air barriers are eliminated. The problem with both natural fibres is that they lose some utility when they get wet—cotton more than wool, but wool still functions best when dry.

As we saw in Chapter 1, compared with cotton and wool, the new synthetic fabrics such as fibre pile (or fur fabric) and fleece, made from materials like polypropylene and polyester, insulate

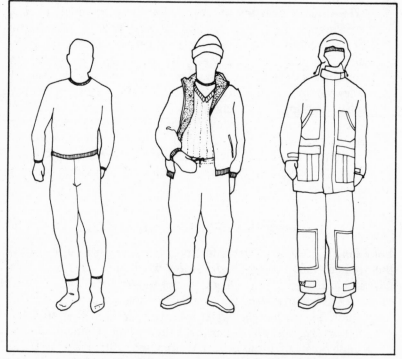

Layer you clothes when dressing for cool- wet weather (left to right). Start at the skin with polypropylene long underwear and socks, then add a woollen sweater, fibre pile or fleece top and trousers, woollen socks, a woolly watch cap, and fleece-lined water-resistant gloves. To keep water out, top everything with foul-weather gear and seaboots.

better when they are wet, dry more quickly, and are more able to wick dampness from the skin and up through adjacent layers. Instead of a big bag of woollen long johns, shirts, and sweaters, an ocean-going sailor now carries along one or two pairs of polypropylene long johns (one light and the other medium or heavy) and fleece and fibre pile jackets and trousers, all of which he or she will wear in a variety of layering combinations, depending on the weather. From underwear out, here is how the clothes may be layered:

Layer 1. Warm, mildly damp weather. Synthetic-cotton blend shorts and T-shirt worn under foul-weather gear.

Layer 2. Warm, very wet weather. Thin polypropylene long johns and socks, which wick sweat from the skin, worn alone (or under layer 1) under foul-weather gear. People who are especially sensitive to cold and not very active on deck may prefer medium-weight polypropylene if the wind-chill factor is great. Fishnet underwear is a natural-fibre alternative to the long johns, providing an air barrier through which perspiration can flow to the shirt and trousers.

Layer 3. Cool weather. Fleece jacket and trousers worn over layers 1 and 2 and, if spray or rain is flying on deck, under foul-weather gear. Fleece also wicks perspiration away from the body and dries quickly. A natural-fibre alternative is cotton fishnet underwear under a wool shirt or wool-cotton blend long underwear. Add fleece lined gloves and a woollen watch cap to keep warm air from pouring off hands and head.

Layer 4. Cold weather. A fibre pile jacket, trousers, and boot liners for added insulation worn over layers 1 and 2 and, if it is wet, under foul-weather gear. Add a balaclava (knit cap for head and neck) made of polypropylene (warm) or fibre pile (warmest) to forestall heat loss through the neck and head, and wear polypropylene- or pile-lined gloves. Or, wear layers of cotton fishnet underwear and light woollen shirts or sweaters, plus rubber gardeners' gloves over wool inserts.

A Checklist for Packing

As a guide, here is a list of clothing and accessories that I usually carry aboard for four days of cruising in an area where the days are hot and windy, the nights are cool, the seas may be rough, and the air may be damp.

2 pair cotton socks
2 pair wool socks
1 pair polypropylene socklets
3 pair underwear
1 pair polypropylene long underwear
2 pair short pants
2 pair trousers
3 T-shirts
2 long-sleeved shirts
1 fibre pile jacket
1 light woollen or cotton sweater
1 heavy woollen sweater

1 woollen watch cap
Swimsuit
Deck shoes
Sunglasses
A light line to secure eyeglasses

Toilet kit: sun lotion, toothbrush and paste, hairbrush, adhesive bandages, laxative, aspirin, seasickness pills, nail clippers
1 towel
Reading material
Eyeshades (for sleeping in daylight)
Rigging knife
Foul-weather gear and seaboots
Wallet with credit cards, cheque book and £50 cash
A small torch
A plastic bin liner for dirty and wet clothes

Items that might also be included in the seabag are: sailing gloves to protect soft hands, a notebook, and a present for the boat, such as a bottle of wine, some beer, a chunk of good cheese, or fruit.

We have now spent three chapters just talking about getting ready for sailing—chapters that I wish I had read when I first went to sea. Now let us get out there.

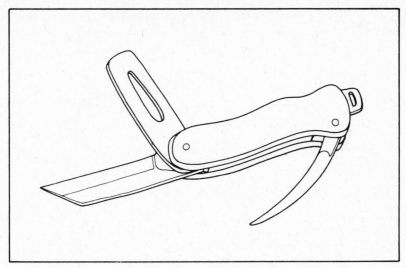

The best sailor's rigging knife has a sharp blade, a spike for loosening knots, a slotted extension for tightening and loosening shackles, and a short tip that can be used as a screwdriver. It should be secured to the owner with a good lanyard.

PART II

Welcome Aboard

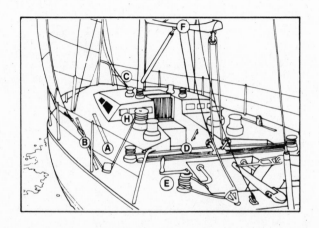

CHAPTER 4

How to
Learn How to
Learn How
to Sail

———

The toughest part of going aboard a boat for the first time is
dealing with lack of confidence, which naturally arises whenever we try something new. This uneasiness can affect experienced
sailors crewing on a new boat just as much as it does converts going
out for their first sail. It is always much preferable to a cavalier
overconfidence, which could lead to crew disharmony, mistakes,
and even more serious problems, yet it can be blown out of all
proportion. The healthiest way to approach sailing on a new boat is
to take for granted the assumptions described in this chapter.

Sailing Is Meant to Be Fun

Even sailing races are meant to be fun. And pleasure in a boat
means enjoying the marine environment, the company of one's
shipmates, physical exercise, and the mastering and performing of
some challenging skills both alone and as a team. Sometimes accom-
plishing a difficult task—especially one that concerns the boat's
safety—may require a decisiveness that can hurt your shipmates'
feelings. A talented helmsman, for instance, may brusquely take the
wheel from a novice in order to steer the boat around a dangerous
shoal area. Remembering that enjoyment is the paramount goal
should help all parties smooth over any hurts later on.

Sailing Well Demands Alertness

Go sailing to go sailing—not to get drunk. Although boozing afloat may not be such a serious problem in British waters, the United States Coast Guard estimates that drinking is a factor in between one-half and three-quarters of boating accidents that lead to fatalities in America. According to the Coast Guard, a blood alcohol level as low as .035 per cent—about one-third the legal limit for driving a car—may severely impair the judgement of a skipper or crew in a boat under way. The average man can attain that .035 per cent limit just by imbibing a couple of beers or a tot of whisky in an hour.

Long ago I learned that drinking even a can of beer will affect judgement and equilibrium even on a relatively calm day. I was sailing in my first long-distance race, from Stamford, Connecticut, down Long Island Sound, around a light tower off Martha's Vineyard, and back. As we approached the tower at about 1800, I joined my shipmates in a happy-hour beer, and then went forward on deck to prepare to lower the spinnaker and set the jib for the long beat back to Stamford. The rolling deck, which had been as firm as the Rock of Gibraltar, suddenly became very unsteady under my legs. Instead of walking I had to crawl on my knees. Every job seemed to take twice as long as it once did, and still my mind could not focus entirely. It was an eerie feeling. For a while I blamed it on my relative youth and inexperience with both alcohol and boats, but it has since come upon me again when cockiness led me to toss down a couple of beers while on watch.

It might be reassuring to hear how much somebody drinks while the boat is under way is a matter best left to personal judgment. Personal judgment, however, is usually booze's first victim. It is better for the skipper to make firm rules before setting out. There will be plenty of time for cocktails once the boat has been safely anchored or docked. During the two Whitbread Round the World Races won by the Dutch yacht *Flyer*, skipper Conny van Rietschoten banned alcohol altogether, despite free and ample supplies offered by the sponsor.

You Will Never Learn It All, but Keep Trying

This is one of the very few sports whose techniques never quite match the demands. Throughout a sailing career we never stop finding new skills to master and problems to solve. This lifelong learning curve is a reason why many sailors stay active well into old age, long after they have given up golf, tennis, and other pastimes. You are a learner, but so is everyone else. Try to learn from your mistakes and from new situations, be tolerant of your (and your shipmates') minor errors, and do your best not to make them again.

Sailing Demands a Routine

Of all the paradoxes and ironies in this extraordinarily complex pastime, the most important is that to enjoy sailing—the most individualistic of all sports—you must standardize your techniques and your equipment and do every job the same way, time after time. One way to keep jobs simple is to do them the same way every time. Standardization permits predictability: every time you do a job, you and your shipmates will know how to undo it. Standardization also leads to good habits of seamanship.

Now, there is often more than one right way to do most jobs in a boat. For example, of the four essential knots described in Chapter 5, two are used to make loops: the bowline and the double half-hitch. For one reason or another, every skipper and experienced sailor has a strong prejudice in favour of one of those knots for certain jobs, like securing the dinghy's painter to the boat. That prejudice may be based on personal experience ('I remember once when a bowline let go in that gale in '73 . . .'), on hearsay ('My dad once told me, never depend on a double half-hitch . . .'), or on authority ('At sailing school, the instructor said . . .'). However it starts, once a conviction or prejudice has laid its foundations into a sailor's memory, it is likely to stay there no matter how many gales try to lift it out. Therefore, 'We always use the bowline in this boat' is not a statement to be contradicted unless you, the new crew member, are an authority in your own right.

So when going aboard a new boat, expect your skipper, no matter how casual he or she may be ashore, to have a fairly firm routine. (More, *hope* that there is a routine.) And do not be surprised if that routine differs from the ones used in other boats you have sailed in. At first, your desire to relax and leave problems and routines on shore may lead you to be somewhat rebellious when you are told exactly how and when you should do a job. You may feel that you have unwittingly stumbled into a slave ship run by a descendant of Captain Bligh rather than a pleasure boat owned by a man or woman who is (or used to be) your best friend. Some of the expectations that you encounter may strike you as unduly militaristic—until you have a frightening experience in which a firm routine makes the difference between order and chaos, ease and disaster. People who make up and impose routines are generally people who, through hair-raising experience, understand how dangerous the sea can be.

On the other hand, you may be right. Maybe the skipper *is* too rigid and insufficiently self-confident and allows no room for relaxation. If so, do your best to keep calm or (if the skipper is a good friend) to suggest tactfully that he or she may be pushing a little too hard. If those tactics do not work, try to distract yourself by getting to know one of your fellow sufferers, reading a book on navigation, or projecting your frustrations on a flight of nasty, scavenging sea gulls—and then turn down the next invitation to sail aboard this *Bounty*.

But then again, allow yourself a moment of reflection. Perhaps you are merely oversensitive. People do not like to think they are being bossed around, especially when they are insecure about their competence. Remember what it was like the time you had to teach a subject you knew well to a raw novice. Orders that appear abrupt to you may simply sound matter-of-fact to the skipper. Give the skipper the benefit of the doubt, and you may soon see him or her coming around. By respecting the boat's routine, you are showing your skipper (and yourself) that you respect the traditional, necessary caution of seafaring.

What Kind of Boat Is the Best Teacher?

To learn how to sail with skill and sensitivity takes a long time and many talents, among them good hand-eye coordination and depth perception and a well developed feel for the wind's changing direction and strength. Some people work at it for years but never really master it; most learn just enough to get by safely in easy conditions and become harried and insecure whenever the wind strengthens and the waves build.

The best way to learn sailing is to do a lot of it in many different types of boats and in many different wind and wave conditions, where the need to 'change gear' in order to adapt to new stimuli will blow away whatever bad habits and false assumptions you may have picked up in one boat or a single type of weather. The variety of boats available is so wide that new sailors are often confused. To clear things up, here is a quick profile of modern sailing, with some concluding comments about which kind of boat is best to learn in.

Day-sailers

These are the simplest boats, ones not equipped with bunks (beds), galleys (kitchens), heads (toilets), and other accommodations for living aboard. But saying what a day-sailer is not is much easier than describing what she is. Some day-sailers are eleven-foot-long sailboards (three and a half metres) on which the sailor stands and holds up the sail. Others are boats between nine feet (three metres) and sixty feet (eighteen metres) long (an America's Cup twelve-metre is a day-sailer) in which the sailor or sailors sit. If she is light enough to be pulled out of the water by a couple of people and carried on the roof of a car, she is called a dinghy, but if she has a heavy keel as a counterweight to keep her from tipping over, she is called a keel boat.

Day-sailers may be raced against each other with or without time handicaps, and some day-sailer classes (or boats of the same specifications) have extremely large racing fleets. But most day-sailers (for that matter, most sailing boats) are, literally, *day-sailed*—casually sailed around on pleasant afternoons with little concern for speed.

Cruising Boats

These are live-aboard boats with all the bunks, galleys, and so on that allow people to stay on board for an extended period of time. If you live aboard and sail from harbour to harbour during the day, you are *cruising*. *Weekend cruising* takes place over short periods of time like a weekend; *long-distance* or *offshore cruising* means taking long, nonstop trips, or passages, from one harbour to another over a large stretch of water (like the English Channel). You can own a cruising boat, or you can charter (rent) one in wonderful holiday areas such as the Mediterranean. Despite their name, cruising boats may also be raced for a few hours, overnight, or for weeks across oceans.

Some cruising boats are only twenty feet (six metres) long, but you need at least twenty-eight or thirty feet (about nine metres) to achieve the volume needed for decent comfort for a crew of three or more people. People who enjoy their privacy prefer not to cruise with more than three people in a boat smaller than thirty-six feet (eleven metres), or with more than five others in one smaller than forty feet (twelve metres). Bill Robinson, my former boss at the old *Yachting* magazine, strongly recommends that if two or more couples are aboard, the boat should have two heads to allow the greatest flexibility for the most private of all functions.

Most of this book is about cruising, on the assumption that cruising is what most sailors want to do.

How to Become a Better Sailor

So what is the best way to learn? You can take all the classroom courses you want, but the lessons really will not begin to sink in until you get out on the water with a standard to measure yourself against. One good standard is an instructor's watchful eye.

In Britain people of any age who aim to crew or skipper sailing craft are lucky to have available a number of training schemes which are administered by the Royal Yachting Association (RYA), the national authority which manages and coordinates all aspects of pleasure boating throughout the country. These training schemes cater for all levels of competence—from the basic handling of a sailing dinghy or sailboard to skippering and navigating a large yacht offshore. Each course can lead to the award of the appropriate certificate of competence. The details and syllabi of the different schemes are contained in the following RYA booklets, obtainable for a small fee from the Royal Yachting Association, Victoria Way, Woking, Surrey, GU21 1EQ.

Booklet G23—RYA National Boardsailing Scheme
Booklet G4 —RYA National Dinghy Sailing Scheme
Booklet G15—RYA National Cruising Scheme (Sail)

The cruising courses give a mixture of shore-based instruction and practical training afloat, to a prescribed syllabus, but before a certificate can be awarded the individual must have had a certain minimum of seagoing experience—defined in terms of days on board, miles sailed, and hours of night watches. For the more demanding certificates the candidate has to take an examination.

The addresses of the many teaching establishments which are recognized by the Royal Yachting Association, together with the details of the courses which they each give, are available from the RYA at the address above.

People who have perhaps learned the basic skills of boat handling in some safe and stable keel boat can either move on to cruising yachts (in which case their skills will probably not improve very rapidly) or find another standard to measure themselves against. One of these standards is the challenge of dinghy or sailboard sailing. Capsizable dinghies are even more unforgiving of mistakes than a tough instructor; trim the sheet a bit too hard, push the helm a few degrees the wrong way, and you are no longer in the boat but swimming alongside her. Although they do not have sheets and rudders, sailboards also make excellent teachers because to sail them you must understand the all-important principle of balance (and I do not mean the balance required to stay standing on the board), which we will explain in Chapter 6. Those small, wet boats will sharpen your wits and techniques and make you a much better all-round sailor.

Finally, you can hone your skills on the race course in any kind of boat. There, a mistake in sail trimming, steering, or wind reading will be noticed immediately when a competitor moves out ahead. As with any competitive sport, there are limits to racing's benefits. You can push yourself to a frenzy and forget completely that this is supposed to be enjoyable, and there is always the chance of excessive risk taking, such as carrying too much sail in fresh winds. But if you can resist the temptation to push yourself, your boat, and your crew to insane limits, you will see your technique and feel for the boat and wind improve in huge steps. In almost every area there are enough different types of racing to allow it to be pursued with varying degrees of intensity. Some classes are very intense, others relatively relaxed; you may quickly find the level at which you are most comfortable.

As we have seen in this chapter, getting started (or getting better) in sailing takes a little time, energy, and attentiveness—not to speak of a good sense of humour. Enough on basic assumptions; let us begin learning how the experts do it.

CHAPTER 5

Six Things
You Should Know
Within Thirty Minutes
of Coming Aboard

―――――

The special demands your skipper will put on you, and you on your skipper, will depend on the people involved, but on every boat there are six things the crew should know about within a half-hour or so of coming aboard. Three of these concern the cabin and its equipment: where to stow your personal gear; how to work the plumbing and stove; and how to keep the cabin tidy. The rest apply on deck: how the sail-handling gear is laid out; how the crew will be organized; and what to do in an emergency. Experienced sailors usually pick up these routines and gear arrangements on their own, taking a few minutes for a self-guided tour of an unfamiliar boat. Less knowledgeable people, on the other hand, should be given a tour during which the skipper outlines the boat's normal routines.

Whether seasoned or just beginning, if you are new on board and are not familiar with any of these areas, be sure to ask questions. This is also a good time for new crew members to give the skipper an honest account of their sailing knowledge and experience, as well as a brief description of their special abilities (say, with electronics) and physical limitations (for example, partial deafness).

A note to skippers: As we mentioned a few pages ago, it is easy to overemphasize on-board routines to the point of spoiling everybody else's fun. While the good habits that we will describe are important (and in the case of lighting the stove, downright vital), the points will usually get across much more smoothly and effectively if they are made in a low-keyed, positive, yet decisive way. In situations like this, experts are always tempted to show off by over-emphasizing dangers, but an encouraging welcome does not have to include a declaration that the boat will immediately sink if a guest does not flush the heads properly. Some of these routines can be established very easily and quickly by setting an example or with an offhand comment—for example, 'You can put your seabag over there on that bunk.' Others may require an item-by-item demonstration or—if the directions (such as those for flushing the heads) are especially important or complicated—written instructions.

Where to Stow Your Personal Gear

As soon as you go below after coming aboard, securely stow your clothing and other personal gear. By securely I do not mean in a safe (presumably, theft is not a worry), but rather in a place where, when the boat heels and pitches, your stuff will not spill out all over everybody else's gear and common territory like the cabin sole (floor). There is so little room in a boat that sailors must follow the advice that 'Good fences make good neighbours.' Relations in such tight quarters, at best the size of a small kitchen or large cupboard, must be governed by an unwritten constitution, the first and most important clause of which is, 'I'll take care of mine if you'll take care of yours.' The second clause is, 'Then we'll both take care of ours.'

Presumably, you have brought your goods in a collapsible sea-bag, duffle bag, or open tote bag. If you are aboard just for a day's sail, you may find that a bunk (also called a berth) has been set aside for it and the bags of other crew members. The bunk should have built-in or cloth restraints called bunkboards or leecloths to keep seabags and, at night, sleepers from rolling out when the boat heels. There are several different types of bunks. Quarter berths are tunnels set into the boat's back part (or quarter) on either side of the cockpit or the engine compartment, whose walls provide a restraint. In the main part of the cabin, a pilot berth is high up on the side, above the cabin seats, which can be converted at night to make settee berths. (The pilot berth apparently derived its name from the fact that professional pilots, who helped navigate ships into port, needed an out-of-the-way bunk for taking naps.) In the forward cabin, there may be a V-berth, which is a V-shaped combination of two bunks jointed at their feet.

This sketch of the interior of a Beneteau cruiser-racer shows a
typical cabin arrangement. In the foreground to port is the galley.
The gimballed (self-levelling) stove has an oven, fiddles to hold
pots, and a strong restraining bar to keep the cook off the burners.
The icebox — its lid has a finger hole — is under the bowl. The
deep single sink has two taps: one operated by the foot pump for
salt water, the other operated by a pressure system for fresh. Note
the high fiddles around the counter, and the corner hole that
facilitates cleaning. In the foreground to starboard is the chart
table. The circular handhold in the dwarf bulkhead and the two
grabrails suspended from the deckhead provide support for people
walking fore and aft. The two vertical pillars in the foreground
support the deck, and the mast is visible beyond the table. The
main cabin table is gimballed so the leaves (which fold down to
provide walking space) remain horizontal when the boat heels. On
either side are settees that can easily be converted to single berths,
and whose backrests cover lockers for clothes and gear. Behind the
port settee is a pilot berth; behind the starboard one are more
lockers. Long windows and a skylight let in plenty of light. Beyond
the far bulkhead are the enclosed heads and a hanging locker, and
beyond them is the forward cabin with V-berths over lockers.

Before a short sail, the whole crew usually put their bags in a free bunk. But if you are staying on board overnight, the skipper should either assign you a bunk or simply tell you to choose one for yourself, most likely making it clear which is his or her own berth. Unless you brought your own bedroll, you will be given a sleeping bag or sheets and a blanket. If there is a shortage of lockers for stowing clothes, you may be asked to 'live out of your seabag,' which means that you will keep your full seabag in your bunk (it can be a good pillow). Otherwise, you will be assigned a locker—a small cabinet with a locking door, usually built into the side of a bunk.

You can store your gear in a locker in one of two ways. The most thorough is to unload your clothes and then carefully stack them in the locker. It is a good idea to first cover the bottom of the locker with the empty seabag or a plastic bin liner, just in case water seeps up from the bilge when the boat heels. This is a problem common to modern boats with very shallow bilges; there is nowhere else for the water to go except into your underwear. The simpler way to pack the locker is simply to squeeze the full bag into it, leaving the zip open on top for ready access. Either way, put clothes that you anticipate needing first near the top, and bunch types of clothes together—say, socks in the righthand corner and sweaters in the left. Some night you may find yourself dressing hurriedly in the dark, and you will not have much time to search for the clothes you want.

Foul-weather gear and seaboots should be left in the hanging locker, with your name or initials clearly visible so nobody else takes your gear. On larger boats, there is usually a special hanging locker called a wet locker reserved solely for foul-weather gear, so that semi-formal and shore clothes can be hung in their own, dry space. If there is only one hanging locker, protect your good clothes with clothing bags or large bin liners.

Toilet kits belong in the heads, or toilet compartments, so that all moist objects are isolated in one place. A decent toilet compartment has several shelves or hooks for these little bags and your towel. Clearly mark your stuff on the outside using an indelible marking pen.

The Biggest Stowage Problem, and How to Solve It
Theft should not be a problem, since you presumably can turn your back on your shipmates (and since you probably did not bring many valuables along anyway). But do not trust the boat with your valuables any farther than you can carry her; just about every small, slippery object you bring aboard is a prime candidate to slide into some inaccessible corner of the bilge.

Some people have problems keeping money where they put it, so they secrete their wallet or small purse deep in the toe of a shore shoe at the far end of the locker or seabag. As for loose change, my friend Harvey Loomis suggests putting coins in a match box secured to the wallet or purse with a rubber band. Eyeglasses can also be a problem, since they will bounce off a shelf. You can hang them by the string used to hold them on your head over the reading light in your bunk. Better yet, put them in a case between the bunk mattress and the side of the boat or in the toe of a hard leather shoe.

Although money and eyeglasses have been the source of many woes over the years, my own big stowage hassle on a sailing boat involves another slippery valuable, keys. They can disappear (and have disappeared) as soon as I take my eyes off them. I cannot sleep if I do not know where they are. You would think that sticking them into a corner of the seabag would be sufficient, but keys (at least *my* keys) simply will not stay in one place until they have settled to a rusty grave in the bilge. My most wrenching experience with boats and keys involved an antique Mercedes that I once borrowed. The Mercedes was in Los Angeles, the boat on which its keys were last seen was in San Francisco, and I did not discover the loss until I had reached my home in Connecticut. The scenario was not pieced together until after I made frantic phone calls to people all up and down the West Coast. The seventh call was to the owner of the boat, who was happy to finally learn who owned those keys he had found while cleaning out the bilge.

Here is my solution to the great key problem: on one of the seabag's handles I keep a fairly large stainless steel screw shackle— the kind you must turn to open and close. After locking my car at the marina or yacht club where I meet the boat for the day's sail, I tightly shackle my key ring to the seabag's handle. There it hangs in rattling security ready for me to inspect at any time of day or night. To lose the keys I must lose the seabag, and while I have known wallets, foul-weather gear, boots, books, clothes, toothbrushes, and, of course, keys disappearing in boats, not once have I suffered the loss of a blue seabag the size of a large dog.

Getting Acquainted with the Heads and Galley

A cruising boat has many of the amenities of a house—a kitchen (called a galley), a bathroom (called the heads), and so on—but you cannot take them for granted the way you do the fixtures in your own home. In many ways, to live aboard a boat requires much the same attention to mechanics, resources, and details needed to live on a farm in the days before electricity and running water. Not only must the cruising sailor adjust to limited supplies of power; he or she must contend with an inhospitable environment and be extremely conscientious about safety.

The toilet compartment is a marine bathroom, containing the heads and, usually, a small washbasin. In some countries, such as the United States of America, antipollution laws require that the heads either discharges into a holding tank (which can be pumped out in a boatyard or marina) or through a small treatment system. Similar regulations apply on most inland waterways, and boats which normally use these are generally fitted with chemical toilets which can be emptied at prescribed places.

In British waters, seagoing yachts have heads which discharge directly into the sea. This type of marine toilet is potentially dangerous because with improper use seawater may flow in through the system, flooding and possibly sinking the boat. They also require regular maintenance and cleaning. If the heads are not used properly there is a real risk of a complete blockage (which usually occurs at the most inconvenient moment, in the middle of a cruise with a full complement on board), requiring the valves, pump and pipes to be taken apart and cleaned by hand—not the sort of chore that most of us relish on or off the water.

So before you use the heads, make sure the skipper has told and showed you how to operate it. In particular, know: (1) how to turn on and off the seacock that closes the water intake valve at the through-hull fitting, where the pipe passes through the boat's skin; (2) what objects may and may not be flushed (sanitary towels, human hair, matches, and cigarettes are normally outlawed); and (3) how many times to pump the manual flush handle up and down (usually twenty or more swings are needed to clear the pipes completely). Find out, too, how to operate the ventilation system—a simple cowl vent or an electric fan—and where the scrub brush, sponge, and cleanser are located so that you can clean up after yourself.

Washbasins and showers use fresh water from the boat's own tanks. The total water capacity varies from boat to boat, and so does the water demand. Since we need only about half a gallon a day, usually there is a large safety factor, but you never know for certain how long it will be before you have a chance to top up the tanks again. If there is a shower, ask how it works and how often you may use it. No matter how liberal the policy is, you will not be allowed to take as many showers as you may be used to, so master the art of taking a sponge bath and learn how to live with a sticky body. When taking a shower, keep the water running only to wet yourself down and rinse off. Long hair may have to be washed on deck in sea water and then rinsed below in fresh (be sure to clean hair out of the drain). Do not despair: you will eventually stop at marinas and harbours, where real showers are usually available for a small charge.

The galley is the boat's kitchen. It has a sink, a stove, possibly a refrigerator, and storage cabinets. Despite its compact size it works much like your home kitchen. The sink may be dual, with two deep recesses for washing and rinsing. There may also be two water taps. One leads from the fresh-water system and so should be used sparingly. The other leads from the sea. As long as it is not polluted, sea water serves perfectly well when steaming vegetables or washing hands and dishes (do the final rinse in the ship's water). As in the heads, these water intakes can malfunction; they should be closed off with seacocks when the crew goes ashore.

The galley stove can be the most temperamental piece of equipment on board—and the most dangerous. In the chapter on the galley we will have a lot to say about stoves and how to light them without starting a fire or blowing the boat up. Do not even think about trying to use the stove until you are told *exactly* what to do.

While showing you the stove, the skipper should point out the fire extinguishers, the number and type of which depend on the size of the boat. Do not assume from looking at it that you know how to turn on and aim the extinguisher. Take it down from its mounting and read the directions. Check the pressure gauge; if it reads low or empty, tell the skipper so that the extinguisher can be recharged before the cruise begins.

Housekeeping Goals and Hints

The boat's housekeeping routines will be governed largely by common sense, but a good skipper will probably assign certain jobs in order to minimize chances of misunderstandings and hurt feelings. Typically, chores that require specialized skills and experience should be left to people who know them and the boat well; cooking and stowing food are two of these. But simple jobs like washing dishes, wiping puddles off the cabin sole, swabbing the deck, dumping garbage, and cleaning the heads should be shared by everybody, much as they would be in a well-run home.

The skipper's style of command will determine how this work is accomplished. Some people prefer to post assignments and job rotations, perhaps after consulting with guests. While that tactic may strike some as unduly regimented, it has the advantage of forthrightness and clarity. Other skippers choose a loose formal arrangement and make verbal assignments.

The third, most usual, and most counterproductive way to get chores done is to wait for volunteers. In the short run it may be the easiest way (since most of us do not like bossing our friends or being bossed by them), yet overall it is less effective than making direct assignments. For a variety of reasons, the same people always seem to volunteer for the grubby jobs, at first cheerfully, later fatalistically, and finally resentfully. They soon begin to feel like martyrs, while those who do not volunteer (for whatever reason) become typecast as shirkers. Hard feelings result and, if the cruise is long enough, may eventually surface in passive resistance and arguments touching about everything except the real matter at hand, which is who is going to do the dishes or clean out the heads. A skipper who does not enjoy giving orders should, if at all possible, be tactfully pinned down on crew assignments before his laid-back style creates an anything but laid-back atmosphere. If you encourage a little decisiveness, you will, at worst, be subject to that old criticism reserved for reformers: 'You did the right thing but in the wrong way'. Yet before the day is up you will probably find your efforts somehow rewarded. At the least, you may not get stuck with the dirty dishes at every meal.

Four Housekeeping Hints

1. Keep your mess to yourself. (You've heard that before, haven't you?) There is so little storage space in the typical cruising boat that you must live as compactly and self-sufficiently as possible. 'Living out of your bag' is the rule of thumb. For weekend and longer cruises, I always take along the largest seabag I own, leaving extra room inside so I can stuff clothes in loosely. For books, games, a bottle of rum, and various loose items, and also for quick stuffing of clothes that I find lying around, I also take along an all-purpose canvas tote bag, 8 by 17 by 16 inches (200 × 430 × 400 mm). (When I was a kid, tote bags were called 'ice bags' because they were used to lug ice from the shore to the boat.) And I also carry one or two large, heavy-duty plastic bin liners for dirty and wet clothes.

Your shipmates are no more keen to live with your socks and underwear than you are to live with theirs, so try to keep track of your own clothes in your own area. Leave the tote bag in your bunk behind a restraint with its mouth toward the side of the hull so when the boat heels your stuff does not pour out. When you find some of your gear loose, just stick it into the bag. Most bunks are long enough, and most sailors short enough, that the seabag and tote bag can be stuck down at the end of the berth at your feet when you are sleeping. One of my sometime shipmates decisively reminds people of their wandering clothes and shoes by hiding them either in the bilge or in the forepeak, with the anchor. A long search for the last pair of socks should remind a careless sailor to keep them properly stowed.

If your clothes get dirty or damp, store them in a plastic bag that you bring or, if there is one, in your seabag's waterproof compartment. If your clothes get soaking wet (at least your socks eventually will), instead of draping them around the cabin, rinse any salt water out and either leave them to dry with clothes pegs on the lifelines on deck or hang them over the door handle of the warm oven. Remember where you have stowed wet clothes; if left too long they will mildew and rot.

2. Never leave an object unrestrained on a flat, high surface. Unlike houses, boats roll, pitch, and heel—and with amazing quickness and force even when lying at anchor. Somebody who was once caught in a storm reported later that even cartons of cheese were potentially harmful as they flew around the cabin. Never put anything down unless you are sure of its stability. Be especially alert about cups of liquids, heavy tools, knives, and glass bottles (glass does not belong in a boat unless it surrounds alcoholic beverages).

Set objects as low as possible, nearest the boat's centre of gravity. The safest, most secure place to put items that you are about to use is the bottom of the galley sink. Experienced sea cooks will put cups into the sink before pouring coffee or hot water into them. If the sink is crowded, either hold onto the object or place it low in the boat. Tool drawers should be low in order to minimize the force of their trajectory should they get loose; knives must be stowed carefully so they cannot fly loose.

3. Offer to help, but never get in the way. You may not be the most qualified person available to deal with the stove's eccentricities, and somebody else may know where the food is hidden in the many lockers. In any case, as a quick glance at the galley will indicate, there is probably only room for one person, so do not feel offended if the cook turns down your offer to help. Perhaps you can scrape vegetables on deck or—most helpful of all—wash dishes when the meal is finished. But do not put them away until told where they belong.

4. Keep an eye out for the vessel's cleanliness and welfare. The ancient seaman's rule 'one hand for yourself, one hand for the ship' applies here: look out for the boat, your shipmates, and yourself with equal attentiveness. This of course means keeping track of your clothes and gear, but it also means that you leave the heads as clean as possible, conserve water and cooking fuel, wash any dishes that you use between meals, shut locker doors before the goods inside pour all over the cabin sole, do not use the last dollop of strawberry jam. In general, be attentive to your shipmates' standards and needs. This rule especially applies to smokers, who, even more than on land, must be especially alert to the fallout of their habit. They should keep track of the mounds of ash that form on deck, particularly along the drain ridges in the cockpit seats. And they should not automatically assume that they may smoke any-where they please. The responsible skipper of a boat with a petrol engine may set severe limits on smoking, but so may somebody who just does not like inhaling another person's exhaust in a cabin on a hot, windless day.

Besides these four rules, the courtesies of common decency will warn people away from obnoxious behaviour such as interminable whistling or humming, irritatingly idle and endless chatter, repeti-tions of the same crude ethnic joke, and other rudeness that you would not tolerate in your own home.

How the Sail-Handling Gear Is Laid Out

You can always spot a seasoned sailor as the person who, after stowing personal gear below, takes a thoughtful bow-to-stern tour (either alone or escorted by the skipper), and, without being asked, helps get the sheets and sails ready for sailing. More often than not, the novices lounge around in the cockpit drinking beer, totally oblivious to the boat and the work that is going on around them. Even if you are not an expert, you might be able to fool everybody else and win a modicum of respect by finding out as much as you can as soon as you can about how the boat is worked—how the sail-handling and anchor gear is organized, where the emergency equip-ment is located, and which crew members are responsible for what jobs.

Do not assume that you will only handle gear in the aft (rear) part of the boat, in the cockpit. You may well be asked to go forward on deck to raise or lower a sail or the anchor. So walk to the bow and work your way aft, taking mental note of where lines are led and cleats and winches are located. As you orient yourself to the rigging, inspect it for looseness or fractures. If something looks loose or frayed, tell the skipper and permanent crew, who may be so familiar with the boat that they do not make a careful inspection as often as they should. If you are confused about anything, ask the

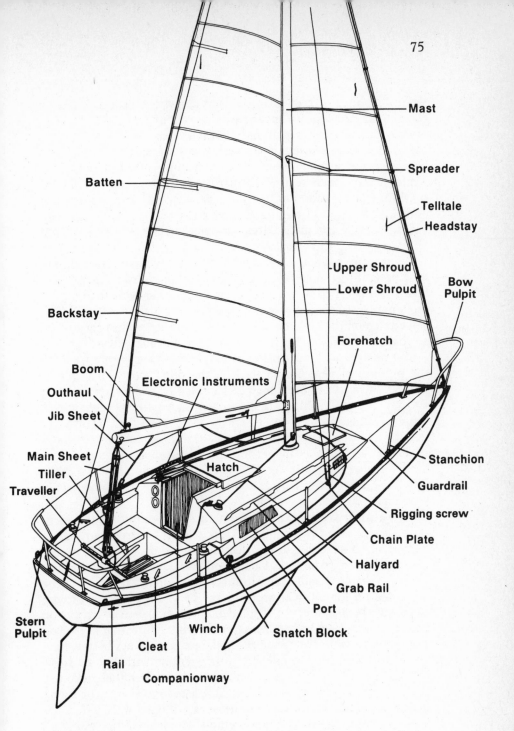

Mast

Spreader

Telltale

Headstay

Upper Shroud

Lower Shroud

Bow Pulpit

Batten

Forehatch

Backstay

Boom

Electronic Instruments

Outhaul

Jib Sheet

Main Sheet

Tiller

Traveller

Hatch

Stanchion

Guardrail

Rigging screw

Chain Plate

Halyard

Grab Rail

Port

Stern Pulpit

Winch

Snatch Block

Cleat

Rail

Companionway

The deck layout of a typical cruiser-racer sloop. Variations include a steering wheel, tracks on deck for the jib sheet leads, halyard winches on or near the mast, and a forestay groove for the jib luff in place of hanks.

skipper or another crew member who knows the boat well. He or she should be happy to answer your questions.

In general appearance and position, fixed and moving gear varies little from cruising boat to cruising boat, and certain conventions are universally observed. For example, the main halyard almost always leads to the starboard side of the mast and the jib halyards (one or more) to the port side. What do vary are the size and exact location of rigging. Larger boats have bigger masts, halyards, sheets, and winches. Item by item, this is probably what you will see as your tour the deck:

The bow pulpit is a stainless steel, cagelike structure on the very bow. It restrains anybody working up there from falling overboard and is especially helpful in rough weather while hauling up (hoisting) and handing (lowering) jibs—the big forward sails. You can crouch on the bow, bracing your leg and hip against the pulpit, so your two hands are free to work with the sail and halyard. Or you can sit on deck with your back against the windward (uphill) side of the pulpit and your feet braced on the other side. The ends of unused halyards or sheets may be shackled or tied to rope or steel eyes on the pulpit so they are visible and easy to find at night and in rough weather. While you are on the bow, push hard against the pulpit's top rail. If the vertical supports, called stanchions, are loose in their bases, ask the skipper for a screwdriver so you can tighten the set screws, that is if the fittings are not through-bolted as they should be. Aft on the stern is another pulpit to which some people have given the ungainly name *pushpit*.

The guardrails run aft from the bow pulpit to the stern pulpit, completely enclosing the deck with two wire guardrails at heights of about one and two feet above the deck. These should restrain anybody who loses balance on deck, and they can also provide a reliable handhold. However, guardrails should not be depended on for ultimate security except in emergencies, as wire can always break. Never sit or stand on a guardrail, and do not clip on a safety harness— a body harness with a long lifeline that keeps you from falling overboard. (Snap the lifeline to the eye at the stanchion base). Guardrails are connected to the pulpits with line or small fittings that should be tight and taped over. Near the cockpit, a section of the guardrails may be detachable to form an open boarding gate; the pelican hooks there sometimes fall open unless they are tightened and taped. Like the pulpit stanchions, the guardrail stanchions must be securely anchored, with their boxes through-bolted to pad pieces under the deck.

On some boats, sail stops or ties (long lengths of webbing) are looped through the stanchion bases forward of the mast before getting under way; they are used to tie down the jib when it is handed (lowered) and lying on deck. Sometimes light line is also woven between the foredeck and the guardrails to make a net that restrains headsails from falling overboard. The line should be replaced when frayed, broken, or rotten.

The anchor may be stowed on deck in a small locker or special chocks, or it may simply be well secured to a small fitting. If not on deck, it may be below in a special locker or other container (such as a plastic laundry basket). In any case, the anchor rode (the combination of line and chain that keeps it connected to the boat when it is on the bottom) should already be secured to the anchor with a sturdy shackle. While you are looking at the anchor check that the shackle pin is securely moused (locked in place) with wire so that it cannot come undone. The rope should be coiled in large loops, preferably with lashings (tape or rode ties) to keep the coil from falling apart. Its inboard (bitter) end should be secured to the boat's structure by a stout lashing, which can be cut in emergency.

The forehatch, giving access to the forward cabin, has two or more latches whose operation you should understand. Some hatches can be unlocked and opened only from below, in the cabin, but others have top- and bottom-operating latches. If it has a good rubber gasket seal to keep water from dripping below, the hatch will lock only when you push or pull down hard on it. Make sure you know the difference between partly and wholly closed; a slightly open hatch will take in water and its lip may snag a flying jib sheet.

The standing rigging includes the mast, boom, shrouds and stays that support the mast. Shrouds hold the mast sideways (athwartships) and stays fore-and-aft. Both are made of very low-stretch extruded stainless steel rod or stiff stainless steel 1×19 wire—one strand with nineteen individual wires. Rigging screws or turnbuckles at the bottom of the forestay and shrouds, on deck, can be adjusted to lengthen or shorten them in order to keep the mast straight or bend it to improve sail shape. Look closely at the rigging screws to check for cotter pins that keep the barrels from unwinding and from disconnecting. Two or three layers of tape should cover the cotter pins so that they cannot rip sails or ankles. A hydraulic adjuster may replace a rigging screw on the backstay, which runs from the top of the mast back to the stern. Also inspect the gooseneck, the large fitting that connects the boom and the mast. Sometimes the pin or bolt that is the main component comes loose or undone.

The halyards, on the mast, pull and hold the sails up. With the sheets, they are the main type of *running rigging*. To cut down on windage, the halyards may run down through the mast, out through holes near the bottom, to geared winches. The typical cruising boat has only three halyards—main, jib, and spinnaker. To speed up sail changes as the wind increases or decreases, many cruiser-racers (cruising boats that may race) are equipped with three combination jib and spinnaker halyards, and the main halyard.

So that sails keep their designed shape, most halyards are made of low-stretch, flexible stainless or galvanized steel 7 × 19 wire rope, which has seven large strands each consisting of nineteen small wires. Wire is hard on hands, so polyester rope is spliced into the wire as halyard tails (ends). Lightweight, low-stretch rope fibres such as Kevlar have come into use in place of wire halyards in an increasing number of racing boats and may soon be standard on cruising boats, too. Kevlar looks like white polyester rope with a yellow or orange fleck, and although it is extremely strong and has very litle stretch it is not very resistant to chafe.

Obviously, it is important to be able to identify and keep track of all these wires running aloft so that you do not tangle them up. Once the halyards are twisted aloft, they will saw away on each other (eventually leading to a break) or jam in the sheave (pulley) at the top of the mast so that they cannot be lowered or raised. Halyards should be colour-coded using plastic tape in the traditional sequence of green for starboard, red for port. The bitter end (very end) of each halyard must be secured in some way or it will accidentally get pulled up and lost inside the mast. Many sailors tie it to a fitting on the base of the mast, such as a cleat or padeye. The only problem is that the bitter end does not rotate as the rest of the halyard twists under torque. Eventually the halyard will develop kinks. By untying the bitter end, you can allow the rope to spin the kinks out. Better yet, instead of securing the end, tie a knot in it. The figure of eight knot is fairly easy to tie but may come loose if it is allowed to flog about; the simple overhand knot is more permanent. Whichever knot you use, tie it several inches in from the bitter end so that if it slips it will not open up.

The halyards should be marked against a reference point with an indelible marker, a piece of tape, or a length of light wire to show when they are fully hoisted. Otherwise, an over-eager crew may pull the shackle into the sheave at the top of the mast and jam it there.

Shackles are small, metal linking devices. The quick-opening ones used on halyards and sheets are called snap shackles; short trip lines make it easier to open the spring-loaded pins. Slower-working but more secure fittings are called screw shackles; they should be tightened more than hand-taut using pliers or a spike.

Blocks are pulleys, either fixed (permanently closed) or snatch (quickly opened). If a sheave sticks, give it a squirt of oil.

Cleats secure halyards, sheets, and other lines. The best are horn cleats—simple metal or wooden bars around which the line is wrapped once, followed by a loop over the top and a locking jam loop. Quick-action cleats, rigged where lines must be freed in a hurry, are the Clamcleat (an open tube with ridges that grip the line) and the cam cleat (with geared locking arms). Of more recent origin are a variety of halyard clutches and stoppers which are lever-operated and can be used for a number of applications in place of conventional cleats.

Winches are geared drums used to pull heavy loads, such as the last few feet of a halyard or sheet. While one person tails (pulls on the line) the other grinds (turns) the winch handle, spinning the

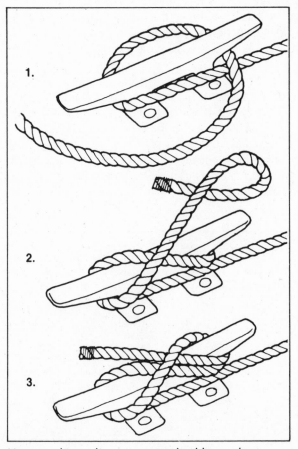

How to cleat a line on a standard horn cleat.

drum. A special type called a self-tailing winch has a built-in cleat on top, eliminating the need for a tailer.

Winch handles are all too often forgotten until they are needed to grind in a halyard or sheet. At least one winch handle must be left near the halyard winches, and at least two should be aft in the cockpit near the sheet winches. They should be stowed in special slots or fabric sacks, into which the halyard tails may also be shoved when the sail is hoisted. You can also put the handles in the cowls (scoops) of ventilators when they are not being used. There are two types of winch handles: lock-in and non-lock-in. A small metal tab on lock-in handles automatically snaps into a recess in the winch when the handle is inserted, and unless you activate a lever the handle will not come out. This provides a great safety advantage over a non-lock-in handle; if a handle slips out while you are turning it, it may well whack you in the face, body, or wrist—and winch handles are both heavy and sharp. If any winch is located in such a way that the handle is likely to fall or slip out, there should be at least one lock-in handle nearby. Care is needed with the type of self-stowing wire halyard winch which incorporates a brake on the drum.

The sheets are, with the halyards, the main part of the running rigging. Almost all boats use polyester rope sheets to pull their sails in and out, although low-stretch Kevlar is becoming increasingly popular. (By the way, *rope* is the stuff on drums before it is cut up and made into *lines* like halyards and sheets). The jib sheets lead from the clew (back corner) of the jib aft through blocks on deck and to winches and cleats. On most cruising boats, the jib sheets are secured to the clew with a bowline, which is both secure and rela-

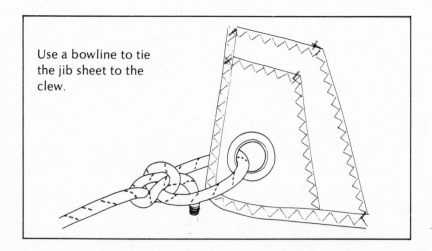

Use a bowline to tie the jib sheet to the clew.

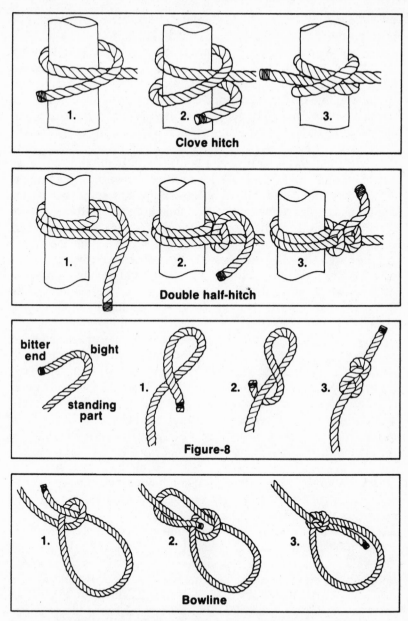

How to tie four essential knots. The bowline is the best knot for making loops; the figure-of-eight keeps line from running out through a block; the clove hitch secures a mooring warp to a post, or a fender line to a guardrail; and the double half-hitch (tied here with an extra turn to absorb some of the load) makes a loop when a line is under load. Leave a long tail on each knot.

tively hard to shake loose. When tying the bowline, make the loop through the clew small and leave about 4 inches in the tail, since there may be some slippage before the knot tightens up under load.

The jib sheet deck blocks (called leads) can usually be adjusted fore and aft on a track. Each jib has a proper lead for every wind condition. The correct leads should be marked on deck with a piece of tape or an indelible pen, or written down somewhere (for example, 'Large genoa jib lead—seven track holes showing forward of block').

The main sheet controls the main boom, while the spinnaker sheets control the spinnaker and are attached with snap shackles. The other, bitter ends of all sheets except the spinnaker sheets should have a figure of eight or overhand knot tied in to keep them from running out of the blocks when they are slack. (In an emergency, you may have to let the spinnaker sheets out all the way).

The sail-shaping controls are lines other than the sheets and halyards that affect the shape of the mainsail and jib. One is the outhaul, which tensions the foot (bottom edge) of the mainsail. The outhaul is eased in light wind to make the sail more full, or baggy, and trimmed (tightened) in fresh wind to make it more flat. Another control is the cunningham, which tensions the luff (forward edge) of the mainsail and jib. It too is eased in light wind and trimmed in fresh wind, not to increase or decrease the sail's draft (or fullness) but to move the point of deepest draft aft (when it is eased) and forward (when it is trimmed). The boom vang is the third of these controls—a tackle or hydraulic adjuster that keeps the boom from rising.

Also on the boom is a set of reefing lines used to decrease the mainsail's area in fresh wind. The reefing lines are often led forward from the end of the boom and down to winches and cleats on deck; sometimes there may be cam cleats called jammers to secure the lines after they have been tensioned, thus freeing the winch for other duty. Another important sail control is the mainsail traveller, a car under the mainsheet blocks that slides athwartships (from side to side). Sailing upwind (about forty degrees to the wind) in light air, the car is adjusted so that the boom is over the centre of the boat. As the wind increases the car is let down to leeward to decrease heeling (tipping). We will have much more to say about reefing lines, the traveller, and sail shaping in later chapters.

The mainsail has three or four plastic or wooden battens that should be inspected when the sail is unfurled (unfolded) from the boom before hoisting. If they are missing, the sail will have a terrible shape; if broken, the sail may rip.

The helm is the last stop on the deck familiarization tour.

Learn how the tiller or steering wheel works and where the helmsman sits. (If you show an interest in steering, you will probably get a chance to do it).

The instruments include the compass, speedometer, wind direction indicator, and other performance-related devices on deck as well as radios and electronic navigation devices below. Most have digital read-outs; some may be interfaced with each other by computer.

The sail and gear lockers may be on deck or below. They are bins and lockers where sails, sail-handling gear, and tools are kept. Sheets, blocks, and other removable items are often stowed below in the locked cabin when nobody is on board; the crew will have to take them on deck and rig them. Since particular gear probably fits and works best in particular places, a newcomer should ask a crew member who knows the boat well for advice on what to rig and where to rig it. All on board should know where to find spare line and blocks, a can of oil, a roll of tape, and basic tools, especially pliers, a wrench, and a screwdriver.

How to Work the Emergency Equipment

By emergency equipment we mean any gear that will help you get out of potential disaster: the engine, the bilge pump, the anchor, man-overboard equipment, safety harness, life jackets, the life raft, flares, and fire extinguishers. While the engine and anchor mainly serve non-emergency functions, you will someday have an emergency if you must quickly start the engine or drop the anchor in order to avoid running aground and you do not know what to do. Unlike sail-handling gear, this equipment is arranged differently on every boat, and sometimes it may require special handling.

Although a newcomer might find out about this equipment on his or her own, the best way is to have the skipper explain it during a briefing both in the cockpit and down below. The skipper should take each piece of gear in hand and demonstrate how it works—starting the engine, pumping the bilge, simulating working the flares, and so on. He or she should show where safety harnesses and life jackets are stowed and how to put them on. This is the best time, too, to explain emergency procedures, for example, how to pick up somebody who has fallen overboard (described later in Chapter 17).

It is important that everybody come out of the meeting not only with a familiarity with the boat but also with a sense of community and mutual trust. The briefing should be presented with authority but without intimidation; much of this equipment, after all, may

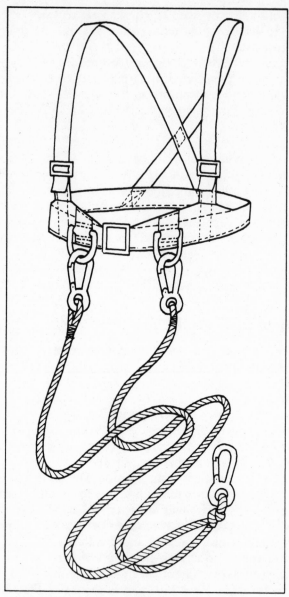

A safety harness provides that 'one hand for yourself' that is so important when working on deck (or just sitting in the cockpit) in rough weather. Hook the lifeline to a secure deck fitting — not the guardrails, stanchions or shrouds — as far to windward (or uphill) as possible, and keep it as short as you can.

never be used. Crew members must be allowed to feel that they can ask any question, no matter how naive it may seem. One of the worst sailing disasters in recent years—a sinking that led to the deaths of three sailors—was probably due partly to an unwillingness on the part of the skipper and the first mate to accept their ship-mates as partners and to respond seriously to their questions about emergency procedures.

Who Does What

Crew assignments should be discussed during the same briefing. The complexity and seriousness of the table of organisation depend on the length of the trip. For a short day-sail, all the skipper need do is offhandedly but publicly appoint a second in command ('Bill's in charge if I'm taking a nap'). On the other hand, a cruise should be preceded by some careful planning of navigating, cooking, and cleaning duties, with primary responsibilities being clearly assigned. Of course, this does not mean that others cannot use the chart table or galley (if they have been briefed about safety problems); it is only a way of clarifying what could turn into a frustratingly unclear situation.

Special skills, interests, and aptitudes can be identified and matched with the many jobs that have to be done. The computer and maths wizard will probably learn navigating more quickly than the poet, the one claustrophobic person on board may not be the best nominee for cook, and a strong, agile college kid might be a better candidate for work on a pitching, heaving foredeck than an awkward sixty-year-old. At the same time, all should remember that this is *fun*—not survival training or warfare—and that all should be given a chance to try out whatever they feel like doing, so long as the boat's welfare is not endangered.

This is the time, too, for some straight talk about routines on deck. If the skipper has strong opinions about some aspect of safety—for example, that all children should wear life jackets, that nobody should sit on guardrails, or that helmsmen should avoid alcoholic beverages—they should be voiced now, firmly but encouragingly. If you are not sure what is expected, ask.

Watch Bills
For overnight sailing—one of the most enjoyable ways to go out in a boat—watches should be assigned and scheduled and watch bills written out and posted. At all times there must be one experienced helmsman on deck and preferably two, since few people can steer well for more than a couple of hours. Besides steering, other con-

cerns are sail-handling competence and keeping a good look-out.
There must be enough people on deck to handle normal chores like
trimming, tacking, and gybing, although somebody from an off-
watch may be called to help reef or change sails. The leader of each
watch is the *mate of the watch* or *watch leader*.

Watch schedules take a variety of forms. The major consideration is allowing those off-watch sufficient time to fall into a deep
sleep (at least 3 hours) while not leaving those on-watch out on deck
so long that *they* go to sleep (no longer than 6 hours in good
weather, but 5 hours in extremely rough, cold, or hot weather).

Using a six-person crew as an example, here are five ways to
organize the watches.

> Two three-person watches, each on for 4 hours. Once a day,
> the watches run only 2 hours usually between 1600 and 2000,
> (the so called 'dog watches') so that the schedule reverses
> every day. The same watch does not stand the murky 'middle
> watch' from midnight to 0400 every day. (Advantage:
> simplicity.)

> Two three-person watches standing 3-hour watches between
> 2000 and 0800, and 4-hour watches between 0800 and 2000.
> (Advantages: short night watches when people lose their alert-
> ness quickly; routine changes daily.)

> Three two-person watches each on for 2 or 3 hours, giving
> those off-watch 4 to 6 hours of sleep. (Advantages: long sleep
> periods and a short time on deck; routine changes daily.)

> Two three-person watches standing 4-hour watches between
> 2000 and 0800, and 6-hour watches between 0800 and 2000,
> with a dog watch once a day. (Advantage: allows one long rest
> period daily.)

> The so-called Swedish system. Two three-person watches on a
> 5-4-4-5-6 schedule: 1900-2400, 2400-0400, 0400-0800,
> 0800-1300, and 1300-1900. (Advantages: variety; short
> watches after midnight, when people are sleepiest; routine
> changes daily.)

An interesting twist on all of the systems mentioned above is to
change half the personnel half-way through the watch and the other
half at the end of the watch. This has two advantages: first, variety of
companionship; and second, less congestion below and in compan-
ionways since fewer people are moving about, changing clothes, and
so on. Sheila McCurdy introduced this system aboard *Wissahickon*

when she (as skipper), her brother Ian, Harvey Loomis, and I sailed to the Azores in June 1985, and it worked extremely well.

On some boats, the cook and navigator stand watches, but if they are especially busy they will need all the sleep they can get, so should be counted on only for back-up calls.

Having used each of these five watch schedules, I have found none to be perfect all the time in all conditions and situations. For a relatively short overnight sail, the first three work best. For voyages running two or three nights or longer, the last two allow both extended time for reading and privacy and a lengthy period for catching up on the sleep that is always lost during the first day of adapting to a new environment. Try them all, or create your own system.

When I began sailing, I quickly noticed that the shipmates who had the most fun as well as the greatest responsibility were the ones who immediately familiarized themselves with the boat and her gear when they first came aboard and who were never afraid to ask questions. This chapter has been about that familiarization tour; the next one is about some of those questions.

CHAPTER 6

'Will This Thing Tip Over?' and Other Reasonable Questions to Ask about How Boats Work

S ailing a boat well is one of the most satisfying of all experiences because it harnesses both natural and man-made elements in a harmony and balance determined as much by the boat as by the way you handle her. The laws of buoyancy and gravity provide a per-formance envelope—a limit of possibilities—and within her built-in limitations every boat, whether a lightweight sailboard or a heavy cruising boat, can tip only so far, sail only so close to the wind, steer only so well, and sail only so fast.

Although many highly skilled sailors can no more explain sail-ing theory than they can the principles of meteorology, during years on the water they have developed an intuition for how boats work just as they have picked up a feel for weather. Taught that way, those lessons come slowly; new sailors do not enjoy the luxury of so much time. While the details of sailing theory are beyond the scope of this book, we can attempt some explanations in the form of answers to four reasonable and commonly asked questions about how boats work.

'Will This Thing Tip Over?'

At one time or another, everybody who steps aboard a boat of any size wonders if she is going to roll over and disappear beneath the surface, crew and all. For many people, that concern long outlives the initial, normal queasiness felt when a heeling boat violently changes tacks or blasts over a wave and drops off its crest, like a falling lift. All new sailors start out in fear of capsize; because they are never convinced of the boat's built-in relative stability, many never graduate from it. Depending on the boat involved, the answer to our opening question is either no or maybe. The 'no' boats (typical keel, monohull cruising sailing boats) are in function and appearance a long way from the 'maybe' ones (dinghies and multi-hulls), and the differences cover a lot more water than whether the boats can or cannot capsize easily.

Stability Through Ballast

Most of the force of the wind acting through the sails is to the side, at about a right angle to the sail's surface. The side force causes the sails and rig to tilt, pulling the hull over on its side, at an angle of heel. Stability is resistance to heeling and it is created by a combination of ballast and hull shape.

Ballast serves as a counterweight to those side forces. It consists of either a large quantity of lead or iron fixed in the keel and bilge, or the weight of the crew moving from side to side on deck, and often both. If the ballast balances out the side force, the boat's heel angle stops increasing; if it is greater than the side force, the heel angle may diminish and the boat may swing back upright. Think of a seesaw: heeling is like the effect of somebody sitting on one end; ballast is another person of the same weight who climbs on the other end.

Fixed ballast in a monohull (single-hull) sailing boat's keel and bilge puts a boat in the 'no capsize' category. Granted, she will heel fairly quickly—in fact there are few times when she will not be heeling—but that does not mean that she will tip over. The angle of heel will gradually stop increasing when it is approximately 25 degrees off the vertical, which is usually when water begins to lap at the leeward (downhill) rail. At that point the fixed ballast deep down in the keel begins to exert maximum leverage on the sails. At an heel angle of about 35 or 40 degrees, which usually is short of capsize, most keel boats will reach the point of ultimate stability. They simply will not heel much farther except in hurricane winds and forty-foot seas (which I assume you will try to avoid).

To be effective, fixed ballast must make up at least 35 per cent or more of the boat's total weight and have a centre of gravity low enough to work as an effective counterweight once the boat has heeled about 15 degrees. The heavier and lower it is, the better. Most cruising boats meet these requirements with ease and, while

they may at first seem tippy and bouncy, are sufficiently well ballasted to be stable even in very strong winds of forty knots and over,
assuming they are being handled with caution and skill.

As we will see in Chapter 16, limiting heel is not difficult. But
if she is being sailed very carelessly, a boat may reach a 30-degree
heel angle. With that much heel, an open boat with a large cockpit
may swamp (fill with water), yet her built-in buoyancy will still
keep her afloat. To keep water from accumulating dangerously on
keel cruising boats, the cockpits drain overboard automatically and
the interiors can be quickly sealed off with hatches and doors. At a
30-degree heel angle, water will come on deck but not pour into the
cabin unless the hatches are left wide open. However, if enough
water gets below to more than half fill the cabin, a keel cruising boat
may sink. Do not hold your breath, though; it takes an enormous
wave to accomplish that disaster.

Movable ballast, as the name suggests, is shifted to keep the

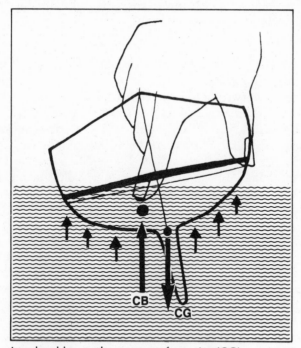

In a keel boat, the centre of gravity (CG),
influenced by the heavy lead or iron ballast in
the keel, acts like a lever around the centre of
buoyancy (CB), which is the locus of all forces
keeping the boat afloat. As long as the CG is to
windward of the CB, the boat will not capsize.

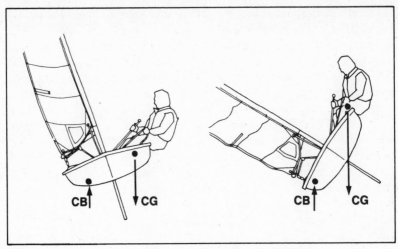

CB   CG   CB   CG

A boat without fixed ballast, like this centreboard dinghy, relies on the movable ballast of her crew to keep the centre of gravity to the right side of the centre of buoyancy.

boat upright. It is used as the primary stabilizing counterweight in light boats without keels—the 'might capsize' boats—and as the secondary counterweight in keel boats. Instead of sitting very low in the keel or bilge, the counterweight is set off to the side, on deck. Movable ballast is effective only when it is off to the windward side of the boat (the uphill side, toward the wind), and the farther it is to windward, the more effective it is. If the boat is allowed to heel more than about 20 degrees, however, the ballast swings up, its leverage against the sails is decreased, and she very quickly capsizes. In the nineteenth century, this counterweight sometimes consisted of sandbags shoved out to windward on boards. Today it is human weight. The heavier it is and the farther it gets away from the lee-ward (downhill) rail, the more heeling force it can resist. Boats with large sails require a greater counterweight than ones with small sails. One type of human movable ballast is the standing sailor leaning back against the pull of a sailboard's sail. Another is the crew in a more traditional boat 'sitting out' as they stretch their bodies over the windward side, their feet held by toe straps in the cockpit. A third—and the most efficient because it moves the weight farthest to windward—is the sailor suspended on a trapeze (a wire and harness hanging from the mast) with feet against the windward rail. Movable ballast is the major resistance to capsizing in the small centreboard boats called dinghies, which will stay upright while under sail in fresh winds only if the human ballast sits to windward.

On some racing dinghies the crew actually outweighs the boat herself, and the ballast they can heave out to windward allows them to carry a lot of sail area in fresh winds at correspondingly high speeds. If crew members move downhill to the leeward rail, the boat will flip right over on them. Even though their glass fibre hulls are heavier than water, dinghies and day-sailers with movable ballast will not sink after they capsize because they are kept afloat by tanks or buoyancy bags full of air, or foam built under their decks; most dinghies may even be quickly righted and sailed away as the water sluices out through automatic drain holes. Obviously, sailing an unstable dinghy is much more of an athletic event than plugging along in a non-capsizable keel boat.

Stability Through Hull Shape

Stability, or resistance to heeling, is affected by the shape of the hull as well as by the amount and location of ballast. Up to a point, the most stable boats are multihulls—triple-hulled trimarans and twin-hulled catamarans—most of which have no ballast at all.

The trimaran carries no fixed ballast, but because she is so big and heavy it would take an enormous crew to provide enough movable ballast to keep her upright. Her stability comes from a three-hulled (actually, one hull and two floats) configuration that may be twice as wide as the beam of a monohull the same length. When she sails, the leeward float acts as an anti-heeling device, its own positive buoyancy counteracting the side force of the sails, like a lever under a weight. When the heeling force exceeds the float's buoyancy, the effect is the same as if a crew hanging out on a trapeze to windward suddenly lets go: the boat quickly rolls over.

The catamaran is another unballasted multihull that is extremely stable up to a point, at which she capsizes abruptly. Length for length, she is less beamy than the trimaran but still considerably wider than a monohull. As she sails, the leeward hull depresses in the water but the weight of the windward hull and the crew sitting on it pulls down against the side, heeling force; the greater the distance between the two hulls, the greater the leverage the windward one has against heeling. The stability of small catamarans, like Hobie Cats, is even greater because their crews hang out on trapezes, allowing them to carry clouds of sail and go extremely fast. Small cats (catamarans) have been timed at over 25 knots, or 28.75 mph, and a large one has gone 35 knots, or 40.25 mph. (A knot is 1 nautical mile, or 1.15 statute miles, per hour. Just say 'knot.' 'Knots per hour' is like saying 'miles per hour per hour.').

The monohull's stability is also affected by her width. If a wide beam helps keep a catamaran upright, it will work for a single-hulled boat, too. Not surprisingly, then, relatively light ballasted keel boats and centreboard dinghies are wider for their length than heavily ballasted keel boats. The cross-sectional shape of the hull is important too. A boat's hull that is as wide near the water as it is on deck will resist the heeling force quite well until the wind is fresh. But if the beam near the water is very narrow, the boat will heel quickly even in light wind.

If stability were all that mattered, boats would be wide and boxy for light winds and have heavy keels to keep them upright in fresh winds. But boxy hulls also have more underwater surface area and make more water-resisting friction than narrow, slim ones. They are slow in light winds. The yacht designer is constantly struggling to find just the right balance between stability (for safety and good fresh-wind performance) and low wetted surface (for good light-wind performance).

The average, relatively beamy, keel cruising boat should not be allowed to heel more than about 25 degrees for two reasons: (1) an increase in heeling over that amount will make her slow and hard to steer; and (2) heeling causes the keel to tilt up, decreasing resistance to side forces under the water and allowing her to make leeway (slide sideways). For the same reasons plus a third—reducing the chances of capsizing—multihulls and centreboard dinghies should not heel more than about 15 degrees.

To bring any kind of boat back upright, you can decrease the heeling force by depowering the sails—a fancy way of saying, 'make them pull less.' The easiest way to depower is to ease the sheets way out and let the sails luff (flap), but you may also reduce the sail area by reefing the mainsail or shortening down (changing to a smaller jib). We will have a great deal more to say about depowering in Chapter 16.

An Example: Why the Winged Keel Worked
The famous 'winged keel' that helped *Australia II* win the 1983 American's Cup match is a perfect illustration of how relatively small changes in a boat's shape can have a large effect on performance. This curious appendage, a fairly small keel sprouting slightly drooping lead wings at its bottom, had these four advantages:

> The wings lowered the centre of gravity of the lead ballast, which increased the keel's leverage over the side forces on the sails and made *Australia II* more stable than her competitors. By heeling less, she sailed faster and made less leeway (side-slippage).

When *Australia II* eventually heeled and her keel tilted up, the leeward wing automatically dropped to near-vertical and added leeway-resisting area.

The wings reduced speed-robbing turbulence at the bottom of the keel.

With the ballast working more efficiently down low, the top part of the keel could be made smaller. This had the joint effect of decreasing friction and making the boat easier to turn sharply.

Leaving aside the controversy over the legality and national origins of the keel's design, *Australia II*'s winged appendage was a remarkable technical achievement. Like most innovations, it was a new solution to a very old problem, solidly based on basic principles that had been well known for many years. Yacht designers had been experimenting with keel shapes for more than a century—adding bulbs of lead on the bottom, changing shapes, reducing or increasing area—but apparently nobody had been able to put so many different pieces together as well as Australian yacht designer Ben Lexcen did in 1983.

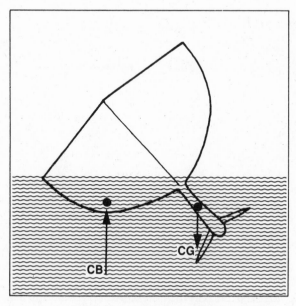

The drawing of this winged keel demonstrates how its weight lowers the centre of gravity.

Twelve-metres are not the only boats that can benefit from a more efficient keel. One of the challenges of cruising boat design is how to provide a keel that both performs well and is shallow enough for sailing in shoal-draft areas like the East Coast of England. For a long time that combination seemed unlikely, since deep keels have almost always provided more resistance to heeling and leeway than shallow ones. A handful of winged-keel cruising boats appeared within a few months of *Australia II*'s victory and perhaps they will prove to be successful. However, wings have been banned by many racing rules because of their expense.

'How Can a Boat Sail into the Wind?'

Square-riggers make perfect sense. Their sails are spread across the sky to catch wind from astern, and like hot air balloons, the sails slide through the air pulling everything attached along with them.

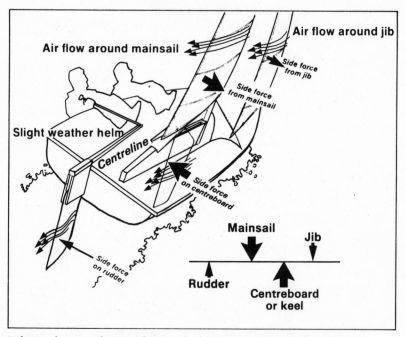

When a boat sails into the wind, the wind and sails combine to create a small forward force and large side forces, which cause heeling (counteracted by ballast) and leeway (counteracted by the centreboard or keel). All those forces combine like weights on a seesaw, and if the sails are trimmed properly and they are in balance over the hull, the tiller or wheel will be centred. In practice, however, it is best to carry slight weather helm.

Likewise, the triangular, fore-and-aft rigged sail works logically when it catches a stern wind. But when it actually pulls or pushes the boat across and even into the wind, the modern sail at first seems to defy reason.

A boat can sail at an angle between 90 and about 40 degrees to the wind because the sails and hull work in partnership to convert the contrary wind into forward thrust. First, the sail, which looks kind of like an aircraft wing, shapes the flow of the wind. Where a plain, flat board provides only abrupt resistance, a wing or sail smoothly redirects the wind to create two forces, one large and the other small. The larger of the two forces pushes sideways to leeward and the smaller one pushes forward.

Speed + Appendages = Low Leeway

If there were no hull and appendages (keel or centreboard and rudder) in the water, these two forces would combine to capsize the boat or, at best, push her like a leaf mainly to leeward and slightly forward. As sailors put it, she would make about 70 degrees of lee-way. For every mile she sailed ahead, she would slide sideways about 1⅛ mile, and the course-made-good (the effective rather than the steered course) would be distinctly crablike. However, with well-designed, aerofoil-shaped appendages resisting most of the side force, the boat would make only 3 to 15 degrees of leeway; her course-made-good would be very near the steered course. The amount of leeway depends on the type of boat and the conditions. All boats make less leeway when sailing relatively fast into the wind in moderate breezes and smooth seas, and more in very light and heavy winds and in rough seas, which slow them down. With her extremely efficient, relatively large appendages, a racing twelve-metre may make 3 to 5 degrees of leeway. On the other hand, the average cruising boat, designed more for comfort than for sailing performance, may slide sideways 5 to 10 degrees; for every mile she sails ahead, she slips between 500 and 1500 feet (150 and 450 metres) to leeward.

So, while the sails actually convert the wind's potential energy into a small, forward-driving force, the appendages almost neutralize the wasteful aspects of the wind's leeway-causing side thrust. If the wind is petrol and the sails are the engine, the keel, centreboard, and rudder act like the wheels to keep the vehicle on track in the right directon. In the next chapter we will see how the sail controls act like the transmission and throttle.

The size and shape of a keel or rudder has a lot to do with its efficiency at resisting leeway. That was one of the lessons of the winged keel. Appendages that are carefully shaped more or less like aircraft wings, with fairly thick leading edges that taper to sharp trailing ones, will resist leeway more efficiently than a flat appendage with squared-off leading and trailing edges. A well-shaped keel or centreboard not only looks but also acts like an orange pip that squirts forward when you press down on it sideways.

'How Does She Stay on Course?'

A boat's balance is the relative symmetry between her hull and her sails. We have already seen two balancing acts—one in which ballast counterweighs heeling forces, the other in which well-shaped appendages resist side forces. Now we will look at a third—the way the sails and hull are balanced so that the boat can be steered. A boat sails more or less in the direction you aim her partly because the appendages work to resist leeway but also because her sails and hull are balanced, allowing her to be steered on a fairly straight course without too much difficulty.

Balance, Heeling, and Helm

A boat is built symmetrically, the two sides of her hull having exactly the same shape. When she is sailing upright, the water should flow around each side at the same speed and with the same volume. If that is the case, the boat is well balanced and has no tendency to yaw, or steer to one side or the other. A balanced boat behaves like a car whose front end is aligned, whose tyres are properly inflated, and whose weight is equally distributed. On a well-balanced boat or car, you turn the steering wheel until it is centred and go straight ahead.

Heeling destroys that symmetry on a boat as quickly as letting ten pounds of air out of a front tyre does on a car. As one side is submerged and the other elevated, the hull's underwater shape becomes less and less symmetrical and the water flows at unequal speeds around the two sides. This imbalance tends to push the bow away from the downhill or leeward side. Heeling also tilts the mast and sails to one side, which creates a twisting force thrusting in the other direction. So when the boat heels to leeward, the two forces combine to push the bow to windward. (When she heels to windward, which is rare, the bow is pushed to leeward). Just like the unbalanced car, the unbalanced boat tends to yaw (steer off to one side) and the steering wheel pulls in the opposite direction. To get both vehicles back on course, the steerer must counteract the wheel's pull.

Windward or weather helm is a pull on the tiller or wheel that shows that the boat is yawing to windward. It almost always

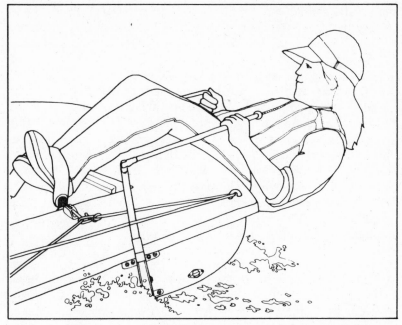

The girl sitting out this dinghy should pinch or ease the mainsheet a little to decrease heel and weather helm.

occurs when the boat is heeled to leeward more than about five degrees, but it may also occur if the mainsail is trimmed too much and the jib is eased out too far. To counteract it, the tiller must be pulled up to windward or the wheel turned down to leeward.

Leeward or lee helm is the opposite. The heel is to windward, or the jib is trimmed in too far and the mainsail is eased out too far. The helmsman must counteract it by pushing the tiller to leeward or turning the wheel to windward.

How the Helm and Rudder Work
Adjusting the helm to turn the boat or to counteract weather or lee helm creates its own asymmetry. As the tiller or wheel changes angle, so does the rudder connected to it. Down below the surface, water builds up on one side of the angled rudder and pushes it and the stern in the other direction. The stern is one end of a seesaw, the bow is the other end, and the fulcrum is about half-way between. So if the stern goes one way, the bow will go the other. Turn a steering wheel in the same direction you want to head, but push or pull a tiller in the opposite direction. Therefore, to turn the

boat to starboard (the right) in order to counteract a yaw to port (the left), either rotate the steering wheel to starboard or push the tiller to port. This angles the rudder to starboard. Hold the wheel or tiller firmly to resist the pressure of the mound of water on the starboard side of the rudder blade. In a moment, the rudder and the stern to which it is attached are pushed to port, and the bow swings to starboard. (To turn to port or counteract a yaw to starboard, angle the rudder to port.) As the bow reaches the course, check (or stop) its swing by oversteering in the other direction; heavy boats need an earlier and more decisive check than light ones.

The helm works fastest and with least strain on the helmsman when the boat is moving fairly fast through the water. Obviously, when the boat is stopped there is no water flow to pack up on the angled rudder. The technical term for sufficient speed to steer is *steerageway;* without it, a boat is uncontrollable.

A Touch of Weather Helm

A slight amount of weather helm is a good thing when sailing close-hauled (into the wind) or on a reach (across the wind). On a run with the wind, the boat rarely heels far enough to develop helm. Extreme weather or lee helm can make a wrestling match out of steering, which is neither fun nor safe; with hundreds of pounds of water packed up on the rudder, not only is steering exhausting but also the boat is sailing very slowly. What you want is just a bit of weather helm, with the rudder angled only about three degrees to leeward. With this three degrees of weather helm, the rudder is working as efficiently as it can to steer the boat and resist leeway. A touch of weather helm also provides a reference point so the helmsman can steer without constantly looking at the compass or the sails. Do not worry too much about having the exact angle. What is more important than the numbers is the feel of the helm. If the helmsman has to fight the tiller or wheel, there is too much helm, and that means four things:

> The rudder and sails are fighting rather than cooperating with each other and you are wasting considerable energy that could go into forward drive.

> The rudder is making too much resistance and slowing the boat down.

> The boat is probably heeling too far and making much more leeway than she has to.

> It is time to depower the sails to ease the helm and bring her back upright by changing the trim, reefing, or shortening sail.

The greater the angle of heel, the greater the amount of weather helm—and the more the sail area must be reduced.

We said earlier that boats with wide beams resist heeling better than narrow boats. But like all advantages, this one has its price. Because their underwater shapes change very quickly when they heel even slight amounts, beamy boats tend to go out of balance more quickly than narrow ones. In sailor's parlance, they are not very forgiving. So their helmsmen and crews should be especially wary of setting too much sail and heeling too far.

'How Fast Can We Go?'

Speed is a relative thing; compared with most other means of conveyance, a boat is ridiculously slow. The world sailing speed record is only about 40 miles per hour, and most boats that sailors call fast, like big trimarans, are lucky to break 20 knots, or about 23 mph. The average sailboat is a turtle even compared with humans; a good runner can do a 26-mile marathon in under three hours, but most sailors would be happy if their 35-foot (11-metre) cruising boats could cover the same distance in four.

Despite its relative modesty, a boat's speed is important, if not vital, in several ways: (1) Steering is more sure and rapid when water is moving quickly over the rudder than when the flow is languid. (2) Sailing fast is the best way to minimize the effects of contrary tidal streams. (3) A fast boat can make longer legs and cover more distance on a cruise. (4) A fast boat can beat a storm to port at shorter notice than a slow one. (5) And, being human, most sailors have more fun going fast than slow. Racing, for many, is what sailing is all about; besides the competition, it offers what many consider to be the best classroom for learning the skills of steering, sail trimming, and boat handling.

Planing and Hull Speed

The main limit on a boat's potential speed is the resistance of her hull against the water, resistance that is increased by waves that the hull stirs up. Most boats create waves until they seem to be riding in the trough between two crests, one at the bow and the other at the stern. In a wind of 12 knots or more, a light boat with a large sail area can accelerate up and over the bow wave, slipping across it with her bow flying free and only a bit of her stern digging into the water, like a carpenter's plane sliding across a board. This exhilarating experience is called planing. Dinghies, sailboards, and some lightweight keel boats plane. A few heavier boats have been

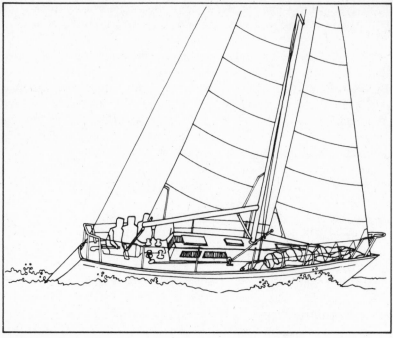

At hull speed, a keel boat creates a wave about as long as her
waterline length. She cannot climb up and over it unless boosted
by a wave from astern.

known to plane briefly in strong winds, and they can also reach
high speeds while surfing down the faces of big waves. Multihulls
do not plane but rather owe their tremendous speeds to their slim,
low-resistance hulls, which create relatively small, non-limiting
waves.

The maximum speed of a non-planing boat is a function of her
length, and for that reason it is called her hull speed. A wave (and
any object on it) can only go at a speed (in knots) equal to the product of 1.34 and the square root of the distance between its crests
(in feet). To use that formula when figuring hull speed, take the
square root of the boat's waterline length—the distance between the
forwardmost and aftermost points where the hull normally touches
the water, measured in feet—and multiply it by 1.34. Granted, a
heavy boat may exceed her hull speed when surfing or planing
down a wave or when sailing in perfectly smooth water, but most of
the time the best she can do is the result of the following formula:

$$\text{hull speed in knots} = 1.34 \sqrt{\text{waterline length in feet}}$$

The waterline length (abbreviated LWL for *load waterline*) is one of the dimensions listed with a boat's plans in the design sections of many boating magazines. If it is 33 feet (which is about right for a boat with an overall, or on-deck, length of 40 feet), the square root of its LWL is 5.75 and the hull speed is 7.7 knots. If 25 feet (the LWL of a modern-day 30-footer), the hull speed is 6.7 knots.

The hull speed, remember, is the maximum theoretical speed of a non-planing (or displacement) monohulled boat. It applies neither to a boat that is planing nor to a multihull, whose performance is limited by whether the crews can keep it from capsizing. When well sailed by expert crews in optimum conditions, both those types may sail faster than twice the square root of their overall length.

How to Predict Average Speeds

Because the typical cruising boat rarely sails in enough wind or is pushed sufficiently hard by her crew to achieve her hull speed, an estimated average speed is more indicative of her performance. In his exhaustive treatise on modern yacht design, *The Offshore Yacht*, AT Thornton figures that the average speed of a cruising or racing monohull or cruising multihull may be between 0.8 and 1.0 times the square root of the waterline length, or:

$$\text{average speed in knots} = 0.8 \text{ to } 1.0 \sqrt{\text{waterline length in feet}}$$

For a boat with a 33-foot waterline length, that is 4.6 to 5.8 knots; for one with a 25-foot LWL, it is 4 to 5 knots. For racing multihulls, Thornton estimates an average speed of between 1.2 and 1.5 times the square root of the waterline length of the longest hull.

Keeping in mind that the engine is powerful enough to push a cruising boat at about that speed in a calm, the lower ranges of Thornton's figures for cruising monohulls sound about right for cruising under power or sail (or both) in average conditions. If you are racing or doing a lot of sailing off the wind in fresh breezes, the higher figure may be more accurate.

So much for theory. Now let us trim the sails.

CHAPTER 7

The Wilful Wind

and

How to Use It

A little theory goes a long way towards developing an under-standing of how a sailing boat works, but getting in the boat and actually going sailing is more fun. In this chapter we will climb into the cockpit, get our hands on the sheets and the helm, and trim the sails and steer the boat. We will see how the sail controls work and what to do with them to shape the sails properly for fast, con-trolled sailing in light, medium, and fresh winds. Using step-by-step instructions we will tell how the helmsman and crew handle the boat, sailing both into the wind and with it. First, though, we will have to understand how to look at the wind and its effect on the sails—and the sails' effect on it.

The terminology may at first sound unfamiliar. I will try to define terms as I go along, but if you get confused, stop for a moment and consult the glossary.

The Infuriatingly Variable, Absolutely Essential Apparent Wind

Many sailors, even experienced ones, never come to understand sail trim because it is so maddeningly variable in its demands. The wind (to quote Scripture) 'blows where it wills,' the boat's course is rarely steady, and the relationship between the sails and their spider's web of lines is complex. All in all, the wind is much less reliable than, say, the numbers shown on the magnetic compass, which mirror the almost immutable relationship between the globe and the earth's magnetic field. From year to year, the compass direction from any point on earth to the locus of the magnetic field, which is called magnetic north, varies by less than one degree, or 0.2 per cent of the 360-degree-card. On the other hand, the angle between boat and wind is rarely stable from second to second; it can and frequently does change 180 degrees (one-half the 360-degree sweep of the compass card) in a matter of moments, leaving the sail-trimmer to try to pick up the pieces. Coping with this variability is often frustrating, but it lies so close to the soul of sailing that we must try to come to terms with it and identify what few constants are hidden deep within it.

True Wind + Course + Boat Speed = Apparent Wind

The main ingredients of the unstable sail-wind relationship are the true wind and the boat's course and speed, which combine to create the all-important apparent wind.

The true wind is the one blowing across the earth and sea. It is indicated by stationary flags and seagulls, which always stand and take off into the wind. This is the wind direction and strength reported by meteorologists, the wind you feel when you first go aboard a moored boat.

The boat's course is the direction in which she is moving, under power or under sail, either into, across, or away from the true wind.

The boat's speed is just that—how fast she is moving.

The apparent wind is the marriage of all three in the wind felt on board the moving boat.

Moving vehicles like cars, bicycles, and boats make their own wind. Obviously, this created wind does not disappear when a true wind is blowing. Depending on whether the boat is heading into or away from it, the boat's speed augments or decreases the force of the true wind as it is felt on board. If the boat is not heading directly into or away from the true wind, the boat's speed will change the direction of the apparent wind, as well as its strength. For example, the crew on a boat doing 5 knots under power feels a different apparent wind depending on the strength and direction of the true wind:

> In a flat calm (when there is no true wind), they feel
> a 5-knot apparent wind from dead ahead (head
> wind).

In a 5-knot true wind from dead ahead, they feel a 10-knot apparent head wind.

In a 5-knot true wind from dead astern, they feel no apparent wind at all.

In a 5-knot true wind from abeam (at a 90-degree angle), they feel a 7.5-knot apparent wind from 45 degrees off the bow.

The Five Points of Sailing

Besides being the wind that the sailor feels on the face, the apparent wind is the one that fills the sails and creates the side and forward forces that make the boat move. It is the breeze that we trim our sails by. When a sailor says 'wind,' almost all the time he or she means 'apparent wind.' Conceivably, there are 360 different apparent wind directions in constant flux as each of the variables—true wind, boat speed, course—alters. Yet over the years mariners have, with typical practicality, reduced these directions to five points of sailing—each a family of angles between the apparent wind and the sails. There are many terms in the sailor's glossary that you can forget, but these five are part of the essential vocabulary of sail trimming and steering.

> **Head to wind (also dead into the wind)**—with the bow aimed into the eye of the wind.
>
> **Forereaching**—with the apparent wind just either side (10–30 degrees) of the bow.
>
> **Close-hauled (also beating, sailing to windward)**—the closest angle to the apparent wind at which the sails are full and not luffing (flapping), 30–50 degrees either side of the bow.
>
> **Reaching**—across the wind; either a close reach (apparent wind 50–80 degrees either side of the bow), a beam reach (80–100 degrees), or a broad reach (100–170 degrees).
>
> **Running**—with the wind on the stern or 10 degrees on either side of the stern.

The five points of sailing break down into two families—*upwind* (also *into the wind*) and *downwind* (also *off the wind*). The first family includes head to wind, forereaching, close-hauled, and close reaching; the second, beam reaching, broad reaching, and running.

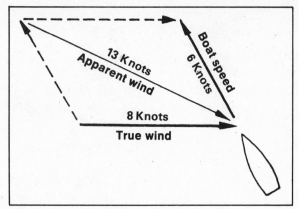

The apparent wind is created by the true wind
and the boat's speed. Close-hauled or on
reaches, it is further ahead and stronger than
the true wind.

Eight Ways the Apparent Wind Works

The apparent wind's effect on the boat's performance varies predictably with the point of sailing and the wind strength according to these eight rules of thumb:

The apparent wind is the wind felt on the moving boat, but the true wind makes the waves. Often the two will differ and the waves will come at an acute angle to the apparent wind.

When she is sailing upwind (close-hauled or close reaching) or on a beam reach, a boat's apparent wind is greater and further forward than the true wind. As she accelerates, the apparent wind increases in speed and draws forward (or 'heads' her). As she decelerates, the apparent wind decreases and draws aft (or 'lifts' or 'frees' her).

When she is sailing directly downwind (running), a boat's apparent wind is less than, but from the same direction as, the true wind. When she accelerates, the apparent wind decreases in speed; when she decelerates, it increases.

If the difference between the boat's speed and the true wind speed is small, the apparent wind will vary greatly from the true wind in speed and/or direction. If the difference is great, the variation will be small. Therefore, relatively fast boats change light true winds dramatically and fresh true winds slightly. Relatively slow boats change light true winds less dramatically and fresh true winds hardly at all.

In light winds (1–8 knots true), most boats will sail fastest on a close reach.

In moderate winds (9–15 knots true), the fastest point of sailing usually is a beam reach.

In fresh winds (16–22 knots), a boat usually sails fastest, and under the most control, on a beam to broad reach.

In strong and gale-force winds (23–40 knots true), the fastest and most controllable point of sail is usually a broad reach.

As you sail, keep asking yourself, 'Where is the true wind? What is the boat's effect on apparent wind? How does the apparent wind change as I head up or bear off? How could I be sailing faster or more comfortably?' Experiment with different courses and note your impressions of their effects. If you keep these guidelines in mind and stay alert, you will soon find yourself developing a sixth sense for the boat and wind that will make sailing even more pleasurable and safe.

How to Trim Sails

The sails must be shaped properly to use the apparent wind well. They have a shape built in by the sailmaker as panels of Terylene (polyester), Mylar, Kevlar, and nylon cloth are sewn together, but since changing wind strengths and points of sail require different sail shapes, and since sailcoth stretches, several ingenious but simple adjusting devices called sail controls have been devised to help the crew make the sails work most effectively. Back in Chapter 5 we took a tour on deck and looked at the maze of lines and other equipment used to hoist and trim sails. Now let us see how they affect sail shape. Line by line, here are the sail controls and how they can be adjusted on each point of sailing in light, medium, and fresh winds:

Mainsail Controls
The main sheet is a line that runs from the boom to the cockpit through several blocks, which decrease the load and facilitate adjustment. The sheet pulls both sideways and down on the boom. Trimming the sheet pulls the boom to windward until it is over the main sheet blocks on deck; then, further trimming pulls down on and flattens the sail. Easing the sheet lets the boom out to leeward

and makes the sail more full, or round. These rules of thumb usually apply in light to moderate winds (1 to 15 knots true):

Running and reaching. Ease the sheet until the luff (forward edge) of the sail luffs (flaps or flutters), then trim it back until the flap or flutter is barely eliminated.

Close-hauled. Trim the sheet until the leech (aft edge) twists (curves to leeward) about 5 degrees. The twist is right if the top batten is about parallel to the boom. The luff of the sail may be just fluttering.

The traveller is an athwartships (sideways) running deck track in which the mainsheet blocks slide back and forth on a car. Adjusting the car changes the angle the boom and sail make to the wind when sailing close-hauled or on a close or beam reach, and provides the quickest way to decrease heel and weather helm and so bring the boat back into balance. The traveller has no effect on the other points of sailing when the boom is eased well out to leeward.

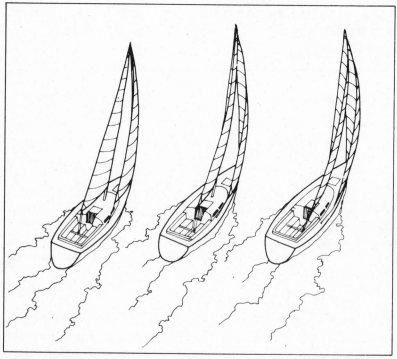

(Left to right) Close-hauled sail trim for light, medium and strong winds. As the wind strengthens, the sails are trimmed farther outboard with more twist.

Beam and close reaching. Keep the traveller car under the boom as the sheet is eased in order to keep the boom from lifting.

Close-hauled. In light and moderate apparent winds, pull the traveller car up to windward so the boom is over the centreline (the imaginary line running fore and aft between the centre of the transom and the forestay). But ease the car to leeward if the boat slows or if weather helm increases beyond about 3 degrees; in fresh to strong apparent winds, adjust the car until the helm is right, trimming the main sheet slightly as you ease the traveller car down.

The boom vang is a tackle or adjustable rod that controls the rise and fall of the boom. Close-hauled, it should be slack so that the main sheet can pull the boom down or ease it up. Otherwise, it should be tight enough so that the leech twists off about 5 degrees —slightly more in light wind and slightly less in fresh wind.

The outhaul is a line running from the aft end of the boom to the clew (aft lower corner) of the sail; it is used to adjust the shape of the foot (bottom one-third) of the mainsail. When tightened, it flattens the sail and decreases side and forward forces. When loosened, it makes the sail fuller and increases side and forward forces. For best performance, the sail should look as follows:

Running. Moderately full with the outhaul eased some of the way (the foot should have shallow wrinkles).

Broad reaching. Very full with the outhaul eased almost all the way (the foot should be wrinkled).

Beam and close reaching. In light and moderate apparent winds, moderately full; in fresh apparent wind, slightly full with the outhaul eased a little (the foot should not be wrinkled).

Close-hauled. In light apparent wind, moderately full; in moderate apparent wind, slightly full; in fresh apparent wind, flat with the outhaul pulled out all the way (tension lines should appear along the foot when the sail is luffing).

The cunningham is a line used to increase or decrease tension along the luff of the sail. Unlike the outhaul, the cunningham does not control the amount of draft, but rather affects the fore and aft position of the point of deepest draft. The mainsail is built with this point about half-way between the luff and the leech (its forward and aft edges), but a high apparent wind—the kind that occurs when a boat is close-hauled in moderate to strong winds—causes stretch in the sail, which blows the draft too far aft. Tightening the cunningham pulls the draft back forward again. Two guides to use are the wrinkles in the luff and the angle of the battens: tighten the cunningham until the luff is just free of wrinkles and the cloth curves smoothly from luff to leech without a knuckle at the forward edge of the battens.

Reefs decrease the sail area in fresh and strong apparent winds, when the angle of heel and weather helm are extreme. A reef is taken in by lowering the halyard several feet, tying the bottom part of the sail to the boom with reef lines led through cringles (steel-reinforced holes in the luff and leech), and pulling the sail up tight again. Most cruising boats carry two or three sets of reef cringles, allowing the sail area to be decreased by almost one-half in a matter of minutes.

The topping lift (which holds up the boom), while not a sail-shaping control, should be loose after the sail is set. If it is tight, the main sheet cannot be trimmed in far enough.

Jib Controls

The jib sheet is a draft-adjusting line that works like a combined outhaul and main sheet. It pulls the jib's clew (aft corner) aft and the leech (aft edge) down to flatten the sail.

> **Running and reaching.** Ease the sheet until the luff starts to flutter, then trim it back in until the flutter just disappears.
>
> **Close-hauled.** Trim the sheet so that there is about 5 degrees of twist (curve) along the leech and so that the sail is very full (light apparent wind) to quite flat (fresh apparent wind). An overlapping genoa jib should not be trimmed closer than about 2 inches off from the tips of the spreaders. If the mainsail is properly trimmed but luffing over its forward one-third, the genoa sheet is probably trimmed too tight and the sail is backwinding the mainsail (directing the wind into its leeward side and making it luff badly). Ease the jib sheet slightly.

The jib sheet leads are adjustable blocks through which the sheets pass. They determine the relative amount of aft and downward pull by the sheet and its athwartships angle. When the jib lead is adjusted properly, the jib should luff (flap) at the same time all along its luff as the boat heads up into the wind or the jib sheet is eased. If the top of the sail luffs first, slide the jib sheet lead slightly forward. If the bottom luffs first, slide the lead slightly aft. On reaches and runs, move the jib lead outboard to the rail and forward. Upwind in light wind, move the jib lead as far inboard as possible; as the wind increases, move it outboard toward the rail to decrease heeling forces.

The jib halyard, besides hauling and keeping up the jib, can be used like the mainsail's cunningham control. Tighten the halyard to move the point of deepest draft forward and ease it to allow the draft to go aft. The jib's point of deepest draft should be just forward of halfway between the luff and leech, and there should be tiny wrinkles all along the luff.

Reefs decrease the area of some specially-designed jibs, either by bunching up the bottom part of the sail or by rolling up some of the luff area.

Steering and Boat Handling on the Points of Sailing

The points of sailing make many demands on crews. Here is some advice on the advantages and challenges of each point.

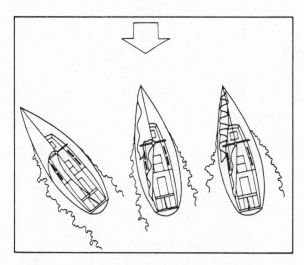

Hoisting or lowering the jib (left to right). The best way to hoist or lower the jib is to head up from a close-hauled course until the boat is fore-reaching. However, the mainsail should not be dropped until you are heading directly into the wind.

Head to Wind and Forereaching: The Utility Headings

These two points of sailing do not provide speed. Rather, they are utility headings that either stop a boat or slow her down so that the crew can set and lower sails, anchor, pick up a mooring, or rest.

Head to wind, as the name suggests, leaves the bow pointed directly into the eye of the wind with the sails luffing (flapping); the boat has no way on (is stopped dead in the water). Heading into the wind is the best way to stop a boat quickly in order to anchor, dock, or pick up a mooring. It is also the point of sailing to be on when hoisting and lowering the mainsail. Watch out, though: the sails can bang around quite violently, and somebody may be whacked by the flying boom, sliding traveller car, or flailing jib sheet.

Once she is stopped dead into the wind with mainsail and jib hoisted, getting her moving again with steerageway (enough speed to steer) requires getting the bow to swing about 40 degrees either side of the true wind's eye so the jib can fill. A full jib will create some steerageway. When leaving a mooring under sail, back the jib (pull its clew to one side to catch the wind and push the bow off the other way). Gathering steerageway with only the mainsail hoisted may be difficult. Try to back the mainsail by pushing the boom to one side. Once she is sailing astern, steer the bow either side of the wind's eye by adjusting the helm *opposite* to the way you would push or pull it when sailing ahead (think of turning a car's steering wheel when backing into a parking space).

Forereaching is the point of sail just either side of head to wind. This is when the bow has fallen off 10 to 30 degrees from the true wind and the boat is jogging along slowly on port or starboard tack with her sails partially filled, partially luffing. Forereaching is the best point of sail to be on when hoisting and lowering the jib, since the sail will bang around the mast violently if you are head to wind. This is also the best point of sail for slowing the boat down without absolutely stopping her: just head up from a close-hauled course until the sails luff a bit. Be careful not to tack accidentally and be caught aback (with the jib trimmed on the windward side).

Close-Hauled Sailing: Hard on the Wind

When you are sailing at a narrow angle to the apparent wind and the sails are trimmed almost flat, you are close-hauled. Your own speed is augmenting the true wind, and with all that apparent wind whistling through the rigging you may think this is the fastest point of sailing. But because the sails' forward force is very small compared with the side forces, and because the boat must climb not only into the wind but also through waves coming at her, sailing close-hauled is almost always slower than reaching and running (except when sailing in light wind and smooth water). Other terms for close-hauled sailing—*on the wind, upwind, beating to windward,* and *working to windward*—tell how a close-hauled boat is not only sailing toward the wind's source but also doing it with some effort.

Close-hauled means 'with sheets and sails trimmed tight'. The sails have to be pulled in pretty far and set quite flat because the angle of attack to the wind is narrow (generally speaking, the farther off the wind the boat is sailing, the farther out the sheets are eased and the fuller the sails are set). The optimum angle of attack varies from boat to boat and condition to condition. Relatively fast boats, such as racing dinghies and catamarans, sail well at fairly wide angles of attack—about 40 degrees to the apparent wind. Non-planing boats, like the average cruiser-racer or cruising boat, sail narrower—about 35 degrees. And boats with extremely efficient rigs and appendages, like twelve-metres and ocean racers, can sail closer still.

When sailing close-hauled in a moderate to fresh apparent wind, do not become so obsessed about optimizing sail shape that you forget about balance. If it is trimmed too flat or if the traveller is pulled too far to windward, a sail—no matter how terrific it looks —may cause excessive heel and, consequently, unmanageable weather helm. A good way to guard against overtrimming is to remember that touch of weather helm on the tiller or wheel that we talked about in Chapter 6. Keep it slight. The helmsman can report how the helm feels, or a crew member can watch it. If the tiller is up under the helmsman's chin, there is too much weather helm and something should be eased.

With the sails trimmed correctly, the sheets are cleated (except in fresh winds in dinghies, which might capsize if sheets are not quickly let out) and the helmsman steers by the jib, not by the compass or any other indicator. The challenge is not simply to sail as close as possible to the apparent wind but also to keep the boat sailing fast. It is an endlessly fascinating problem demanding patience, concentration, and alertness. Helmsmen on racing boats get some help from sophisticated electronic instruments that calculate and display the apparent wind angle and boat speed, and from microcomputers that factor the two against each other to indicate sailing efficiency relative to a theoretical optimum. The average boat, however, may have only a boat-speed indicator, leaving the helmsman to steer more by feel than by the numbers.

How to Steer Upwind with Jib Telltales
Whether or not he has electronic assistance, the helmsman's best

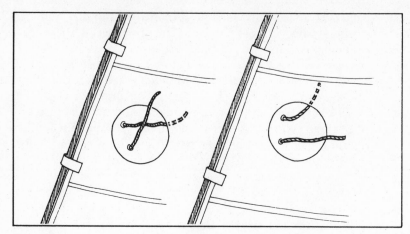

(Left) If the jib telltales look like this, with the windward one lifting about half the time and the leeward one streaming, on a close-hauled course you are sailing about right and on a reach the sails are trimmed correctly. (Right) But if they look like this, either you are sailing too far off the wind or the sails are trimmed too tight. Use green yarn on the starboard telltale and red on the port one in order to eliminate confusion.

guide is the luff (forward edge) of the jib, which he steers by (uses as a steering reference point). The helmsman wants to sail at an angle of attack where the sail is completely full but just on the edge of luffing (flapping and spilling wind). By sitting or standing on the windward side, a helmsman will be able to watch the approaching waves and steer around the bad ones.

In the days of cotton and early Terylene sails, the soft cloth fluttered visibly just as it began to luff. Today's hard-finished, stiff, low-stretch sailcloth is less sensitive and harder to read, so sail-makers and sailors attach simple wind-flow indicators called tell-tales near the luff on either side of the sail. There should be three pairs of telltales distributed at equal intervals up and down the luff. Telltales may be made of yarn or ribbon (ideally, green on the star-board side and red on port) taped to or sewn through the sail cloth on both sides 6 to 12 inches aft of the luff. They should be short enough not to wrap around the stay but long enough to be visible from the helm. Sometimes a plastic window is sewn into the sail's luff to facilitate reading the telltales.

This is the story the telltales recount:

If the leeward telltale is streaming straight aft and the wind-ward one is streaming half of the time and just lifting half of the time, you are sailing perfectly—neither *footing* (sailing too wide) nor *pinching* (sailing too close).

If the windward telltale is lifting straight up and the leeward one is streaming aft, either the jib is eased too far or you are pinching (sailing too close to the wind). To make the jib work at optimum again, trim the sheet a couple of inches. But if it is already trimmed hard, bear away a couple of degrees until both telltales are streaming. Pinching is not all bad, since it can be a quick way to make the sails less efficient and spill wind when a sudden gust hits. (For some reason, pinching through a gust is called *feathering*.)

If the leeward telltale is lifting more than about 20 degrees and the windward one is still streaming, the angle of attack is too broad. This is called 'sailing stalled' because the air flow is stalling on (or stagnating and separating from) the sail. To get the air flowing properly again, head up. Or ease the jib sheet until both telltales are streaming and foot (sail a little broader than close-hauled).

The goal, remember, is to sail as close to the wind as is efficiently possible. Although footing takes the boat through the water faster, in most conditions most boats lose too much ground to leeward to make footing pay off. The major exception is when sailing in a rough sea, where you want to be moving fast in order to slice through waves without being stopped by them.

The helmsman should never become complacent. Like a fly fisherman teasing a line across a stream's surface, he or she keeps testing the angle of attack, constantly edging the boat closer to the wind until the windward telltale lifts about 20 degrees, then nudging the bow off a bit. The course may waggle, but the sails will always be trimmed at or near peak efficiency.

Reaching: Sailing Fast

On a reach, the helmsman usually does not use the jib luff telltales as the steering guide. Rather he steers either by the compass (with the lubber's line, over a specified degree mark) or by a buoy, star, harbour, or landmark on shore, keeping the bow aimed at the object. Meanwhile, whoever is in charge of trimming the sails adjusts the jib sheet until both the windward and leeward telltales are streaming aft. If the windward one lifts, the sheet is trimmed until they both stream; if the leeward one, the sheet is eased. After the jib is trimmed correctly, the main sheet is trimmed or eased to keep the mainsail from luffing. Tighten the boom vang until the boom is about horizontal to the deck with the mainsail leech twisted off about 5 degrees.

When reaching in fresh and even moderate winds, as when sailing close-hauled, it is easy to forget about heel angles and weather helm as you trim the sheets to optimize sail shape. Sure, keep the sails pulling hard as possible, but if this means sailing way over on the boat's ear with her leeward rail under water, ease out the main sheet (and even the jib sheet, too) and let the sail luff a little to bring the boat back up to a heel angle of under 20 degrees (10 degrees for a centreboarder). Already sailing fast, the boat will seem to take off as soon as her decks are dry.

Running: Easy Street, Mostly

When the wind comes over the stern and the mainsail is eased out until the boom is almost at a right angle, the boat is on a *run* (sometimes called *running free*, a *square run*, or a *dead run*). The jib will be blanketed by the mainsail; to make it fill with wind, pull it around to windward and set it 'goosewinged' to windward, either with or without the spinnaker pole. Set the pole about perpendicular to the apparent wind, and trim the sheet so that there is a constant but small curl in the windward leech.

If you have a spinnaker and the crew is sufficiently large and talented and the wind not too strong, set it to increase your speed. Hoist it behind the jib, which blankets it, pull the guy (windward sheet) around through the spinnaker pole, let the sail fill, and lower the jib. If the big sail threatens to take charge of the boat, release the sheet and either let the sail luff, or release the guy and pull the sail around to leeward of the rehoisted jib before dropping it. A special cruising spinnaker is not set on a spinnaker pole but hoisted like a jib, only it is not hooked to the forestay.

Sails do not produce much forward drive on a run; they are simply pushed by the wind, and as they are pushed they pull the hull along. In light and moderate winds, therefore, a run may be even slower than sailing close-hauled. To speed up, head up to a beam reach and, as the speed of both the boat and the apparent wind increases, gradually bear away, keeping on a slightly broad reach with the wind at about 110 degrees off the bow, or slightly abaft the beam. 'Head off in the puffs and up in the lulls' is a time-honoured, proven rule of thumb for keeping the sails working well when sailing downwind. As the wind freshens (strengthens), it will kick up waves down which the boat may surf at high speeds. Yet the same waves may also cause her to roll violently. To stop the boat from rolling, head up to a broad reach and trim the mainsheet; the side force on the sail will steady her.

On a run, the helmsman may steer by the compass or by an object off the boat, simply aiming the bow at the destination. But he must keep track of the wind to avoid sailing by the lee (with the wind shifting to the leeward side of the stern). If that happens, there will be an accidental gybe, and the mainsail may be slammed across the boat unexpectedly, possibly injuring crew members or breaking gear. A good way to avoid sailing by the lee is to sit or stand facing forward and keep the wind pressure equal on the backs of both ears, with your hood or hat off. Another way, when running under jib and mainsail, is to keep the jib hanging across the centre of the foredeck. If it blows to windward, you are by the lee; to leeward, you are safely broad reaching. With the spinnaker up on a run, steer the bow under its centre like a seal keeping its nose under a ball. If the spinnaker sways to windward of the bow, you are by the lee and must head up; to leeward, you are broad reaching and may bear away (head off).

Changing Tacks the Right and Wrong Way

By heading up or bearing off, the helmsman can alter course through about 150 degrees, from a run to close-hauled. Sometimes, however, a more drastic course change is called for, and he or she changes tacks by steering the boat through the eye of the wind so that the sails must be trimmed on the other side. The windward side becomes the leeward and the leeward side the windward. The two tack-changing manoeuvres are tacking and gybing. Tacking is a turn made into the wind; gybing is done facing away from the wind.

Tacking

To tack, head up to dead into the wind from a close-hauled course, and then bear away on the other tack until close-hauled again. It may help to preselect a reference point on the compass for the new tack before you start the manoeuvre. Say, for example, that on starboard tack the compass course is 150 degrees. The true wind is 195 degrees, which indicates that you are sailing 45 degrees off the true wind. Therefore, when close-hauled on the *port* tack (after you change tacks), you will be steering 240 degrees—or 45 degrees the other side of the wind direction. Keep the helm over through the tack until you are near that course and then check her swing.

Tacking is often called 'coming about,' and the skipper's warning is 'ready about.' When that command is given, one crew member uncleats the jib sheet and checks to see that the sheets and sail are clear; he or she then answers 'ready'. Next, the helmsman heads up by sharply pushing the tiller to leeward or turning the

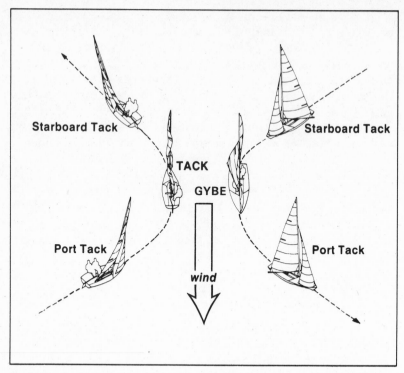

(Left) To tack or come about, head up into the wind and off on the other tack, easing and trimming the jib sheet. (Right) to gybe, bear away and ease sheets. When the wind is astern or just beyond it, quickly trim the main sheet and throw the boom across as the jib sheet is eased and trimmed.

wheel to windward, and says 'lee-oh' (meaning, 'the helm's to leeward'). When the jib begins to luff, the crew lets go the jib sheet, making sure it is not tangled or kinked. As the bow swings through the wind's eye, a shipmate trims the jib sheet on the other side, starting with one or two clockwise turns on the winch and adding more as the strain builds. When the trimmer can pull no more, somebody grinds the sheet in with the winch, watching the sail to make sure it is not trimmed too flat (a common occurrence with today's big, powerful winches). The jib should be trimmed almost as far as it was before the boat changed tacks and then pulled in to where it was as she gains speed.

Before the tack, the mainsail traveller car should be put in the centre of its track with its two control lines tight to keep it from banging around as the sail luffs. Otherwise, the mainsail tends itself during the manoeuvre.

Most bungled tacks are due to one or more of the following mistakes:

The helmsman stops turning the boat too soon and the boat is left hanging dead in the water head to wind.

The helmsman turns her too far and ends up on a beam reach with the sails trimmed for a close-hauled course—a sure invitation to an unpleasant knockdown (sudden heeling) in a gust of wind.

The helmsman allows the boat to be stopped and lose steerageway during the tack because she was turned too fast or because she was slammed by a wave. Adjust the helm firmly but smoothly, and choose a relatively flat spot of water between waves before beginning the manoeuvre.

The old leeward-side jib sheet is let out too slowly, or it kinks and jams up in a block leaving the jib backed (trimmed to windward) on the new tack.

The crew member trims the jib much too far on the new tack, perhaps tearing it on a spreader, because he or she is not looking at it.

Gybing

Gybing is altering course away from the wind. A gybe is usually slower and takes up more water than a tack; since the mainsail must be trimmed most of the way, it may be more physically demanding, too.

Before gybing, get on a broad reach or run. The skipper warns 'stand by to gybe.' When the crew is ready—one or more on the jib sheets and another on the main sheet—they respond 'ready.' The helmsman commands 'gybe-oh' and bears off in a smooth, gradual turn as the main sheet is trimmed rapidly to keep the boom from wildly banging across. The boom should be over the boat's centreline when the stern passes through the eye of the wind. To avoid an accident on deck, be sure the traveller is centred and its control lines are tight. Then the main sheet is eased out very rapidly. In a very light wind, the main boom may be allowed to swing across the boat on its own without trimming the sheet. The old leeward jib sheet is let go just as the stern swings into the wind's eye and the new leeward one is trimmed.

In any wind stronger than moderate air, the boat may broach (suddenly head up uncontrollably and heel violently) as she finishes the gybe. Here is a simple way to avoid this: just as the sails fill and the boat begins to heel on the new tack, the helmsman sharply bears off about 5 degrees to check the spin of the bow; when the boat has levelled off, he or she heads up to the new course.

In fresh and strong winds, a poorly executed gybe can lead to serious trouble since (unlike on a tack, where the boat is luffing dead into the wind) her sails are always full and there is no way to spill wind. Here are the typical causes of a bad gybe:

The helmsman loses track of the wind direction and heads up too rapidly on the new tack. Before the gybe, find a couple of reference points that will help locate the wind—its feel on the back of your neck or your ears, a telltale on a stay, a masthead fly (wind indicator at the top of the mast)—and refer to them as you bear off, gybe, and head up on the new tack.

The helmsman does not adjust quickly to the boat's new orientation to the waves and loses control after the gybe. This is why the best and most experienced helmsman should be steering during a gybe in rough seas and fresh winds. (Often the most qualified downwind helmsman on board is a young dinghy sailor who has developed a good feel for the wind while avoiding capsizes in a tippy little boat).

The main sheet is not trimmed far enough before the gybe, so it bangs across violently, perhaps injuring a crew member or filling so quickly that it causes a broach.

After the gybe, on the new tack, the helmsman tries to head up onto a reach before the main sheet is eased. With the sail trimmed tight, the boat will broach when she comes up.

The jib sheet is eased too far before the gybe and the jib wraps itself around the forestay (wire running from bow to mast).

Gybing in light wind is easy, in moderate wind a handful, in fresh wind a real challenge, and in heavy wind a major risk. When in doubt about your ability to handle a gybe, swallow your pride and tack.

Those are the fundamentals of boat and sail handling—all easier to describe than accomplish. The very best way to learn and master them is to go out and practice them, preferably in a light, quick boat whose relatively small gear will not bruise you too badly when you make a mistake (and you will) and whose sensitivity sets a challenging standard. The next chapter may answer some of your questions (and cries for help).

CHAPTER 8

Tricks of the Seaman's Trade for Better Steering, Easier Trimming, and Safer Sailing

Seasoned sailors have spent years accumulating a repertory of rules of thumb that make handling and living aboard a boat more efficient, safe, and enjoyable. Here we will summarize the most important tricks of the trade, opening with ways to improve steering and sail trimming, moving on to hints for safe sail handling, and closing with some important advice on how to walk around on deck without losing your balance.

Five Hints for Alert Steering and Sail Trimming

As with all skills, sailing competently begins with alertness. Yet it is harder than, say, driving a car safely, because the indicators a sailor must be alert to are not part of modern everyday experience, which is far removed from the forces of nature. In order to evaluate those forces, we must consciously retrain our senses to feel and interpret subtle changes in the relationship between wind, water, sail, and helm.

First, always know the direction from which the wind is blowing. That advice may sound elementary, but it is amazing how many people need a weatherman or electronic instrument to tell which way the wind blows. Develop a feel for the wind on your face and body. Take off your hat or hood and face the wind; when the pressure is equal on your cheeks and ears, you are facing directly into it. Refer to wind indicators—the telltales on the jib luff and the shrouds, the masthead burgee or flag at the top of the mast, and the luffs of the sails. Indicators off the boat can be helpful, too. Among them are smoke or flags on shore, other boats under sail, and the directions of waves, clouds, and bird flights. Whichever reference point you use, you should be able to point in the direction of the true and apparent winds, as well as sense when the velocity has increased or dropped.

Second, develop a feel for the boat's performance relying on the one indicator that mirrors all the boat's forces, the helm. If there is a lot of weather helm—more than a slight touch or about three degrees of rudder angle—the boat is heeling too far to leeward or the mainsail is trimmed too flat and the jib too loose. If there is lee helm, the boat is heeled to windward or the jib is trimmed too tight

Reliable wind indicators include (for the apparent wind) the wind arrow or burgee at the masthead, and (for the true wind) a flag or smoke from a chimney ashore and seagulls (which always stand facing the wind).

and the main sheet is eased too far. Correcting excessive helm *always* improves speed and comfort. Besides being attentive to the helm, the helmsman and sail trimmers will do well to learn to estimate the boat's speed and angle of heel, using a speedometer and an inclinometer (a kind of curved spirit level), if they are available.

Third, look at the sails. Too many people try to steer by the compass while the sails luff inefficiently. Regardless of the compass course, the sails are the boat's engine. You do not have to stare at them; just keep your eyes moving around the boat from sail to sail, then to the helm, then to the compass. The good sailor is the person who comes on deck and immediately looks up at the sails; who can have a pleasant conversation and still know if the trim is right because he or she is facing forward; who can tell whether the helmsman is steering well simply by the feel of the boat.

Fourth, do not trim the sails too flat. 'When in doubt, let it out' is an old sailor's dictum worth writing down and taping where everybody can see it. Flat sails provide little forward drive, while full ones (even if they are luffing a little) shape the wind so it can produce drive. If the speed is low and the helm feels wooden, ease the sheets a couple of inches and let the mainsail's traveller car down to leeward a bit. If you are close-hauled, bear away a couple of degrees. An experienced crew will know to ease the sheets by the feel of the boat's heel decreasing in a wind lull and to trim them again when the heel increases.

Fifth, realize that the *goal is not to sail the boat but rather to help the boat sail herself.* There is no way that a well-designed boat can sail fast and comfortably unless the crew takes advantage of, and is attentive to, her inherent seaworthiness, speed, and seakindliness. Granted, some boats are faster and more weatherly than others, and it is important that you do not try to exceed built-in limitations. For instance, a heavy cruiser with a small sail area and shallow keel cannot be made to sail close-hauled in light wind as fast as a modern ocean racer. But you *can* help her sail up to her own potential if you are alert to all her indicators.

If you have to fight the helm, if the boat is heeling right over, if the sails are luffing wildly, if the speed is low, if she is bouncing up and down violently or wallowing in waves instead of sailing over or through them—in brief, if the boat is not moving comfortably where is is aimed—then something is wrong. In fresh wind (over 16 knots), the culprit almost always is bad balance brought on by too much heel. In light (0-8 knots) and moderate (9-15 knots) wind, it is usually trying to sail too close to the wind with sails trimmed too flat.

Even when the solution is unclear, simply identifying the problem is an important first step. This ability is what mariners call 'a feel for the boat,' and despite the common wisdom, it is something you can develop. Open your mind, use your eyes, and above all, stay alert.

What the Helmsman and Trimmer Do

The helmsman steers the boat and the sail trimmer—usually another crew member but sometimes the helmsman as well—adjusts the sheets to make the sails pull and the boat balance. The two sailors should keep up a running conversation about the boat's performance.

The Helmsman

The person who is steering lets eyes and senses roam alertly around the sails, the compass, the water ahead, and the various wind and speed indicators, both natural and electronic. He or she should sit or stand in a position that provides a clear view of the luff of the jib and any obstructions or big waves to steer around, and has the right to ask shipmates to move out of the line of sight. Every experienced helmsman has a favourite position. Most prefer to sit or stand up to windward, where the visibility is better, but sitting to leeward has its appeals—among them an enthralling sense of power and speed as the water races by just inches from your elbow.

When you steer, do not just grab the wheel or tiller in a tight grasp. Hold it gently with your fingers and move it smoothly but firmly with wrist action. As the wind strengthens, tighten your grasp but avoid getting into a wrestling match. Downwind in rough weather, you may have to make very abrupt helm changes, especially if the boat is light and unstable. Yet turning the rudder too sharply will cause the blade to stall, which means that the water flow becomes detached from the blade. To get the flow attached again, pump the helm back and forth several times. Counter a roll to the side by steering slightly into the roll, heading up as the boat rolls to windward and bearing away as she rolls to leeward.

Good steering depends on quick reactions, mental alertness, and good hand-eye coordination—all of which alcohol impairs. Almost as harmful as excessive drinking are exhaustion, over-confidence, and an inflated, euphoric feeling of heroism. Whenever I have got into trouble on the water, it was because I either pushed myself beyond my physical limits or overestimated my abilities. If you begin to get weary or bored at the helm—and most people do after an hour or so—ask somebody else to take it. Before a long sail, the most experienced, skilled helmsman should be identified and

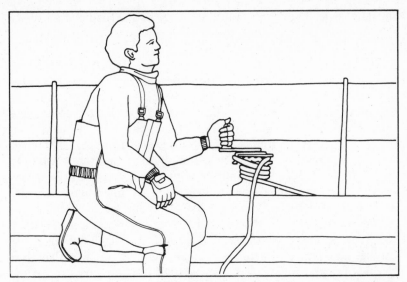

While trimming the jib, sit facing forward near the sheet winch. As shown here, the sheet must lead up to the winch so it does not form riding turns on the drum. This trimmer is wearing leather sailing gloves to protect his hands.

assigned to tricks (turns) at the helm at regular one-hour intervals. Perhaps the conditions will be easy enough to allow everybody to steer, but at least the crew will have a routine to fall back on if conditions get rough.

The Sail Trimmer

It may seem at first that the person trimming the sails is playing second fiddle to the helmsman, but he or she has an important role in making the boat sail fast and comfortably. Like the helmsman, the trimmer should be alert to every part of the boat and, especially, to changes in wind velocity that might require adjustments to the sheets. He or she should sit to leeward when trimming the jib and to windward when trimming the mainsail, in each case watching the sail's luff while adjusting the sheet. Because the helm is generally the best indicator, whoever is steering should have last say on sail trim. However, a good sail trimmer glances at the helm occasionally to see if the boat is balanced. Being tuned in to the helm also allows the trimmer to see when the helmsman is getting careless. The speedometer, if available, is a helpful auxiliary guide that both sailors can refer to, but with practice they should be able to judge the boat's speed with reasonable accuracy by the rush and gurgle of the passing water.

Coordination and Teamwork on the Points of Sailing

On a reach or run, when sailing a compass course, the best procedure is for the helmsman to get the boat on that course, shouting 'on course' when the lubber's line (vertical post) on the compass is right over the designated number. Next, the crew trims the jib properly for that heading so that its windward luff telltale lifts when the helmsman steers a few degrees too close. Then the mainsail is trimmed so it luffs at the same time that the jib telltale lifts. If this trim causes too much weather helm, the trimmer must ease the main sheet slightly.

Using this system, the sailors have complementary guides—the compass and the luff of the sails. If the sails luff when the boat is on course, they should be trimmed; if they do not luff when she is a couple of degrees high of course (upwind of course heading), they should be eased. On racing boats, a couple of crew members watch the sails like hawks and everybody keeps exchanging information about balance, speed, and trim. But when cruising or day-sailing, the helmsman might be able to check on trim and, when adjustments must be made, let go of the helm briefly to make them her- or himself.

Close-hauled sailing, when steering by the sails rather than by the compass, is a bit more dependent on alert steering than reaching and running. When the wind direction changes (as it does every few minutes), the helmsman simply heads up or bears away to keep the jib's luff telltales streaming. While the compass is not the primary guide, he or she should keep an eye on it. If a close-hauled boat is heading more than 45 degrees off the direct course to the destination, it usually pays to come about; the heading on the other tack will probably aim the boat closer to her destination and get her there faster.

When the wind changes in velocity rather than direction, or when the sea condition alters, the sail trimmer makes small alterations in the sheets and other sail controls. If the wind lightens or the waves get bigger and threaten to stop the boat, make the sail fuller by easing the sheets a couple of inches and slightly letting out the outhaul, cunningham, and jib halyard; do not try to point too close to the wind. Later, if the wind freshens or the sea gets smoother, flatten the sails by trimming the sheets and controls back and point a little higher. Of course, be attentive to the boat's balance through the helm.

On breezy days, you will find that the quickest and easiest way to adjust heel and helm angles is to depower the mainsail by playing (constantly adjusting) the main sheet traveller car. Letting it down usually decreases heel and weather helm. Pulling it up increases both heel and helm. On many boats the traveller control lines are handy to the helmsman so that he or she can make quick adjustments in gusts and lulls. We will cover other ways to make sailing in strong winds more comfortable in Chapter 16.

Safety Guidelines for Sail Handling

Although there are occasional disasters—like the 1979 Fastnet Race in England, in which I sailed and about which I wrote a book— remarkably few serious accidents occur in sailing boats. In almost thirty years of serious sailing I have yet to suffer an injury worse than a cracked thumb bone (caused by a fall) and I have seen only one accident that put a sailor in the hospital (he let go of a handle on a reel-halyard winch, a winch with a take-up like a fishing reel, which spun, broke his wrist, and inflicted concussion). But lesser accidents occur all the time. These include badly rope-burned

To control a line that is under load, take some turns around a winch. When grinding, lean over the winch and use your back muscles.

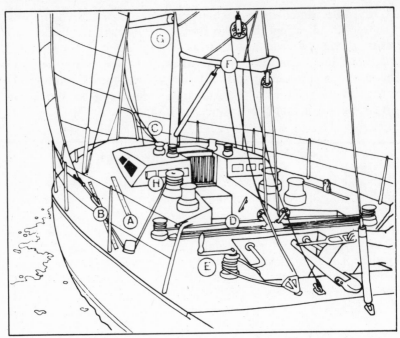

A sailing boat is crowded with potential dangers. You can trip over deck tracks (A), sheets (B), and guardrails (C), or be whacked by the traveller car (D) or a spinning winch handle (E). A swinging boom (F) or spinnaker pole (G) may fracture your skull if you do not duck in time, and the sheet on a winch (H) could pinch your fingers or snag long hair.

hands, deep welts, huge bruises, minor concussions, wrenched shoulders, broken teeth, and other mishaps that may leave you or a shipmate in pain and the crew shorthanded.

You can avoid these accidents if you follow some simple guidelines for safe sail handling, a few of which I was lucky to learn in my mid-teens from a couple of experienced seamen who, no doubt nervous about my adolescent recklessness, took me aside and gave me some succinct warnings. As I gained experience, the list gradually lengthened to ten guidelines that should be observed on any boat, and most assiduously on cruising boats larger than 35 feet (11 metres). Follow these rules as automatically as possible, and insist that your shipmates follow them, too.

> Before a line comes under load, snub it. Preferably, take at least three turns clockwise around a winch, but a turn around a sturdy cleat may do. Otherwise you will lose control of the line and probably suffer a bad rope burn.

Stay out of the way of moving objects. During tacks and gybes, dodge the main boom swinging over the deck, the traveller car banging across the cockpit, the jib clew whipping across the foredeck, and the winch handle whirling around a winch. Sailors have lost eyes to flying bowlines tied into jib clews.

Never step or sit on a loaded line or in the V formed by a line running to and from a block. If the line or block breaks, you will be lashed overboard or into the rigging.

Remove a winch handle not in use. It may fall out, trip somebody, or snag a line. And always remove the handle before letting go the brake on a reel-halyard winch.

Never be a hero by trying to do difficult tasks singlehanded. Two-person jobs like lifting a heavy spinnaker pole or gybing the main boom in a fresh breeze are just that—two-person jobs.

Keep all lines coiled and under control in pouches or corners of the cockpit. Square up after every manoeuvre by recoiling

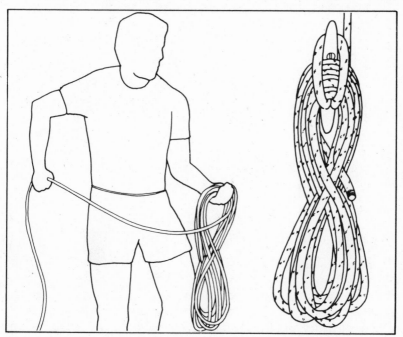

This is how to coil a braided line, which is generally used everywhere except in the anchor rode. It should hang in loose figures-of-eight.

any line that has been used. To avoid kinking, always coil line properly: braided line is coiled in loose figure of eight's; laid three-stranded line is coiled with a slight clockwise twist of the wrist at the end of each loop so that it ends up hanging in a loose oval.

Keep kinks out of sheets and halyards. Braided line can twist badly, and the resulting kinks will stop it running through a block. Either milk (ease) the line through your hands to clear it of kinks, or cleat one end and heave the rest overboard (unless the propeller is turning!) to spin them out quickly.

Look at the sail you are adjusting when trimming or hauling on a sheet, halyard, or other line.

Take nothing for granted. Just because shipmates say they are performing a job, do not automatically assume that they are actually doing it. Double-check cleated and coiled lines. Triple-check for lines dragging overboard before putting the engine in gear (or you will need a hacksaw to cut away the tangle around the propeller).

'One hand for yourself, one hand for the ship.' This means that you give equal attention to your own safety and that of the vessel and your shipmates. If you are secure and doing your job well, the odds are that the vessel is safe.

There is no way to guarantee that following these rules will keep you free of injury; if perfect security were all we wanted out of life, we would never leave the house. Bad luck, sudden weather changes, broken gear, a careless shipmate, and other forces beyond your control may have more say about your fate than your own alertness and self-sufficiency. But if you follow these guidelines, you are at least giving yourself every possible chance to stay healthy and your boat every opportunity to sail efficiently.

How to Feel Secure on Deck

Handling a sailing boat in rough weather is like steering a roller coaster through a tropical rain forest while standing on one foot. Working, walking, and even sitting on the deck of a heeling, bouncing boat make near-impossible demands on even a good athlete's balance and strength. Some gymnasts quickly learn how to keep their feet under them; the rest of us must gradually become accustomed to the boat's motion over a couple of days on board. But most people at one time or another worry about losing their balance, and since that one time or another usually appears just when you are least expecting it—say, when a powerboat races by as you are stepping out of the companionway—an attitude of supreme caution should always prevail.

The constant refrain 'one hand for yourself, one hand for the ship' neatly summarizes the best approach to staying vertical; as you move around the boat, give equal attention to your job and your own safety. Whenever possible, be within arm's reach of a guardrail or grabrail. Below, lean against cabin furniture and, if possible, swing from one grabrail to another like Tarzan moving through the jungle on vines. Only at anchor or in the marina—and then only in flat water—should people with doubtful balance walk across an open area like the foredeck without a hand on a support.

As you stand or walk, keep your weight low and well distributed in a boxer's wide crouch. Absorb the deck's rise and fall in your bent knees. If the boat is rolling violently from side to side, stand with your feet spread crosswise; but if she is pitching, with her bow and stern lifting and falling violently, turn and face to leeward. The safest thoroughfare from the stern to the bow is along the weather, uphill deck. Up there, you can walk with dry feet and with one or both hands firmly on the windward guardrails, in full view of the rest of the crew. Always stay inside the guardrails. Few things frighten a responsible skipper more in rough weather than losing sight of somebody who was 'just there a moment ago' and who may have fallen overboard. It can be a long fall from the windward rail to the leeward one, so hang on tight if you are moving. If the weather is bad, put on a safety harness and clip its lifeline onto a deck fitting—not the guardrails themselves, which may break under a heavy, sudden load—and shorten the lifeline as much as possible to limit the length of a fall.

Sitting for Security

If you feel unsteady and are not doing anything, *sit down*. Do not let false pride or an exaggerated eagerness to be involved keep you standing any longer than necessary. A standing crew member obstructs the helmsman's vision and is extremely vulnerable to toppling when the boat makes even small rolls and pitches. Sitting is also the most secure position on board for doing many jobs, among them pulling down a jib, trimming a sheet, and hauling up the anchor. Not only is your centre of gravity lower when you are sitting, but with a three-point foundation you can wedge your feet against the leeward rail or some other object. In rough seas, you may find that the best way to get around is either to crawl on your hands and knees or to slide around on your bottom.

When working on the foredeck, use the guardrails and the pulpit for support. Sitting down is the most secure position, but be cautious about sitting (or walking) on slippery sails.

It is remarkable how little time sailors spend actually doing anything. Mostly, we are just sitting there. The average cruising boat's cockpit can seat half a dozen people comfortably, half on one side and half on the other. When she is heeled far over, however, sitting on the leeward seat and facing to windward may inspire the less than pleasurable feeling that the boat will soon roll over on top of you. Then you can sit on the windward seat, facing to leeward and sheltered behind the cabin to avoid flying spray. If the cockpit is full of your shipmates, find a perch on the windward deck with your back against the guardrails and feet braced against the cabin.

Now that we have seen how to get around on deck, let us look at getting the boat around in open water—the art of navigation.

CHAPTER 9

How to
Find
Your Way

═══════════

In this chapter we will lay out a quick and simple summary of the tools and skills of coastal navigation. Navigation is the nautical art (and sometimes science) of knowing where you are, determining where you are going, and avoiding running into land. The navigator's guides include the magnetic compass; electronic instruments like the echo sounder and various kinds of radio receivers; and navigational aids such as buoys and lighthouses. Data concerning these guides are printed in miniature on a nautical map called a chart, on which the navigator plots the boat's position and progress. This scale model of the vessel's surroundings and manoeuvres is often supplemented by written entries in the log, a book like a kind of diary. Between the two written histories of the journey, the navigator has enough information not only to determine present position and a safe course to the boat's destination but also to backtrack to a previous position should he or she get lost. Fascinated by these tools and the skills that go with them, many sailors find that navigation can be one of the most enjoyable and rewarding aspects of cruising.

The Navigator's Tools and Skills

The navigator relies on four simple tools to perform the basic skills of position finding and course planning. These are the magnetic compass, which is used to steer courses and take bearings of (determine directions of) objects; the chart; the plotter or parallel rules, which transfers bearings and courses to and from the chart; and dividers, which measure distances on the chart.

Compass Courses and Bearings

The heart of the magnetic compass is a circular card (dial) showing the four cardinal compass directions (north, east, south, and west), and which is graduated into 360 degrees. Magnets attached to the underside of the card orient it to the earth's magnetic field so that no matter which way the boat is headed, the north arrow points to magnetic north, situated in northern Canada. The card sits on a fine-jeweled pivot point in a pool of light oil (which dampens its

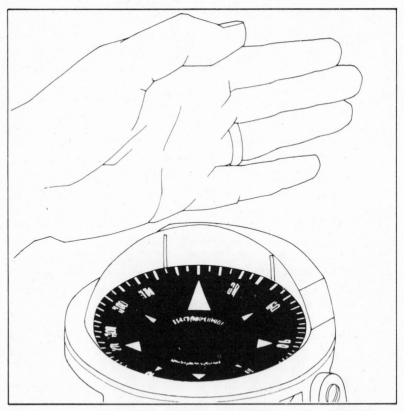

The course is the compass direction in which the boat is heading, as indicated by the reading of the card at the forward lubber's line. A bearing is the compass direction of another object. Cut a bearing across the compass with the hand or use a hand bearing compass.

rotation as the boat turns) under a plastic dome that magnifies its print and allows it to be read from the side. Vertical sighting sticks called lubber's lines provide reference points for steering or taking bearings, and they and the card are gimballed so they stay level when the boat heels or pitches.

Local magnetic fields surrounding nearby metal objects—like a torch, a tool, another compass, or a wrist watch—may deviate the compass so that the north arrow points off to one side of magnetic north. Deviation can be eliminated by removing the metal object or adjusting compensating magnets in the compass base. If the deviation remains, a correction sheet called a deviation table should be constructed to allow the navigator to compensate for errors. All this work is both difficult and important, and is best left to a professional compass adjuster.

The reading of a corrected or undeviated compass is the single constant on board a boat. Regardless of the wind direction and visibility, north is north and 170° is 170°. Like death and taxes, a correctly installed and compensated compass can always be depended on to provide an accurate course and bearing.

Compass courses are courses steered by the compass, in which the steerer uses the compass rather than the sails, a buoy, or some other object as his or her reference. To steer a course, say, of 170 degrees (170°), the helmsman adjusts the helm until the forward lubber's line is directly over 170. Depending on her size and the wind and sea conditions, even a well-steered boat will wander several degrees either side of that heading. Since it is easier to steer by the thick lines at 5- or 10-degree intervals on the compass card than by the thin ones every 1 or 2 degrees, the navigator will help the helmsman by giving the course in 5- or 10-degree increments (for example, 095° instead of 093° or 097°).

Compass bearings are the compass directions from the boat to another object, and are normally taken with a small, portable instrument called a hand bearing compass. This will also serve in emergency as a steering compass, and can if necessary be transferred to a dinghy or liferaft. When taking bearings be careful to keep it away from magnetic objects. Modern hand bearing compasses use optical systems that enable the compass to be held close to the eye, so that the degree scale is seen together with whatever is being viewed, removing any error due to parallax. In the absence of a hand bearing compass, an approximate bearing of an object may be obtained from the boat's steering compass: for greater accuracy aim the boat right at the object and read the heading on the forward lubber's line.

Compass bearings or courses can be expressed as magnetic

(M)—the actual reading of the compass card corrected if necessary for deviation—or as true (T)—where allowance is made for variation at the place concerned. Variation is the angle by which magnetic north is displaced from true north, and is expressed as west (W) if magnetic north is west of true north and as east (E) if it is to the east. Variation changes across the surface of the globe, and also to a lesser extent with the passage of time. At present in the British Isles it varies from about 5°W in the extreme south-east to about 10°W in the Outer Hebrides.

So in British waters it is easy to remember that a magnetic bearing or course is numerically greater than the true one. For example, if variation is 7°W a true bearing of 105° is equivalent to a magnetic bearing of 112°. This becomes very clear if a simple diagram is drawn, showing the direction of true north (straight up the page), of magnetic north (displaced 7° to the west), and of the object concerned. The figure to be applied for variation is always given near the centre of the compass rose (the circular 360° scales which show both true and magnetic norths) on the chart in use.

When necessary, exactly the same rules apply for deviation as for variation, remembering that deviation may be either east (E) or west (W). It is sometimes convenient to add variation and deviation together to determine the total correction to be made. Thus if variation is 7°W and deviation is 2°E the total correction to be made is 5°W.

To summarise—when converting true courses or bearings to magnetic, add westerly variation or deviation and subtract easterly. When converting magnetic to true, subtract westerly variation or deviation and add easterly.

Most navigators prefer to work with true bearings and courses, rather than magnetic, if only because information given on the chart or in sailing directions (for example the line of leading lights, the set of tidal stream or the bearing of a rock from some fixed point) is invariably expressed in true nomenclature. It is however perfectly acceptable to plot on the chart with magnetic bearings and courses, provided that you stick to that method, using the inner of the two concentric rings of the compass rose which takes care of variation (but not deviation).

Compass bearings can be either actual or relative. The actual bearing is the number on the card or in the viewfinder of the hand bearing compass. A relative bearing is the included angle between the boat's compass course and the absolute bearing. For example, when you are sailing a course of 100° and take a bearing of 150° of a lighthouse, the absolute compass bearing is 150° but the relative compass bearing is 050° (150° − 100° = 050°).

The Chart

Knowing the compass course and taking bearings of suitable marks or lights opens the door to the chart, that scale model of your surroundings on which your pencil mimics your every move in miniature. The modern chart is a wondrous thing, beautiful in its colour and its logical, clear expression of mounds of information. Admiralty charts are widely used by yachtsmen as well as by professional seafarers, and cover most of the world. Those for the British Isles and north-west Europe are listed in a special catalogue, available from Admiralty chart agents in all major ports. Things are always changing at sea, and charts soon get out of date as (for example) channels alter and buoys are moved to new locations. One particular advantage of Admiralty charts is the correction service offered by *Admiralty Notices to Mariners*. These are published weekly, but a specially edited edition of those corrections which affect yachtsmen is published every two months during the summer. For smaller yachts the folding charts produced for yachtsmen by Stanford or Imray have some attraction.

The most obvious difference among individual charts is the scale, or the size of the area of land and sea that they cover, and the amount of detail that they show. The scale is given near the title of the chart, and is the relation between a distance on the chart and the actual distance it represents on land or sea. Small scale charts cover large areas, like Admiralty chart 2675 which shows the whole of the English Channel on a scale of 1:500,000. Charts of coastal areas are typically to a scale of 1:150,000. Large scale charts are used for the approaches to harbours, say 1:10,000, while harbour plans giving the greatest detail may be 1:3500. Remember that the largest scale charts have the smallest numbers, and vice versa, and always use the largest scale chart available, because much detail has to be omitted from small scale charts. It would be pointless trying to find your way around London on a road map covering all southern England.

To make the best use of the available space the information on a chart is displayed by symbols and abbreviations, which must of course be understood if they are to be interpreted correctly. They are explained in detail in an excellent booklet NP 5011 (*Symbols and Abbreviations used on Admiralty Charts*). It is wise to carry a copy on board.

Modern charts have depths (below a level called chart datum) and heights (above the level of Mean High Water Spring tides) shown in metres, but there are still some charts in existence where these are shown in fathoms (units of six feet) and in feet. Make sure you know which units apply. On Admiralty metric charts the land is tinted buff, and areas which dry between high water and low water are shown green. Areas where the depth is less than five metres are blue. Certain features such as navigation aids, traffic schemes, prohibited anchorages, submarine cables etc are shown in magenta.

Scattered over the chart are soundings, showing the depth of water at each place so indicated. Places with equal depths are joined by depth contours, just as the contours of a hill are shown on a map. The ten metre contour line has a ribbon of blue tint.

A chart has to display on a flat sheet of paper the curved surface of the earth, which involves some compromise. Most charts are constructed on Mercator's projection which has certain advantages for navigation. In particular, angles on the earth's surface correspond to angles on the chart, and the scale of distance is given by the latitude scale which runs up and down each side. One nautical mile (n mile) equals one minute of latitude at the place concerned. The actual length of a nautical mile varies somewhat because the earth is not a perfect sphere, but for practical purposes such as calibrating marine instruments it is taken as 6076 ft (1852 m), and therefore can be seen to be a bit longer than a land (statute) mile. A cable (ca) is one-tenth of a nautical mile—about 200 yards (183 m).

The compass rose is a chart's most important feature for normal navigation. It is a replica of the card in the cockpit compass and it serves as a sailor's Rosetta Stone to translate courses and bearings onto paper. The compass roses on a chart actually include two concentric compass dials. The outer dial is oriented to polar or true north—the spot that geographers have decided is the top of the world and toward which, at least in the Mercator projection used on most charts, the vertical meridians of longitude ascend in parallel. The rose's inner dial, like the compass on deck, is oriented to the earth's magnetic field and so is usually skewed to the meridians. The angular difference between north on the true, outer dial and north on the magnetic, inner dial is the magnetic variation, as already described. Since variation alters slightly from year to year, as well as from place to place, the small annual changes in variation are also labelled.

The Plotter and Dividers

All right, you have your course and some bearings on deck, and you have got your chart spread out on the chart table below, well out of the spray and crew traffic. Now you need some tools to help convert deck compass degrees to chart compass rose degrees, and to display distances to scale. Start out with a soft 2B pencil sharpened to a fine point. Then get out a plotter and a pair of dividers.

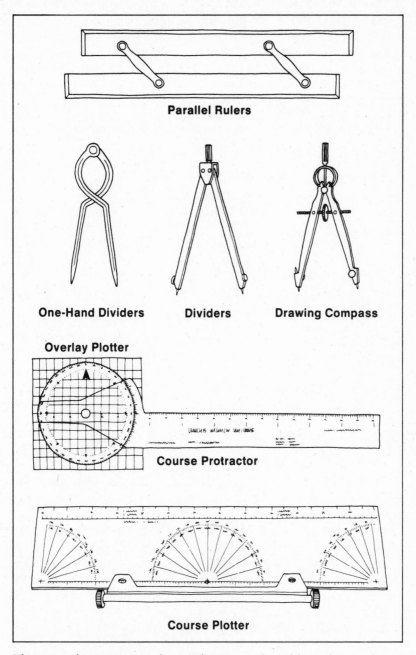

Parallel Rulers

One-Hand Dividers   **Dividers**   **Drawing Compass**

Overlay Plotter

Course Protractor

Course Plotter

These are the navigator's basic plotting tools. Add a soft pencil,
calculator, watch, cruising guide and the necessary charts,
almanac with tide tables and other navigational information, and
you are ready to go.

The plotter provides both a straight edge to draw courses and bearings and a way to duplicate them on the chart. There are different types of plotters. Some, called parallel rulers (or rules), are laid across the compass rose to find the course or bearing that has been reported from the cockpit, and are then slid (or 'walked') across the chart to the boat's approximate position. When plotting a course, a plotter's edge is laid over the last known position and a course line is drawn from it. On the other hand, when plotting a bearing, an edge is placed over the symbol of the sighted object and a bearing line is laid off on the chart.

Since parallel rulers can slide around when the boat is rolling or pitching, many navigators prefer to use another type of plotter—a 360-degree protractor with an adjustable arm. The protractor is laid over an intersection of a north-south running meridian of longitude and then turned until it mimics the local variation as shown on the closest rose. The protractor is adjusted until the arm passes at the reported compass course through the last position, or at the reported bearing through the sighted object. Then the line is drawn.

Dividers—a drawing compass with a point at each end—are used to measure distances on the chart, referring to the latitude scale on the side (since the scale varies due to the distortion of the Mercator projection, be sure to use the latitude scale exactly alongside your position).

Understanding the Tides

In some parts of the world yachtsmen need give scant attention to the tide, but around north-west Europe and in many other places it deserves careful study since the rise and fall every 12 hours or so can be four or five metres—and sometimes a great deal more. What looks an inviting stretch of water can soon become an expanse of sand or mud, or perhaps disclose dangerous rocks. In many harbours boating is governed largely by the tide, and plans need to be made accordingly. So it is essential to be able to discover the times and heights of high and low water, and to have some insight into what happens in between.

The ups and downs of the sea bed are shown on charts by depth contours, linking places with the same depth, while actual depths are also recorded at many places. These depths are all measured below a horizontal plane called chart datum, normally Lowest Astronomical Tide (LAT) or in other words the level below which the tide does not fall under normal weather conditions. Points which are covered at high water but exposed as the tide falls are

shown as drying heights above chart datum, with their figures
underlined.

Tidal Terminology
In order to understand the use of tide tables you need to be familiar
with a few of the terms which are used:
  Height. The height of sea level at any moment, above chart
datum.
  Range. The difference in height between high and low water.
  Depth. The depth of water at any time is the charted sounding
(below chart datum) plus the height of the tide (above chart datum)
at that moment: or, if a drying height is shown for that place, the
height of tide minus the drying height (if the result is positive that
place is submerged, if negative it is exposed).
  Springs. Tides are caused by the gravitational effects of the
moon and the sun. When they act together, near new moon and full
moon, they cause spring (big) tides.
  Neaps. The opposite of springs, when tides are small, near the
first and last quarters of the moon.
  Standard Ports. Those selected ports for which daily tidal
predictions are published in tide tables (see below).
  Secondary Ports. Other places for which tidal information
can be obtained from time and height differences applied to the
predictions for the appropriate Standard Port (see below).

Tidal Predictions—Standard Ports
Predictions of the times and heights of high water and low water for
Standard Ports are given for each day of the year in tide tables pub-
lished in nautical almanacs (or *Admiralty Tide Tables, Vol 1* for
European waters).
  Note that the times are expressed in Greenwich Mean Time
(GMT). During summer months one hour must be added to convert
to British Summer Time (BST).
  It is however often necessary to calculate what the height of the
tide will be at a certain time between high and low water, or the
time at which the tide will reach a certain height. This is done by
means of tidal curves which are drawn for each Standard Port. An
explanation of their use is given in the tide tables concerned.

Tidal Predictions—Secondary Ports
For a Secondary Port the approximate time and height of high
water or low water can be found by adding (when +) or subtracting
(when −) the time and height differences shown for that port to or
from the predictions given for the associated Standard Port.

It will be seen in the tide tables that time differences are given (only) for selected times of high and low water at the Standard Port. For intermediate times the time difference must be interpolated (or adjusted) to suit. This can usually be done well enough by eye, but a mathematical procedure is given in the tide tables. Although time differences are quoted to the nearest minute it should not be assumed that the resulting predictions will be quite that accurate.

The same principle applies to the height differences for Secondary Ports. For each port these are given in turn for Mean High Water Springs (MHWS), Mean High Water Neaps (MHWN), Mean Low Water Neaps (MLWN) and Mean Low Water Springs (MLWS). For dates between springs and neaps the height differences must be interpolated, in the same way as time differences.

Plotting: The DR, EP and Fix

Standard Terms

In recent years an attempt has been made to standardise the terminology used for chartwork. Since it is important to know certain terms in a boat, or if attending navigation classes, these are given below.

Track—the path followed or to be followed between one position and another. This path may be that over the ground (ground track) or through the water (water track).

Track angle*—the direction of a track.

Track made good—the mean ground track actually achieved over a given period.

Heading—the horizontal direction of the ship's head at a given moment. (This term does not necessarily require movement of the vessel).

Course (Co)—the intended heading.

Course to steer—the course related to the compass used by the helmsman.

Set—the direction towards which a current and/or tidal stream flows.

Drift—the distance covered in a given time due solely to the movement of a current and/or tidal stream.

Drift angle*—the angular difference between the ground track and the water track.

Leeway—the effect of wind moving a vessel bodily to leeward.

Leeway angle*—the angular difference between the water track and the ship's heading.

Dead Reckoning—the process of maintaining or predicting an approximate record of progress by projecting course and distance from a known position.

DR position (DR)—(1) the general term for a position obtained by dead reckoning; (2) specifically a position obtained using true course and distance run, the latter derived from the log or engine revolutions as considered more appropriate.

Estimated Position (EP)—a best possible approximation of a present or future position. It is based on course and distance since the last known position with an estimation made for leeway, set and drift, or by extrapolation from earlier fixes.

*The word angle will be omitted in normal use unless there is a possibility of confusion.

Dead Reckoning (DR)

The DR plot is the best way for the crew to stay in tune with the boat's progress without relying on external aids to navigation. *It depends solely on information found on board:* the boat's course, read off the compass and reported (accurately, we trust) by the helmsman; and the distance she moves through the water as measured by the log (distance-run indicator). Just as a compass must be checked for deviation, a log should not be relied on until it has been calibrated by runs in each direction up and down a measured distance. If the boat does not have a log, her speed through the water must be estimated for DR purposes. With experience this can be done reasonably accurately by eye, or it is possible to use what is called a Dutchman's log—by throwing a floating object overboard at the bow and measuring the time it takes to reach the stern. Knowing the length of the boat, the speed can be calculated.

No matter how you calculate speed, you may determine the distance run (how far you have sailed at a known speed for a certain time) from the formula:

$$\text{distance run} = \frac{(\text{speed} \times \text{time})}{60}$$

where distance is in nautical miles, speed is in knots, and time is in minutes.

If you have sailed at 6 knots for 28 minutes, you have covered 2.8 nautical miles; for 70 minutes, 7 miles; and so on.

With course and distance run known, you can plot the DR. Let us use this example; it is 1934 (the 24-hour clock is always used at sea) and since you last plotted your position at 1900 you have averaged 5.5 knots on a compass course of 165°. What is your new DR position?

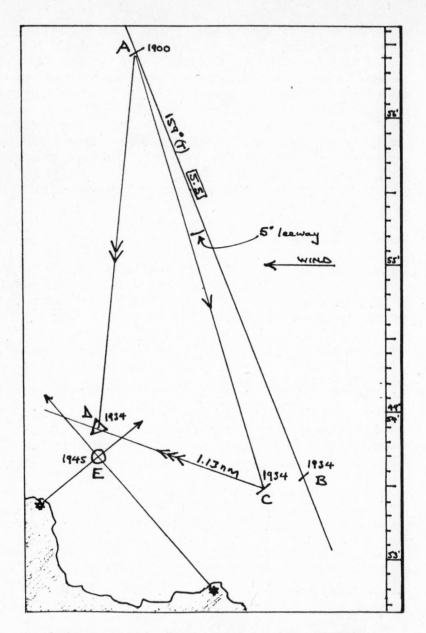

A is the boat's original position at 1900. B is the Dead Reckoning (DR) position at 1934, from course steered and distance run. C is the corrected DR to allow for five degrees of leeway. D is the Estimated Position (EP) at 1934, allowing also for tidal set. E is a Fix obtained from bearings of two shore objects at 1945 and is a separate procedure.

Here are the steps you take:

1. Calculate the distance run. Read the log at 1934 to determine distance run since 1900. If these readings are not available, calculate distance run from the average speed during that period (5.5 knots) and the elapsed time (34 minutes) according to the formula given above. It comes to 3.12 (say, 3.1) nautical miles.

2. Plot the course. From your last position, use the plotter or parallel rule to draw a short, light line on the chart at 165°, being careful to use the inner, magnetic circle on the compass rose. (Alternatively, apply variation to the compass course and use the outer, true circle. If for example variation is 6°W, the true course will be 159°. Against the course print 165°(M) or 159°(T) as appropriate. By convention the average speed (5.5 knots) is inserted in a square box as shown in the diagram.

3. Plot the distance run. Using the latitude scale alongside the position, spread the dividers over 3.1 miles, pick them up, and place one point at the 1900 position (A) and the other point on the course (or its extension) steered since 1900, just pricking the paper. Remove the dividers and, if necessary, complete the line to the prick.

4. Label the DR. Put a pencil mark across the course line at the prick, and label it 1934. This is point B in the diagram.

With the DR position plotted you now have at least some idea of where you are. But if there is any tidal stream or wind-driven current, leeway, unreported wandering from course on the part of the helmsman, or mistakes in figuring out the distance run, this position will be wrong.

The Estimated Position (EP)

The DR position can be improved by making allowance for any leeway and for drift due to the effect of tidal stream between 1900 and 1934 in the example above. The amount of leeway a boat makes depends on the characteristics of the individual boat, the conditions of wind and sea, and the point of sailing. As already discussed in Chapter 6, it is likely to be 5–10 degrees for the average cruising yacht going to windward in normal conditions, decreasing to zero when the wind is right aft, and can be gauged fairly accurately with a bit of experience. Let us assume that in the situation we are discussing the wind is easterly, and that leeway is estimated as 5 degrees. This means that if the course steered is 165°(M), the water track will be 170°(M). Thus at 1934 the boat would have reached C, and not B.

Tidal stream predictions can be obtained either from the chart or from a tidal stream atlas for the area concerned. In the first case predictions are shown at a few selected places, giving the set and rate at each hour before and after high water (HW) at a nearby port, both for spring and neap tides, which are discussed more fully later. A tidal stream atlas gives a dozen maps of the area, one for each hour before and after HW. Each map depicts by arrows and figures the set and rate of the stream at numerous places throughout the area. Select the appropriate map and estimate set and rate for the position concerned.

One way or the other you can decide the approximate set and rate of the tidal stream between 1900 and 1934. For the sake of argument let us assume it is running 290° at 2 knots. So for the 34 minutes concerned the drift will be $\dfrac{2 \times 34}{60}$ = 1.13 n miles.

Commonsense then tells us that the effect of the stream during these 34 minutes will be to move the boat 1.13 n miles in a direction of 290°. Draw a line on a bearing of 290° from C, and mark the distance along it, giving point D.

D is then the Estimated Position (EP), which by convention is marked by a small triangle round the point, with the time 1934 alongside. Other conventions can be noted in the diagram. The boat's water track (AC) is marked by a single arrow, the drift due to tidal stream (CD) is marked by a triple arrow, and the track made good (AD) is marked by a double arrow.

To summarise the steps to be taken in plotting EP:

1. Estimate leeway. Apply it (in the right direction) as a small angle to the course steered to give the water track, and mark this new line with a single arrow. Along it step off with dividers the distance run—as already obtained when deriving the DR, above.

2. Estimate tidal stream. Obtain the best possible predictions for set (direction) and drift (amount of tidal stream during the relevant period.)

3. Plot tidal stream vector. From the new position obtained in 1. above, construct a vector (line) representing in direction the set and in length the drift from 2. above, and mark it with triple arrows. Label the end of that line as a small triangle (EP), with the time alongside.

4. Construct track made good. Join the EP to the original position to show the track made good, and mark it with double arrows.

Any EP can be improved by a position line obtained, for example, from a compass bearing of a charted object—a buoy, beacon, lighthouse, church spire or whatever. Another kind of position line may be provided by a succession of depth soundings, compared with the figures on the chart. Major changes in depth can provide good evidence of your position. In fact, an excellent tactic when sailing in fog is to get over a depth contour and, using the echo sounder as your eyes, follow it to your destination.

A single position line does not tell you how far you are from the sighted object; but it does allow you to picture a clear, straight, and repeatable path to it. Your position is somewhere along that path. Not the least of the virtues of a single bearing or depth sounding is that it will give you a fairly clear picture of where you are *not*, which can be comforting when sailing near rocks and land.

The Fix

If there were some way to measure exactly how far along the single position line you are, you could improve on that estimate with a fixed position (called a fix). Of course, you can guess the distance, but poor visibility or eyesight usually make that unreliable. Better to find another position line (from another charted object) that crosses with the first one—preferably at as near right angles as possible so that any errors made in taking or plotting the bearings are minimized. When using three position lines, try to cross them at 60-degree angles.

To take a fix, follow these steps:

1. Update the DR or EP. This will be a check against the accuracy of the bearings.

2. Note the time.

3. Take and plot two or more bearings. They should be taken as near simultaneously as possible. Plot the position lines, clearly indicating the objects that the bearings were taken on.

4. Take and record the log reading. This is important for subsequent navigation, and is easy to overlook.

5. Label the fix. Where the position lines intersect or form a small triangle (called a cocked hat), draw a small circle and mark the time. If you are using two position lines and one of them puts the boat surprisingly far from the DR or EP, retake them both. If one of three position lines skews the fix by making a large cocked hat, either consider this an area of position rather than a fix or retake the bearings.

The new DR plot then begins at the position and time of the fix. If the difference between a reliable fix (with a reasonably small cocked hat) and the last DR is large—say one mile after ten miles of sailing—try to figure out why. The cause could be as simple as a log or speedometer over-reading, or a helmsman too optimistic about his ability to hold a course. Maybe the boat is making a lot of leeway, and you should compensate when you set the new course.

(Sailing close-hauled or on a reach in rough weather, most cruising boats make 10 to 15 degrees of leeway). Or perhaps the tidal stream shoved the boat to one side, forward, or backward.

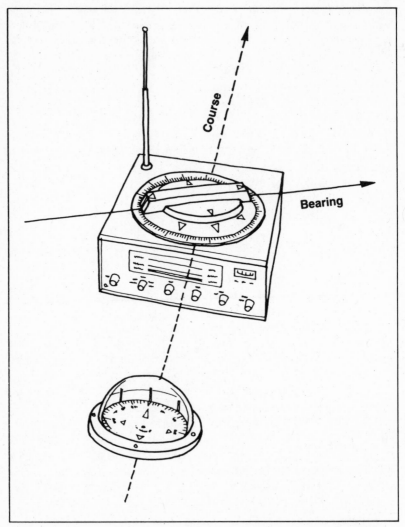

The radio direction finder (RDF) takes bearings of radio beacons. First tune to a nearby station and align the outer ring with the compass heading (dotted line) — but keep it well away from the cockpit compass. Then rotate the pointer until the dot-dash signal is inaudible (solid line). That is the null. Read the bearing off the ring. Many modern sets have a hand-held aerial with its own compass.

Electronic Navigation: RDF and Decca

The two electronic navigation instruments most commonly used in yachts for coastal cruising are the radio direction finder (RDF) and Decca. The former is less expensive and less accurate; the latter costs somewhat more and is very precise. They have one problem in common—performance falls off at night and they tend to go haywire during thunderstorms.

The Radio Direction Finder (RDF)

RDF works like a long-range, hand bearing compass, picking up and taking bearings on radio signals from beacons 100 miles or more away (although most radiobeacons only have an effective range of about 50 miles, some less). RDF receivers fall broadly into two types:

1. With a hand-held, directional aerial which incorporates a small compass—similar to a hand bearing compass—enabling a (magnetic) bearing to be taken directly of a radiobeacon, regardless of the course of the yacht at that time.

2. With a directional aerial incorporated into, and rotating on, a fixed set. In this case the resulting radio bearing is relative to the ship's head, and the helmsman must note the compass course at the moment the operator takes the bearing, which is sometimes difficult to achieve.

In both cases the procedure is similar so far as the operator is concerned. He or she tunes the receiver to the frequency of the radiobeacon required, as shown in nautical almanacs or *Admiralty List of Radio Signals, Vol 2*. Marine radiobeacons mostly transmit at fixed intervals, often for one minute in every six, but some are continuous—like certain aeronautical beacons which (being on the coast) are suitable for marine navigation. Each beacon is identified by its individual Morse call sign, followed by a long continuous note during which the aerial is rotated until the signal is minimal or inaudible. This point is called the null, and at that moment the bearing is recorded.

Often half-a-dozen radiobeacons share a common frequency, each transmitting for one minute in turn. In this way two or three useful bearings can often be acquired within six minutes, without any need to re-tune the set.

Radio bearings give a position line, just like visual bearings of shore objects, but they are usually less accurate particularly at night, and even more so near sunset and sunrise. At least three should be taken for a reliable fix, and they should be plotted like visual bearings, showing the time they were taken and were they originated.

Decca Navigator

The Decca Yacht Navigator is a receiver which accepts signals from a chain of Decca transmitters and continuously calculates the boat's position, which is displayed as a digital readout of latitude and longitude. The system works (like other electronic aids such as Loran-C and Omega) on the hyperbolic principle. A hyperbola is constructed from points whose distances from two fixed points always differ by the same amount. By measuring the phase difference between synchronised transmissions from two fixed stations on shore, the receiver can identify its appropriate hyperbolic position line. Similar measurements from another pair of transmitters give a second position line, and hence a fix. A Decca Navigator chain normally consists of four transmitters—a master station and three outlying slave stations designated Red, Green and Purple. The range of a chain is about 350 nautical miles from the master station by day, and about 250 miles by night.

Since World War II commercial vessels have hired Decca Navigators for use in European waters and in other parts of the world. These commercial sets use special Decca charts, overprinted with a lattice grid on which a vessel's position can be plotted from readings on the Decca receiver, and allowing for corrections to be made for both fixed and variable errors in the system from Decca Data Sheets. The Decca Yacht Navigator, with its direct readout of latitude and longitude, does not have this facility and is therefore slightly less accurate. In general an accuracy of 0.1 to 0.2 nautical miles can be expected, but under adverse conditions (at night, in winter, and at higher ranges) this could well increase to 0.5 nautical miles.

Other position-fixing systems available include Loran-C, Omega and satellite navigation. Each has its advantages and disadvantages for particular applications. It is possible that Loran-C may come into more general use for European waters, while the new Navstar GPS (satellite system) will give continuous, accurate fixes in any part of the world.

With the advent of electronic navigation instruments came the term waypoint, meaning any selected position along a vessel's intended track. A waypoint may for example be a convenient position for altering course round a headland, or a departure point or final destination—or anywhere in between. Instruments such as a Decca Yacht Navigator can store several waypoints, entered with their latitudes and longitudes. The set will then provide distance and course from the present position to a selected waypoint, or if required from waypoint to waypoint which can be useful for passage planning.

Other benefits from these remarkable gadgets may include displays of cross track error (the distance off track for the next waypoint, and the course to steer to return to track), average course and speed over (say) the last four minutes, the time that will be taken to reach a selected waypoint at present speed made good, and an alarm in the case of poor reception of Decca transmissions or on close approach to a selected waypoint. When outside the range of Decca

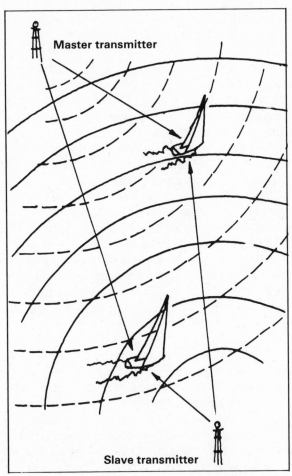

Decca, like Loran-C and Omega navigation systems, works on the principle of the hyperbolic position line, illustrated here. For each point on the hyperbola the difference in time between the receipt of synchronised signals from the master station and the slave station is the same.

transmissions the set operates as a DR computer, from manual inputs of speed, course and tidal data. All this is yours for well under £1000.

Old-time navigators become very squeamish when they hear praise for devices like Decca and satellite navigation, which are quickly making obsolete many traditional skills, including celestial navigation. Like everything else (celestial navigation included), these remarkable devices have their limitations and their place, yet they should not be blithely ignored by *anybody* who cares about knowing where he or she is on the water. A selling point that I have only recently discovered is that, unlike celestial navigation or complicated pilotage, electronic instruments fascinate many bright people who find nothing else of interest in a boat.

Nonetheless, too much can be made of a good thing. It is fine to use these magic boxes as long as you do not *depend* on them. They are only aids, and must be backed by a proper knowledge of standard navigational techniques. Radio waves are not infallible. Besides being vulnerable to reception errors, electronic addicts are open to two other dangers which I call the fallacy of precision and the fallacy of completeness. First, the instrument's reputation for precision can lower the navigator's guard. You read the little green numbers; you plot your position and mark it as a fix. There—precisely, exactly, indisputably *there*—is where you were when you read the numbers. No doubt about it. The machine told you so.

Well, yes and no. There are some necessary compromises in the system, as already explained. The readout of latitude or longitude may be given in 100ths of a minute, but this does *not* mean that the set is as accurate as that. Your dividers or straight edge may be a fraction off, and even a pencil line has a certain thickness. So you are probably not *there*, after all, but rather *about there*—somewhere within a couple of hundred yards (or maybe even a quarter of a mile) of *there*. Instead of marking a precise spot, the fix identifies the reliable area of your position.

The second fallacy, the fallacy of completeness, assumes that the machine is telling you all that you have to know to get from where you are to your destination. You go below and push a few buttons; within seconds the machine tells you something that would take five minutes to figure out on the chart: your destination is 10 miles away on a course of 323°. So you tell the helmsman to steer 323° (or, if you are thoroughly automated, you dial 323 into the autopilot). Somebody asks when you are going to get there, so you push a couple of other buttons to learn that at your present speed of exactly 5.38 knots over the ground, you will reach your destination in precisely one hour 51.52 minutes. You have just enough to time to finish reading your book. You lean back on the settee and open it up. That is how simple it is. You do not have to look at the chart or plot your position or take a depth sounding or even go to the considerable effort of asking a shipmate sunbathing up on the foredeck to roll over and take a glance ahead. And then, Wham! The rock that the chart or a depth sounding or a lookout would have warned you about—an obstruction that a Decca receiver has no capability of discovering—suddenly appears in precisely the wrong place, through the cabin sole.

So while electronic instruments can tell you a lot that is important and helpful and accurate, they do not and cannot tell you everything that is relevant to your situation and your intentions. It is a truism of our age that to depend too much on a machine, to expect a gadget to do more or better than it is capable of is to risk idolatory and invite disaster. Every time a navigator turns on one of these extraordinary machines, he or she must consciously declare the limits of his or her reliance on it, and be prepared to assume personal and human responsibility for safe navigation.

Keeping Up the Log

The log is the 'ship's journal or day by day record of events, observations, courses steered, weather experienced, etc.' according to the *Encyclopedia of Nautical Knowledge*. It can be a simple, ruled notebook or a fancy, leatherbound volume with the boat's name embossed in gold leaf. Plain or fancy, either way it should have enough room for the crew to record what is important to the boat's and their own welfare.

What information should be recorded? Some navigators put information such as courses steered, log readings, bearings taken (and the times for these various events) directly onto the chart, so that dead reckoning and fixes can be worked up without having to refer elsewhere. This however is often less than satisfactory, since for DR purposes it is desirable for the helmsman to assess and record the course steered at regular intervals (say every half-hour) together with the relevant log readings, while it is also wise to keep a permanent record of more important changes of course, bearings of shore objects, the times at which they occur, and the log reading in each case. The navigator, is then free to work up the DR as is seen fit. This might be in 30 minute steps, but more likely he or she will choose to average the course steered over a period of one or two hours before plotting on the chart accordingly.

So prime headings in the log are time, course ordered (as a reminder to the person on the helm), the estimated course actually steered, and log readings. The skipper should ensure that these are always entered at regular intervals, no matter what other distractions there may be. Gale force winds or fog are just the occasions when it is important to keep as accurate a plot as possible.

Barometer readings should be recorded regularly so that any rising or falling trend is quickly identified. By the same token it is helpful to note any build-up of heavy clouds (or a clearance), an increase in swell or wave size, or a change in visibility.

With regard to other entries it is useful to have one wide column for general remarks which might include the bearings of shore objects (or of other vessels, to identify risk of collision), RDF bearings, the times of starting or stopping the engine, sail changes, times of anchoring or getting under way, and any other matter of navigational significance. Maintenance observations should be recorded in much the same way that you write grocery lists on the backs of envelopes: a change of engine oil; clearing a blocked filter; a shortage of toilet paper or of marmalade; a lost mainsail batten. Announce a strange clank in the engine, a frayed halyard, a drop in voltage, or a shortage of fresh water.

But the log need not be all business. It is a place to wax poetic about a glowing sunset, to repeat a joke that deserves immortality, to tell about the porpoises that slipped under the bow wave all afternoon, to list the ingredients of a memorable drink, or to tease the seriousness out of the skipper at the beginning of a cruise.

The Navigator's Mind and Routine

Like any sort of detailed calculating, navigation is only as accurate as the data used. 'Garbage in, garbage out' applies here just as it does in computer programming. There is one big difference, though: the navigator can often get into trouble by having too much faith in the accuracy of his information, which for a variety of reasons usually has some errors and occasionally a downright blunder. Though many sailors aim for pin-point navigation, they rarely achieve it. Expecting too much accuracy will lead to frustration, time-consuming repetitions of bearings and calculations, and optimistic projections that may cut corners and leave the boat high and dry. Experienced navigators know that although the tiny circle they draw on the chart looks like a precise position, it is more like a probable area of position. Rather than drawing a small circle and saying, 'We're right there!', the navigator is better off saying that there is a 95 per cent chance of being within two miles of the fixed position. Once made, promises are hard to go back on.

A good navigator also knows that even in calm weather nobody can steer a course or take a compass bearing of an object a mile or more away with an accuracy better than plus or minus two or three degrees; when the boat is rolling in steep waves, the error expands to five or even ten degrees. Therefore, depending on the conditions, a 'spot on' course or bearing of 270° might actually be anywhere between 265° and 275°. At a range of one mile, that is an error of 300 yards; at five miles, three-quarters of a mile. Obviously, then, the navigator should take every opportunity to check his position.

Stick to a Routine

The lowest common denominator of good navigation is to keep in safe water. There are other reasons for taking bearings and plotting positions, but none is better than that one. Good navigators may not always know precisely where they are, but they usually know where they are not—and that is where rocks, shoals and other hazards are. Only a fool would be under way in fog or heavy weather without such a conservative approach, but defensive navigation should be standard procedure all the time. The many groundings and collisions that occur in perfectly clear weather suggest that even expert mariners let down their guard when the sailing becomes easy. Somehow, the routines that we follow so rigorously in poor visibility are forgotten when the sun comes out, and we cut corners and take other risks that may well pile us up on the nearest rocks. So it is desirable to establish a reasonable ship's routine, to be followed all the time she is under sail. Here is the one I like to use:

> At all times one person is assigned as navigator and has the primary responsibility for taking bearings, plotting positions on the chart, and advising the skipper about the boat's position and progress. The navigator may be the skipper or somebody with less experience (over whose shoulder the skipper takes an occasional peep). The actual mechanics of navigation are simple enough for anybody to do; it is the interpretation of apparently contradictory evidence that requires some experience. The essential skills can be mastered by anybody who can focus the mind, concentrate for extended periods of time, read a map, draw a straight line, and perform elementary mathematics.

> All potential problems must be anticipated and talked through before they appear. For example, the times of tide changes should be calculated ahead of time, and charts should be arranged in the probable order of use.

The plot and log must be kept up to date. The boat's position is noted regularly in clear weather. Near shore, this means plotting the position at every turning point and inspecting the future route on the chart (to save chart wear and tear, the position need not be written down). In bad weather, the position is always written down on the chart at every turning point near shore and at every hour (or more frequently) offshore. In addition, the most important courses, distances run, and turning marks are listed in order in the log. That way, the navigator can backtrack to find mistakes.

A little system, care, and routine—that is all we are encouraging. In the long run, the five minutes you spend over the chart and tide tables every hour will save you many hours of worry. Much of the time, what worries a navigator most is the threat of running into something—either land or another vessel. In Chapter 10, we will see how the risk of collisions can be minimized.

How to

Avoid

Running into

Things

International agreements have resulted in the creation of two legal systems which, when observed by mariners, keep vessels from colliding with the land and with each other. They are the buoyage system of the International Association of Lighthouse Authorities (happily contracted to IALA for general use), and the *International Regulations for Preventing Collisions at Sea*—more conveniently referred to as the Collision Regulations (COLREG) or the rule of the road. These two sets of regulations feature visual and sound signals that warn which kinds of hazards to anticipate and indicate how to avoid them. Once you have taken the time to learn these two systems, you will find them ingeniously unambiguous.

Avoid Running Aground:
The IALA Buoyage System (Region A)

Up to ten years ago there were more than 30 different methods of buoyage used by countries all over the world. But since 1977 a new system has been gradually introduced so that (with one notable exception, described below) mariners now need to memorise only the one IALA system. It applies to all fixed and floating marks (except lighthouses, sector lights, leading lights into harbours,

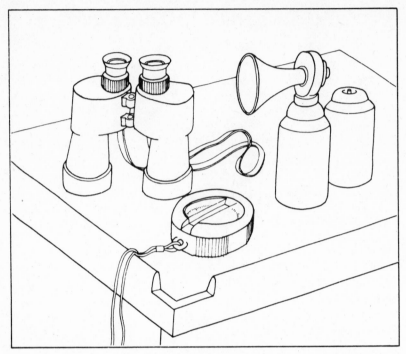

Besides the chart and a knowledge of the rule of the road, these three items may be your best protection against running into land or another boat: binoculars for identifying distant objects, a hand bearing compass for taking accurate bearings, and a horn for making the required signals.

light-vessels and large navigation buoys) used to indicate navigable channels, dangers (including wrecks), and other important features. It embodies five types of marks, which can be used in any combination.

Lateral Marks (Region A)

Lateral marks are used with a conventional direction of buoyage to indicate the port and starboard sides of a channel which should be followed. The direction of buoyage is shown on the chart by a special arrow, and in harbours or estuaries it is normally the direction followed when entering from seaward: but in channels around the coast of Britain the general direction of buoyage is from SW to NE.

A port-hand mark (to be left on the port side of the boat) is red. If a buoy, it is can-shaped (with a flat top) or a spar buoy. Any topmark fitted is a single red can. Any light shown is red.

A starboard-hand mark (to be left on the starboard side of the boat) is green. If a buoy, it can be conical (with a pointed top) or a spar buoy. Any topmark fitted is a single green cone, point up. Any light which it shows is green.

The above system of lateral buoyage applies to much of the world, including the whole of Europe and the Mediterranean, in what is designated Region A. However, in American and Japanese waters (designated Region B), the characteristics of port and starboard-hand lateral marks are reversed, so that America retains her traditional system of 'red, right, returning'. The rest of the IALA buoyage system, described briefly below, applies equally to Regions A and B.

Cardinal Marks

Cardinal marks show navigable water and dangers in relation to the compass. A cardinal mark is named after the quadrant in which it is placed relevant to the danger it marks, and should be passed on the named side. Thus a N cardinal mark is placed north of (say) a shoal, and vessels should keep to the north of it.

All cardinal marks are pillar or spar buoys, painted black and yellow, and with double cone topmarks. Their different characteristics are shown in the accompanying table. To help identify

Cardinal marks	North	East	South	West
Colour	Black over yellow	Black over yellow over black	Yellow over black	Yellow over black over yellow
Topmark—two black cones, one above the other	Points up	Base to base	Points down	Point to point
Lights (white) Q—Quick flashing (50-60 per min) VQ—Very quick flashing (100-120 per min) LFl—Long flash (not less than 2 secs)	Q or VQ	Q(3) 10s or VQ(3) 5s	Q(6)+ LFl 15s or VQ(6)+ LFl 10s	Q(9) 15s or VQ(9) 10s

Cardinal marks are named after the quadrant in which the mark is placed, in relation to the danger concerned. They all carry double-cone topmarks, as shown in the table above, and are all painted yellow and black in different combinations. Lights, where fitted, are white — either quick flashing or very quick flashing.

their topmarks, note that for a N cardinal mark the cones point up (north) while for a S cardinal mark they point down (south). The cones on a W cardinal mark (point to point) can be thought of as 'waisted'. Some people remember the E cardinal cones (base to base) as 'expectant'. The directions in which the cones point also indicate the location of the black markings on the marks: for example with a N cardinal mark where the cones point up it is the upper part of the mark which is painted black.

Lights on cardinal marks, where so fitted, are always white, either quick flashing (about one flash per second) or very quick flashing (about two flashes per second). It will be seen that the number of flashes resembles the face of a clock—three at three o'clock (east), six at six o'clock (south) and nine at nine o'clock (west). To help distinguish it, a S cardinal light also shows a long flash of not less than two seconds.

Isolated Danger Marks

Isolated danger marks are placed on or over a danger such as an isolated rock, which has navigable water all around it. An isolated danger mark is coloured black with one or more red bands (in buoyage and lighthouse terminology bands run horizontally, and stripes vertically). It carries a topmark consisting of two black spheres, one above the other. If a buoy, it is pillar or spar shaped. Any light fitted is white, group flashing (2)—that is to say two flashes followed by a period of darkness, two more flashes, and so on.

Safe Water Marks

Safe water marks indicate that there is navigable water all round, and are used for landfall buoys or mid-channel marks. They are spherical, pillar or spar buoys with a red spherical topmark. Any light fitted is white and is isophase (equal periods of light and darkness), occulting (longer flashes of light than periods of darkness), or one long flash every 10 seconds.

Special Marks

Special marks are not primarily for navigation but indicate special features such as spoil grounds, cables, exercise areas, water ski areas etc. They are all coloured yellow. If they have a topmark it is a yellow X. Any light fitted is yellow, with a rhythm which is distinctive from navigational marks.

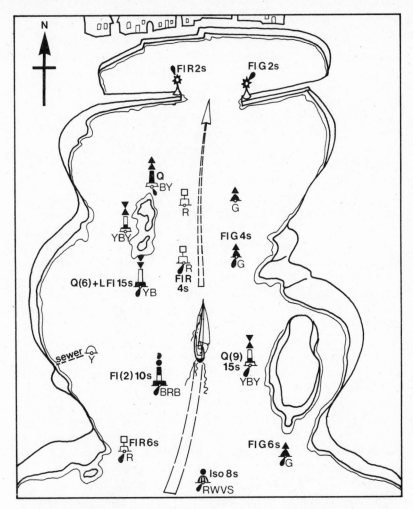

Entering harbour, a boat is guided by the various marks indicated
on the chart by the symbols shown above. First comes a fairway
buoy (safe water mark, red and white vertical stripes, with isophase
light); the land each side of the entrance is marked by port and
starboard lateral buoys, to the east and west respectively in the
diagram; proceeding inwards, a rock surrounded by navigable
water is marked by an isolated danger mark — black, red, black
and surmounted by two black spheres with a light (where fitted)
which is white with two flashes; an island on the east side is
marked by a west cardinal buoy; the navigable channel to the east
of the island in the middle of the harbour is marked by lateral
buoys, as is the harbour entrance at the top of the diagram. The
direction of buoyage here is from south to north.

Hints on Using Buoys

The beauty of the IALA buoyage system is that it *is* a *system;* all its pieces intermesh to define 'roads' around hazards or 'no-go' areas. Lateral (channel) buoys are often numbered or lettered in sequence: once you are on the road keep track of your position by following the numbers or letters. Where the water is shallow and the channel is twisting, it is easy to get confused unless you plan and trace your progress on a large scale chart. Be attentive to soundings marked on the chart, and give yourself a safety factor of at least a metre below your keel.

Many buoys in large, deep stretches of water are laid out for commercial shipping and may safely be passed on either side by a shallow-draught yacht. Usually it is best to avoid the main, deep-water channel, which should be reserved for large vessels which are forced to use it. But in the confines of harbours and in shallow bays most buoys should be passed on their correct side. In winding rivers, swing towards the outside of bends to keep in deeper water, but always keep a good watch for any traffic coming the other way.

In poor visibility you may have trouble locating or identifying buoys and lights. When looking for one, keep your eyes moving across the horizon—staring invites double vision—and do not panic if it does not immediately appear where you think it should. Land, another boat, or waves may be obscuring it, or your eyes may be tired. Slow the boat down and rest for a moment, or get a fresh pair of eyes working on the problem.

The authorities sometimes relocate buoys and alter their characteristics, particularly in places where channels run through banks and are liable to change. Your best protection is an up-to-date chart, kept corrected from *Notices to Mariners,* as already described in Chapter 9. Important changes to navigational aids—such as a light extinguished or a buoy out of position—are broadcast by coast radio stations as Navigational Warnings, along with Shipping Forecasts and Gale Warnings. These can also be received as a print-out from a special Navtex receiver, a sort of miniature radio Telex which avoids constantly listening to radio broadcasts and which is rapidly gaining popularity.

Avoiding Collisions:
The Rule of the Road

Over the centuries, each maritime community developed its own driving rules to keep vessels within sight of each other from colliding. These rules have gradually been standardized, and are now published as the *International Regulations for Preventing Collisions at Sea*, abbreviated to COLREG or often referred to as the rule of the road. They apply to all vessels on the high seas and in waters connected therewith which are navigable by seagoing vessels. Local rules and bye-laws may also apply in harbours and on inland waterways. The rule of the road is published in full in various books, some of which contain explanatory notes and diagrams. It is as well to get hold of one of these and to study it in some detail, because any person in charge of a seagoing boat should have a good working knowledge of the regulations, which can only be summarized here in broad outline. Since dimensions under the international regulations are expressed in metres, metric figures are used below with the equivalent Imperial measurements in brackets.

Definitions, Signals and Navigation Lights

A few rules apply all the time in the form of definitions, required signals, and lights when sailing by night.

Give-way vessels are responsible for staying out of the way of *stand-on* vessels. When a collision threatens, the rules specify which boat is the give-way vessel and must alter course. While the give-way vessel changes course, the stand-on vessel must do what the name implies—continue on her course so as not to confuse the give-way vessel.

A power-driven vessel is a boat whose engine is running and in gear. Even when your sails are set, if your engine is in gear, your boat is a power-driven vessel under the rules, and to show that you are motor-sailing you are required to exhibit a cone, point down, somewhere forward of the mast.

Signals between vessels are made by horn or loud whistle in short blasts of about one second or prolonged blasts of four to six seconds, or in combinations of the two. Whenever there is any risk of imminent collision, the danger or warning signal of five or more short blasts is sounded.

Navigation lights must be turned on from sunset to sunrise. Different combinations and types of lights identify different types of vessels. Sailing boats smaller than seven metres (23 ft) in length need only carry a bright torch, although this is not recommended. Larger craft must carry and show the following lights:

Sidelights showing red to port and green to starboard, aimed ahead and to a point slightly abaft the beam each side. Sidelights (as the name implies) are placed each side of larger vessels, usually each side of the bridge structure. In boats less than 20 metres (65ft)

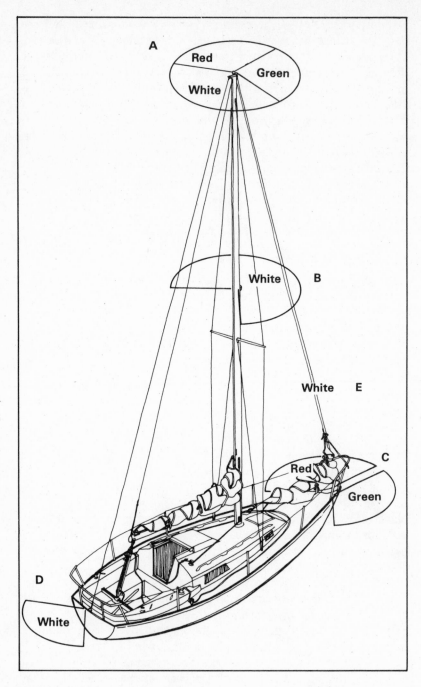

These navigation lights must be shown at night by sailing boats
over 7 metres (23 feet) in length (and by smaller sailing craft where

possible). As explained below, there are certain optional arrangements. A — masthead tricolour lantern, comprising red and green sidelights and white sternlight (only used under sail — not when under power). B — white masthead light. C — sidelights in a combined lantern. D — white sternlight. E — white, all-round anchor light.

A satisfies all requirements under sail, and is the best arrangement in terms of visibility and battery drain; C and D provide a stand-by. B, C and D are used under power. For boats less than 12 metres in length an attractive extra is a white all-round light at the masthead, separately switched, which can be used as both a masthead light and sternlight under power (with C), or instead of E as an anchor light.

overall, sidelights may be mounted side by side in a combined lantern on the centreline of the boat, usually on the bow pulpit.

A white sternlight that aims astern and slightly to the sides, over an arc of 135 degrees. In sailing yachts less than 20 metres (65ft) in length this white sternlight may be combined with the red and green sidelights in a single tricolour lantern at or near the masthead, which is more visible and reduces battery drain.

A white masthead light (usually in fact about two-thirds of the way up the mast of a sailing yacht) showing ahead and to each side over the same arc as the two sidelights, which must be shown (*only*) by a power-driven vessel. Large vessels, over 50 metres (164ft) in length must show two masthead lights, the forward one lower than the aft, on two separate masts. Motor boats less than 12 metres (39ft) in length may combine their white masthead light with the white sternlight in a single all-round white light—plus of course their red and green sidelights.

A white anchor light, an all-round light that is turned on when the boat is anchored at night. This may be anywhere in the forward part of the boat, where it can best be seen.

General Rules
Certain rules of the road apply all the time, regardless of how boats are approaching each other.

When sailing boats (with their engines off or out of gear) are near each other:

- On different tacks, the give-way vessel is the one on port tack (the one with the wind coming from her port side). If a collision threatens, she must alter course to

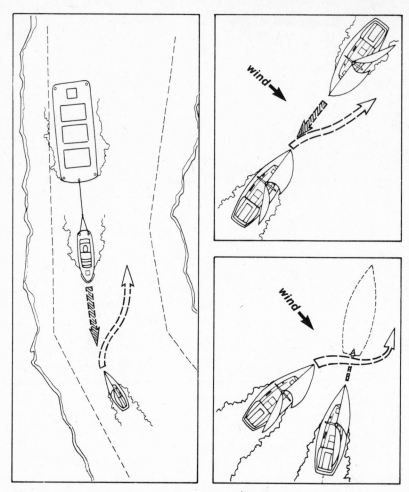

These general rules of the road always apply: avoid unmanoeuvrable power vessels; port tack keeps clear; windward boat keeps clear.

avoid the stand-on, starboard-tack boat, which must continue on her course. *'Port tack keeps clear.'*

● On the same tack, the give-way vessel is the one to windward, or upwind of the stand-on vessel. *'Windward boat keeps clear.'*

In all other situations, as a general rule, the boat with the better manoeuvrability—the one most able to change course quickly—is the give-way vessel, and the less manoeuvrable boat is the stand-on vessel.

For example:

- When a power-driven vessel is near a sailing boat, the power-driven vessel is the give-way vessel. *Exceptions:* a sailing boat must give way to large, power-driven vessels in narrow channels or using a traffic lane; to any vessel she is overtaking; to vessels which are fishing; or to any vessel which is not under command (control), restricted in her ability to manoevure (such as vessels towing), or constrained by her draught.

  A moving vessel must stay out of the way of an anchored, moored, or otherwise stationary vessel.

When Power-driven Vessels Meet

Certain rules apply when power-driven vessels (including sailing boats under power) meet. To help avoid collisions the following sound signals by horn or whistle apply when vessels are in sight of one another:

One short blast (of about one second)—'I am altering course to starboard'.

Two short blasts—'I am altering course to port'.

Three short blasts—'I am operating astern propulsion'. (Note that with a large vessel this does not necessarily mean that she is moving astern).

Five or more short blasts—'I am doubtful of your intentions' or 'I am doubtful that you are taking sufficient action to avoid collision'.

The actions required by each vessel are summarized as follows:

When two power-driven vessels are meeting bow to bow, so that there is likelihood of risk of collision, each is a give-away vessel with responsibility for altering course, preferably sharply to starboard so that they pass port side to port side at a safe distance. At night, you know you are in this situation if you see the other vessel's red and green sidelights, and her masthead light (or lights).

When two power-driven vessels are on converging or crossing courses, the one to port (on the left side) of the other is the give-way vessel. At night, you know you are in this

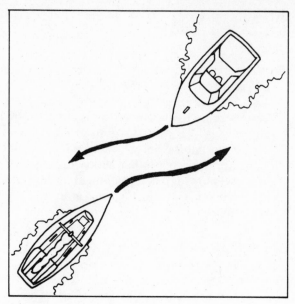

Sound one short blast if you intend to alter
course to starboard, and two if you plan to alter
course to port. Three short blasts mean that you
are going astern, and five short blasts is the
danger signal. These rules apply when the two
vessels are in sight of each other, whether you
are overtaking, meeting (shown here), or
crossing another boat.

situation if you see a green light to port or a red light to starboard. If the compass bearing of the other vessel does not
change appreciably, there is risk of collision. The action
required by the give-way vessel is neatly summarized in the
phrase 'If to starboard red appear, 'tis your duty to keep clear'.
The give-way vessel's turn should be abrupt, and normally to
starboard in order to pass astern of the other vessel.

When one power-driven vessel is overtaking another—
passing from astern but not yet level—she is the give-way
vessel and the boat ahead is the stand-on vessel. At night, you
know you are the stand-on vessel if you see red and green
lights approaching from astern. You are the give-way vessel if
a white sternlight ahead seems to be getting nearer. Confusion
sometimes exists as to whether another vessel is converging on

your starboard side, or whether she is overtaking somewhat at an angle. If the other vessel is approaching just to one side or another of your bow, at between 11 o'clock (just off the port bow) and 1 o'clock (just off the starboard bow), she and you are on a converging course. If she is to port, she is the give-way vessel; if she is to starboard, *you* are the give-way vessel. However, the other vessel is overtaking if she is coming up from astern between 7 o'clock and 5 o'clock. (Legally, the bearings are 22½ degrees, but you probably will not be debating half-degree differences when another vessel is in your neighbour-hood.)

Anticipating Possible Collisions

Always proceed at a safe speed, taking into consideration the visibility, depth of water and amount of traffic. A sailing yacht running under spinnaker at 8 or 10 knots in poor visibility is contravening the rule of the road. Keep your eyes and ears open; a big problem is seeing the other boat in the first place. You must be able to answer these questions within a minute of spotting another vessel: How big is she? In which direction is she headed? How fast is she moving?

At night, analyse her lights and their arrangement. If all you can see is a red or green sidelight, she is probably a boat under sail; a white masthead light higher than the sidelight indicates that she is under power. Commercial vessels such as tugs, supertankers, dredgers and fishing boats show special light combinations by night and special shapes by day. These are described in various seaman-

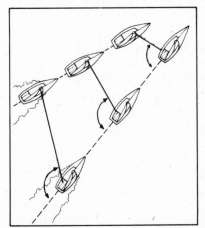 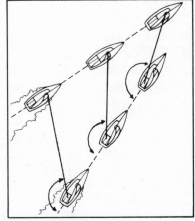

(Left) If bearings taken of another boat move aft, you will pass ahead. (Right) If they move forward, she will pass ahead.

ship and navigation manuals—such as *The Macmillan & Silk Cut Yachtsman's Handbook*. After a few minutes of this hard work, your eyes may get tired and your mind may turn to jelly; if this happens, ask somebody else to study the other boat. Anybody taking over as lookout or helmsman must be carefully briefed about nearby boats and possible collision situations.

Be extremely cautious when near big ships, whose manoevrability is limited (if there is nobody at the helm, it is non-existent) and whose speed is greater than you may at first think.

When you see another boat coming towards you, try to figure out her heading. Study the arrangement of her rigging, and, at night, her navigation lights. Unless both boats take evasive action, a collision is certain to occur under one or more of the following circumstances: if her forestay and mast line up; if her stern cannot be seen; if the windward and leeward sides of her sails alternately appear; if her red and green sidelights are both visible; or, on ships, if the two masthead lights—one forward and the other aft—line up.

When another vessel is approaching you, take a series of compass bearings of her. If the bearings do not change, you will definitely converge and collide. When near a boat that is between you and the land, try to determine if the land seems to be moving behind her; if not, you may collide.

If you are the give-way vessel, take abrupt and obvious evasive action. When meeting another vessel, 'show her your port or your red' with a 20° (or greater) turn to starboard. When passing behind the other boat, pass far astern. However, if you are the stand-on vessel, hold your course—unless collision is imminent, when you must take whatever action seems best to avoid it. In keeping clear of one vessel take care that you do not collide with another.

Do not trust the other skipper to know the rules. If there is any question of his competence (or yours), or if you cannot make any sense of his lights or behaviour, either step aside and wait for the other vessel to pass or alter course away from her. Clear-headed caution is your best guide.

CHAPTER 11

Painless Docking and Anchoring

―――――

O nce a boat and her crew have left the mooring or marina, they often proceed, slowly or otherwise, towards a place to stop for the night, a meal, a swim, or just a nap. Here we will talk about the mechanics of anchoring, docking, and using the dinghy. In Part III we will have a lot to say about what to do once you have brought up at your destination.

Before setting sail, the crew should agree on a secure destination (multiply the number of hours you want to be under way by your anticipated average speed to figure how far you will sail) and at least one closer, more protected alternative, just in case the wind dies or the weather worsens. Depending on the area, the destination will be either an anchorage, where you may drop an anchor or pick up a mooring, or a marina or pier, where you will dock. Many sailing areas offer both alternatives, each of which has advantages and disadvantages spelled out in the appropriate pilot or cruising guide covering the area concerned. Anchoring is free and can be done in many places near shore, but it requires some skill, and an anchored boat should not be left unattended longer than a few hours. Moorings and jetties at yacht clubs, boat yards, and town docks are usually secure and provide access to showers, shops, and entertainment, but they are noisy and crowded and can be expensive. In 1985 overnight fees for marina berths in the Solent area were about

25p per foot of overall length per day, plus VAT. This would include water, but not electricity. Many experienced cruising sailors anchor out away from civilization most of the time, breaking their cruise every few days with a night spent on a mooring or in a marina near a town. One money-saving tactic is to anchor at night and, every couple of days, tie up for a short while at a fuel dock (generally at no cost beyond the fuel you purchase) for short shore trips. Remember, too, that you can drop somebody off on a pier for a shopping expedition and slowly circle under power until he or she returns.

How to Dock and Undock

A dock is the spot of water that a boat sit in when she is secured to a pier, pontoon, or wharf, so docking is the act of securing and undocking is the act of leaving.

Docking Equipment

To dock properly you will need two or more fenders (rubber bumpers) to hang between the boat and the jetty or pontoon and four mooring warps, each preferably about 30 feet (9m) long and made of 14 mm or larger nylon rope. Nylon is less expensive, stronger, and more resistant to chafe (abrasion) than polyester, so do not use the jib or spinnaker sheets as mooring warps; they will quickly be worn so badly that they may break when used for their primary purpose. At a pinch, a long nylon anchor warp may be rigged as a continuous mooring warp, but since each of the four lines has a unique function and often must be rigged and unrigged quickly, it is better to have separate short ones. Some warps have large loops spliced in one end to hang over cleats or bollards on the pier, but you can do just as well if you know how to tie a bowline or cleat a line properly.

The four mooring warps and their uses are as follows:

> **The bow line** runs from a cleat on the bow through a fairlead (a metal groove that minimizes chafe) and forward to a cleat or bollard on the pier. The bow line keeps the bow from swinging out from the pier.

> **The stern line** runs from the stern aft to the pier to prevent the stern from swinging out.

> **The fore spring** runs from the foredeck, to a cleat on the pier, somewhere near the stern. The fore spring restrains the bow from surging forward.

The after spring crosses the fore spring in a shallow X. It runs forward from the after deck, to a cleat on the pier, somewhere near the bow. The after spring stops the boat from surging aft.

The bow and stern lines serve mainly to keep the boat parallel to the pier. The main load is taken by the two crisscrossed springs, which should be led around winches or large cleats. All the mooring warps should be dead-ended at (secured with one end at) the cleats or bollards on the pier, pontoon, or wharf, leaving plenty of line at the other end so that they can be adjusted by the crew on board. Lines tied to piers or wharfs, which are not buoyant, must usually be lengthened and shortened as the boat falls and rises with the tide, although spreading them out at very shallow angles may minimize or even eliminate the need for adjustment. (Pontoons, however, rise and fall with the water.) Double up warps in threatening or stormy weather, or where there is a strong tidal stream or river current.

How to Dock
Small, light day-sailers may be docked under sail by jogging toward the pier with sails luffing, then heading the bow into the wind and towards the dock. Do not try to dock on a reach or run, or you will

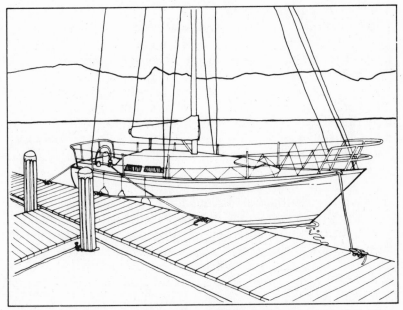

This properly docked cruiser-racer has three fenders over the side, and is secured with bow and stern lines and springs.

ram the pier and scratch the boat's sides. Hang the boat downwind off the pontoon or pier with a bow line.

Most cruising boats come alongside under power. Approach fast enough to have steerageway but not so fast that you cannot stop within about five feet by going astern. Hang the fenders over the side at the height of the side of the pier, tying them to a plastic-coated lifeline or a fitting on the rail using a double half-hitch or bowline, and lay out the four mooring warps on deck. The boat should be parallel to the pier as you make the final approach. Put the engine into neutral or slow astern—shifting suddenly into hard astern may damage the transmission—and heave or pass the bow and stern lines to people on the pier (or have two of your crew step onto it). Adjust the lines at the bow and stern as she slows and stops, and then rig the two springs and adjust them until the boat lies parallel. Heavy boats or boats docking in a high stern wind or rough seas may need the help of the fore spring—that is the one running from the bow aft to the pier—to brake to a stop. Hand that line across and have it cleated first. The stern will swing out as she slows, so rig the stern line next.

Larger boats have boarding gates (openings in the guardrails); they should be positioned as close to the pontoon or pier as possible.

How to Leave the Dock

A boat has no steerageway when she makes a standing start, so getting away from the pier can be more difficult than coming into it. Here the springs are used to aim the boat out into the channel. The basic principle is that *as a boat pulls against a line secured at one end of her hull, the other end swings out.* Therefore, going astern with the after spring attached forces the stern into and the bow away from the pier, and going ahead with the fore spring attached forces the bow into the pier and the stern away from it. Be careful to keep lines from dangling overboard and fouling the propeller when the engine is in gear.

It is best to motor out of a dock in ahead gear since sailing boats go astern erratically and slowly. First, the bow must be swung away from the pier—which means that the stern must be swung into it. Let go the bow line and fore spring (that is the spring running aft from the bow to the pier). Then gently go astern against the aft spring to pull the stern in. When the bow is aimed out, cast off the stern line and aft spring, shift into ahead gear, and proceed out of the berth.

Sometimes, though, you will have to come astern out of a dock, first swinging the bow into and the stern away from the pier. Let go

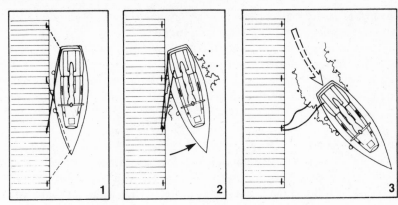

Undocking, use a spring to aim the bow into the channel. First, go astern against the aft spring, then throw off the spring and motor ahead. It is helpful if the spring is rigged as a slip rope (as shown) — taken round a cleat on the jetty with the end brought back inboard.

the stern line and after spring and go slow ahead, against the fore spring. When the stern is aimed out into the channel, let go the bow line and fore spring line and proceed out astern.

Because single-screw boats like the average sailing boat are inherently asymmetrical and therefore handle poorly under power at low speeds, you will never be bored while docking and undocking. Yet while it can spoil manoevrability, the propeller's built-in asymmetry can be a help. When a right-handed, clockwise-turning propeller is put astern and the throttle is given a quick burst, the stern will initially walk (slide) to port more than it will go aft. Left-handed, counterclockwise-spinning propellers will walk the stern to starboard going astern. Used properly, this trick will give you an eggshell landing every time; all you need to know is which direction the propeller turns. Do not try it in forward gear, though, unless you want to ram the boat ahead.

How to Anchor

The anchor and its connecting rode (nylon warp, chain, or a combination of both) are called *ground tackle* because they secure the boat to the ground beneath the water. There are several types of anchor—plough, Danforth, Bruce, fisherman's, and others. Of the more manageable, smaller anchors, the CQR-type plough seems to work well in just about all bottoms and the Danforth-type lightweight and Bruce are especially good in the soft sand and mud found in many cruising areas. The anchor's weight and the rode's strength must be carefully matched to the boat's size. Typically, the rode is a nylon warp except for the last 10 to 16 feet (3 to 5m), where chain cable is used to add weight, improving the horizontal pull down near the bottom. For serious cruising however there is no substitute for chain cable throughout.

Selecting an Anchorage

The anchorage is where you anchor. Local knowledge or reference to the appropriate sailing directions will tell you the better anchorages, where boats need not show white anchor lights at night and where the holding ground presumably is good and will grab an anchor well; these areas are also shown on charts. But you can anchor just about anywhere, so long as you comply with certain important guidelines.

For the greatest possible security when anchoring overnight, the depth of water at high tide should be about one-quarter to one-eighth the length of your rode. If the rode is 160 ft (50m) long, you are entirely safe if you anchor in 20 feet (6m) of water, all right in 30 feet (9m), but tempting fate in 40 (12m). The reason for this is that to make the hook dig in, you must maximize the horizontal pull by narrowing the angle between the rode and the bottom. To do that, you let out much more rode than the water is deep. The ratio of rode to depth is called *scope*. The ideal scope ranges from 4:1 (4 metres of rode for every 1 metre of water) in light conditions to 7:1 or more in storms. To determine the high-tide depth, find the low-tide depth on the chart and add the local tidal range to it.

Choose a soft mud or sand bottom rather than one that has hard rocks, hard mud, or (worst of all) weed. Chart labels show the type of holding ground.

Anchor with some protective land between you and the wind —a shoreline, a peninsula, even a sandbar—so that the waves are broken before they get to you.

Anchor at least 50 feet (15m) from other boats and at least twice that distance in rough weather.

Anticipate changes in wind direction and their effect on your position, keeping in mind a quick escape route if you must up-anchor and leave the harbour in the middle of the night in a rising gale.

Dropping the Hook

Pull the anchor and about 50 feet (15m) of rode on deck and see that all the shackles are tight, and *moused,* or secured with wraps of light wire or line. Lead the anchor so the rode will run smoothly from the anchor winch or mooring bitt, over the stemhead roller and down to the water. Tie the bitter end of the rode to the mast or some other strong, permanently fixed object just in case it runs out all the way. The bitter end of chain cable should be lashed to the boats structure in the chain locker.

Meanwhile, the skipper steers the boat toward the anchorage,

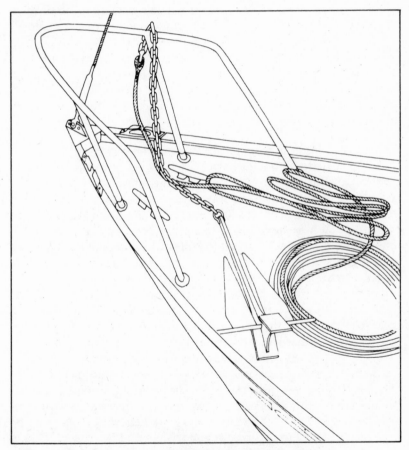

Before anchoring, prepare the ground tackle carefully. Here a Danforth anchor is ready to be dropped. Its chain and rope rode are faked out in long loops, to run clearly. All shackles should be moused (securely lashed) and the rode's bitter end should be secured to the boat with a bowline.

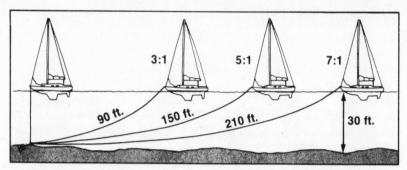

(Left to right) To anchor, first bring the boat slowly into the wind and stop her over the desired spot, then go slow astern and drop the hook. Let out considerable rode, gradually, to make a shallow angle between the rode and the water, so that the pull is as horizontal as possible — up to 7:1 scope in fresh winds. Keep checking to make sure that you are not dragging anchor. To weigh anchor, motor slowly ahead while the rode is pulled up. When directly over the anchor ('up and down'), cleat the rode and motor ahead to pull the hook out of the bottom, and heave in rapidly.

motors dead into the wind to the chosen spot, and goes slow astern to stop her there. (Though power provides better manoeuvrability, you can anchor under sail in light and moderate wind under mainsail alone, beating up to the spot, then heading into the wind). As the boat makes her approach, the crew should quickly check the anchorage. When she falls back about 50 feet (15m), will she swing safely distant from nearby boats? Will she be lying out of a channel? Is this harbour *really* safe? Or does it just seem that way because you are tired? Is the depth of water as expected?

The skipper keeps the bow pointed into the wind and, when the boat begins to drift astern, orders that the anchor be dropped. As it goes over, he or she puts the engine into astern gear (or the mainsail is backed) to gather sternway (reverse speed). The crew on the bow lets out, to start with, about three times as much rode as the water is deep and takes a turn of rode around the mooring bitt or bow cleat. The boat's sternway pulls the anchor back until it digs in. The hook should grab within a minute or two; if not, it may have snagged an obstruction like a cardboard box or a polythene sheet and must be retrieved and cleaned off before you try again. The crew will know by checking for drift relative to anchored boats and the shore; by the motion of the bow, which will bob if the anchor is set but swing to one side if it is not; and by feeling the rode, which will jerk and twitch if the anchor is dragging but quietly stretch and compress if it has grabbed the bottom.

By far the most common mistake made when anchoring is not having enough scope. If the anchor drags or does not immediately catch, let go more rode—several metres of it. The greater the scope, the more horizontal is the rode's pull on the anchor and the more likely it is that the flukes will dig in. If more scope does not stop dragging, haul up and clean off the anchor, move somewhere else, and try again. Once the anchor is set, the scope should be increased to approximately 6:1, or about 120 feet (36m) of rode in water that will be 20 feet (6m) deep at high tide. If you become nervous during the night, and find yourself waking frequently to take bearings on nearby stationary objects to see if you are dragging, the best sleeping pill is even greater scope.

How to Weigh Anchor

It is best to weigh anchor under power. While you can drop a mooring under sail (backing the jib to swing the bow off), few boats under sail can accelerate sufficiently from a standing start to pull the anchor out of the bottom. With a crew member pulling in the rode, motor slowly towards the anchor. Somebody should point down the line of the rode to keep the skipper aimed properly. When the rode is straight up and down, the crew notifies the helm by raising an arm. The engine is shifted into neutral as the rode is cleated on the bow cleat. With a wave, the crew tells the skipper to go ahead, and the boat's momentum trips the anchor from the bottom. The crew then hauls the rest of the rode and the anchor on deck, carefully avoiding scratching the topsides with the anchor's sharp flukes. If the hook is muddy, it may be washed off by bouncing it up and down in the bow wave and scrubbing it overboard or on deck with a long-handled brush. Keep mud off sails and lines. Once on deck, the cleaned anchor and coiled rode should be immediately lashed down and left to dry.

Rafting-Up and Other Anchoring Tricks

A sociable way to spend an evening is to secure one or more boats alongside each other in a raft. The largest boat first drops and securely digs in her heaviest anchor at greater scope than she would use if anchoring alone. Then the other boats secure alongside using fenders and bow and stern lines and springs just as they would when docking. The main danger from rafting-up is that the masts and spreaders may tangle when the boats roll; alert adjustments to the springs should keep the rigging well separated. Another problem is dragging, in which case the raft should be broken up immediately. Caution suggests that raft-ups should not be left unattended and that they be broken up before everybody turns in for the night.

When rafting-up, the biggest boat first digs in her largest anchor, then the other boats come alongside using fenders with bow and stern lines and springs. Be sure to keep the masts well separated so they do not roll into each other when a motor boat passes by.
Break up the raft and go your separate ways if the wind freshens or any sea builds up.

Setting two anchors has the triple advantage of increasing the holding power, using less scope, and limiting swinging around in tidal streams and gusty winds. Two anchors may be dropped over the bow either on the same rode or on separate rodes. With the two-rode system, drop the first anchor the way we described earlier, then using the dinghy set the second anchor so that the included angle between the rodes is 60 to 90 degrees. Dual anchoring over the bow and stern is used in narrow, crowded anchorages where boats may swing into each other. Drop the first anchor over the stern and, making sure the rode does not tangle in the propeller, keep going ahead until the scope is 8:1. Then drop the second anchor over the bow and go astern to dig it in until the scope on both is 4:1. The boat will now lie quietly between the two, like a shirt on a clothesline.

The Dinghy

A great help in an anchorage—for transportation and pleasure—is the boat's dinghy. In British waters inflatable dinghies have largely replaced the traditional solid tender and more's the pity. A solid dinghy is easier to row and some can even be sailed—fitted with centreboard, rudder and a small rig. But they are naturally difficult to stow on board a small yacht. If towed they should normally be allowed to ride comfortably on the second wave astern, except in close quarters (for example, a crowded anchorage), when the painter should be shortened until the bow nudges the big boat's stern. Remove the oars before towing. In fact, for security, keep the oars out of the dinghy except when she is actually being rowed; thieves do not normally walk around with oars looking for a dinghy to steal.

Getting in and out of a dinghy can be the most challenging part of the sailor's day. Keep your weight in the middle of the boat, stepping onto and off the middle of the centre seat and lowering or raising yourself gradually with a hand on each rail. If another person is already aboard, balance his or her weight. For example, if someone is sitting in the sternsheets, lower yourself onto the forward thwart. Never make a sudden move in a crowded dinghy.

An inflatable rubber dinghy under tow can easily capsize in crosswinds and rough seas unless the bow is pulled right up on the big boat's transom with only the after half dragging. Better still,

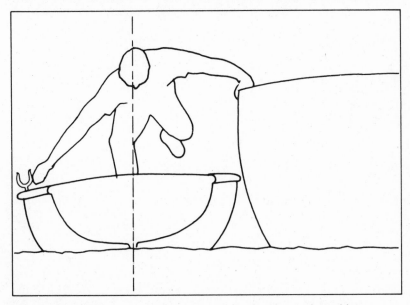

When climbing in or out of an empty dinghy, face aft and keep your weight in the middle of the boat. If somebody is already aboard in the bow or stern, step into the opposite end to balance the weight. Remove the inside rowlock so that it does not scratch the yacht's hull.

partially or wholly deflate it and lash it on deck or, after a thorough drying, stow it below. Inflatables used in salt water should be hosed off with fresh water and then dried before being put below, since dry salt crystals will attract moisture and cause mildew. The advantages of an inflatable are that you do not have to tow it and that, with its buoyant sides, it is much more stable than a hard dinghy when loaded. The disadvantage is that there is not much you can do with it in the water except run it with a small outboard engine. Most inflatables cannot be sailed, and when rowed in rough seas they make very little way unless the wind is from astern.

Dinghy painters (bow lines) are usually made of buoyant polypropylene rope that will not sink and foul the propeller. Unfortunately, this rope is also extremely hard and slippery and, under load, liable to slip off a cleat or cause rope burns.

The last eight chapters have provided a survey of the fundamental skills of sailing, navigation, and seamanship. In Part IV, we will have more to say about the technical side—particularly about getting along in challenging conditions and situations. But the next four chapters are given over to the pleasure of living aboard a boat, which (for me, at least) is what sailing is all about.

PART III

Cooking and Gracious Living Afloat

CHAPTER 12

The View
from
the Galley

F or many people, cruising has very little to do with sailing and a
lot to do with relaxed eating. Even more than life in Ernest
Hemingway's Paris in the 1920s, life aboard a boat on a holiday is a
movable feast. Just how movable and elaborate the feast will be is
up to the crew and, to a great extent, to the cooking tools at hand.
Some people prefer simplicity, others relative luxury. Whichever,
all seasoned sailing cooks and sailing eaters have evolved a system
that meets their needs and that provides nutrition, comfort, a degree of ease, and a modicum of graciousness—the little things that
make living and eating aboard a boat a special pleasure, adding a
touch of quiet elegance to what is, after all, not much more than
camping out. The next three chapters are about the cruising lifestyle below decks: galley equipment, food and recipes, and that
intangible called gracious living. Since children are frequently
aboard, I have appended a short chapter on the challenges and
delights of sailing with young people.

To help with these chapters I called upon fifteen widely experienced cruising cooks (and their mates). Two of them have sailed
around the world, several have crossed the Atlantic more than once,
and one has cruised to the Arctic Circle. I estimate that among them
they have spent a total of three centuries and 200,000 miles under
sail. Responding to a five-page, thirty-nine-item questionnaire,

these experts (whose names are on the acknowledgement page) provided an immense amount of information about life below. While
they agree on many key items, each has her or his equipment
preferences, favourite recipes, and own way of doing things. The
sheer range of opinions and the undisputed success of their sailing
careers suggest that, unlike on-deck routines, the cook's chores
rarely have a right and a wrong way.

The Right Galley Equipment

As when cooking ashore, you must make sure to begin with that
you have the right equipment and know how to use it safely and
efficiently. The main difference between a house's kitchen and a
boat's galley is that limitations on electrical power mean that most
sailing cooks have few equipment options; while large powerboats
with generators may have goodies like electric cookers, freezers,
microwave and toaster ovens and dishwashers, the average 30-foot to
40-foot sailing boat is considered luxurious if she has a refrigerator
(in place of an icebox) and hot and cold running water. For every
appliance a boat carries, the engine must be run another hour or so
a day just to keep the batteries charged to operate it; and while the
cook gains in one way by having the appliance, he or she only
suffers in another since the noisy, vibrating, hot diesel is usually
thundering away right next to the galley. Another difference is that
storage space is greatly limited in a boat's galley. There is not much
room for even a few general purpose tools, much less many
specialized ones. Knives, especially, are at a premium because there
may not be sufficient secure drawer spaces to stow them so that
they cannot fly out dangerously every time the boat heels or slams
into a wave.

The Essential Gear
At the beginning of the questionnaire I asked the experts what
galley equipment they found essential. The answers to this question
reveal perhaps more than any others just how simple a sailing
kitchen can be.

Besides a good stove with at least two burners and an oven, the
'essential' item most frequently mentioned was a foot-operated
pump for the water system, which gives the cook access to water
when hands are full. This is no small consideration in rough
weather, when one hand is seriously engaged in holding on while
the other may be clutching a pot. Some correspondents said they
found hot-and-cold pressurized tap water essential. Many sailors
have strong opinions concerning the design and number of a

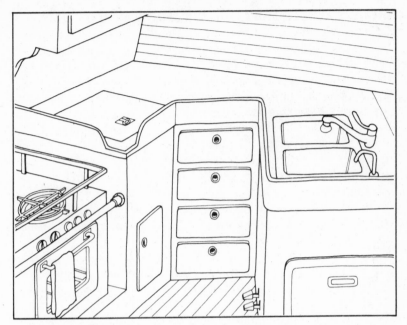

Every cruising cook's dream, this galley has deep double sinks with fresh- and seawater taps worked with two foot pedals, many deep drawers (heavy items go in the lower ones), and high fiddles round the stove and working tops. In rough weather, the cook will be able to wedge in securely and, with the aid of a restraining belt, stay there.

galley's sinks. As several cooks emphasized, a good galley has two deep sinks side by side. *Deep* means sufficiently recessed to hold large dinner plates on-edge while they soak in soapy water or wait to be rinsed or dried. The second sink is then available for rinsing or, on rough days and nights, to hold food, bottles, cups, or other items in the intermediate stage between stowage lockers and a sailor's hands.

Another 'essential' item mentioned was a holder for a roll of paper towels. On a boat, sponges, tea towels, and handkerchiefs (for wiping eyeglasses) are not much help since once used they never dry out entirely in the humid marine environment. Always take one roll of paper towels for every day or two of cruising.

Important—and Not So—Tools and Gadgets
We asked our informants to list five tools that they find indispensable in the galley, as well as any standard home kitchen gadgets that are helpful on board. Many of the tools deal with the never-

ending cruising problems of food preservation and energy conservation. Reflecting how difficult and important it is to save leftovers, two chefs put food storage bags at the top of their lists, and several people advise stocking plenty of plastic containers with lids. Others recommend using pressure cookers, which, because they boil water and cook stews, soups, and vegetables more quickly than regular pots, save on cooking fuel. Cooks who use block ice, which is less expensive and melts slower than cubes, recommend ice picks. Other tools and gadgets mentioned include a sharp knife (with a sharpening stone), several small and medium-sized pots (so you do not have to heat more water than necessary, again in the interest of fuel conservation), a good cookery book, a cavernous six-quart pot for cooking lobsters purchased from fishermen, a big all-purpose iron frying pan, a fold-up metal gadget for making toast over an open burner, and a kitchen timer.

To help decide which kitchen gadgets to take along, transatlantic veteran voyager Sheila McCurdy proposes a simple rule of thumb that is well worth making a commandment:

> Not helpful: anything that takes up space and is not
> used often.

Items that are worth the space they take up include a simple vegetable peeler, a folding dish rack, a wire whisk, a jar opener, a cheese grater, and a coffee pot for brewed coffee (but not a drip pot—'too tippy,' says one expert). Almost everybody agrees that electric gadgets have no place on board. 'Forget about a toaster or blender on a boat,' says one cook. On the other hand, Steve and Linda Dashew, who made a circumnavigation in two boats with good electrical systems (and who wrote an excellent book about world voyaging, *The Circumnavigator's Handbook*), carry an electric blender which on their sloop *Intermezzo II* is used often enough to satisfy the McCurdy rule.

We asked how cooks keep metal cookware from rusting in a salt atmosphere. One answers, simply, 'We don't,' and circumnavigator Mimi Dyer cheerfully responds, 'A rusty tin opener works swell.' Suggested remedies include rubbing cooking oil onto iron pans, careful drying before stowage in a dry locker, and frequent use and washing.

Stainless steel eating implements are vastly preferred to plastic knives and forks. While some cooks use paper plates for sandwiches or other simple meals, paper becomes soggy and takes up too much valuable garbage space to be worth the saving in cleaning time. (These days, is it necessary to say that garbage is dumped ashore, not in the water? I hope not.) Plastic or china plates, bowls, and mugs—preferably with nonskid rubber rings inset in their bases—are the choice on most boats. Any boat going out into rough weather ought to have a big, wide-mouth, flat-bottom plastic bowl for each crew member. You will be eating more than your breakfast cereal out of it in rough going, when nothing stays on a plate.

Other helpful gear includes a good cutting board, preferably one that nests in the sink top (to save space); plastic scrubbers (steel wool corrodes); and an ice cooler with a secure lid, for drinks.

The Stove, a Mixed Blessing

Since it is the largest, most complicated, and most frequently used galley item, we asked several questions about the stove and its use. The two main variables are the type of fuel and the number of burners.

Liquid and Gas Fuels

As all the cooks in our survey acknowledge, there is no one perfect fuel. The main advantages of the liquid fuels—alcohol and kerosene —are that they are very unlikely to explode and their tanks can be located below deck. But to quote one experienced sea cook, they are 'not for the unwary' because lighting them requires an elaborate

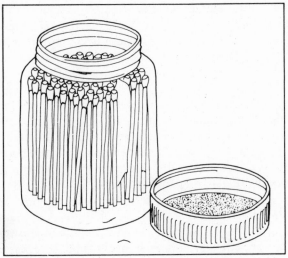

To keep wooden matches from getting damp, store them in a plastic container or an empty screw top jar. Glue a strip of sandpaper into the lid for striking.

routine of priming and preheating to convert the liquid into a gas. If the stove jets clog or the preparations are done carelessly, the equipment may flare up or even cause a bad fire. (Later, we will tell how to light an alcohol stove and look at general cooking safety). Alcohol also heats poorly and slowly, has an unpleasant smell, is expensive and is frequently difficult to find in out-of-the-way places. Since kerosene burns hotter than alcohol and is easier to find and less expensive to buy, it is often the fuel of choice on board boats setting off on very long voyages or circumnavigations.

The stoves on most of today's cruising boats use a gas fuel, either propane or butane. These light with the flick of a match and burn clean and very hot. However, propane and butane are both heavier than air and, therefore, extremely dangerous if their pipes, valves, or on-deck containers leak and drop gas into the bilge; any nearby exposed flame or spark will blow the boat to pieces. More about gas anon.

Burners and an Oven

As to how many burners are needed, and whether an oven is necessary, our panel of sea cooks split into two camps. One favours simplicity: 'Two burners are essential, all else is luxury.' The other side likes a stove with as many as four burners and an oven (at least to heat up casseroles and rolls, warm the cabin, and dry socks). Just how many of these elements are used at once depends on the cook's ambition and taste. Those who like to prepare elaborate meals use all elements most of the time, and those who aim for simplicity use few of them. It is nice, though, to have a choice. Sailing around the world in their 37-footer *Rabbit*, Mimi and Dan Dyer used only one burner 60 per cent of the time and the oven every couple of weeks and on special occasions—'We always had turkey for Christmas.'

No matter how many burners it has, an alcohol or kerosene stove will rarely have them all lit at once both because fuel is expensive and because safely lighting a new burner can be complicated and time-consuming. One fuel-conserving alternative is to move pots around from active to inactive burners; another is to double-deck pots in an actual or improvised double boiler—say, one of rice or potatoes below another of vegetables. Unfortunately, since liquid fuel does not burn very hot, ovens in alcohol and kerosene stoves may not be very efficient. Yet even the 300 to 350 degrees that they can produce is enough for most purposes.

Most stoves are gimballed, which means that a hinge and counterweights allow them to self-level when the boat heels. Still, the stove's swing may be slow or fast and containers may fall off unless they are secured on the burners with metal fiddle rails and in the oven by a securely locked door.

A one-burner stove is usually the primary cooker on boats smaller than about 25 feet (8 metres) and can also be a helpful backup for heating water on a larger boat. A few members of our panel say they use these single-burner stoves at night, others prefer to make hot water on the big stove and store it in insulated bottles (obviously ones without glass liners) for night use.

How to Use a Liquid-Fuel Stove Safely

An alcohol stove can be dangerous. The cooks agree with Betty Noyes that 'only people who are *thoroughly* familiar with the stove may light it.' In some boats, only the cook and captain are allowed to apply match to burner. If liquid-fuel stoves are not lit correctly, there may be a dangerous flare-up.

Alcohol and kerosene stoves are lit by preheating (often called priming) the burner jet so the liquid fuel passing through it is vaporized and can burn evenly. If the preheating is incomplete, liquid fuel instead of vapour will spurt out and cause a flare-up or fire.

This is how to light a liquid-fuel stove:

1. Fill a medium-sized pot or a kettle with water and put it on a spare burner. In case of fire, this may be the first and only extinguisher you will need (although a regular fire extinguisher and an asbestos fireproof blanket, for smothering flames, should also be within reach).

2. Open the valve from the tank to the stove (ideally, the cook should be able to turn this valve without reaching through a stove flare-up or fire).

3. Pump the handle in the fuel tank to build up sufficient pressure to force fuel to the stove. If the pump has a pressure gauge, it probably is marked at the proper pressure. If not, keep pumping until you meet some resistance.

4. Slightly open the burner valve handle for a couple of seconds to let some drops of alcohol drip onto the cup under the burner until there is a very shallow pool of alcohol. With a kerosene stove, use a funnel to drip a bit of alcohol into the cup. Close this valve.

5. Double check that the burner valve is closed completely. Then

ignite the alcohol with a long wooden match or a commercial gun-shaped spark-making instrument.

6.   Watch the alcohol burn. When it is just extinguished—*and no sooner*—open the burner valve about a quarter-turn.

7.   If the preheating has been successful, you will hear a low hiss of pressurized alcohol (or kerosene) vapour escaping. You may light it with a match or the spark-maker. When you are sure that there is a flame and that no liquid fuel is gurgling or spurting out of the jet, you may safely start cooking. *However, if drops of liquid appear, the jet has not been sufficiently preheated and you must immediately shut off the valve and return to step 5.*

Lighting an oven is generally more difficult since the burner, jet, and preheating cup are usually all but inacessible. You may have to lie on the cabin sole (floor) and remove a part of the stove in order to get a clear view. Follow the same step-by-step procedure described above (or the instructions that, frequently, are printed on the stove), keeping all distractions at bay until the oven is going properly.

When you have finished cooking and want to turn off the burners, first shut off the fuel-line valve closest to the tank. This allows the fuel between it and the stove to be burned off so none remains to leak onto the preheating cup through an accidentally opened burner valve. Once the fires are out, turn off the burner valves.

Why Alcohol Fires Occur

Fires and flare-ups happen when large amounts of standing liquid alcohol, or small amounts of pressurized fuel, are suddenly ignited. Five sources of trouble are:

Too much alcohol is allowed into the cup, and it spills over, ignites, and spreads flames across the stove.

The valve is not completely shut before the cup of alcohol is ignited for preheating, and liquid fuel spurts out into the flame to spread the fire. This may happen because the handle is loose or the valve is stuck; do not use the burner until you have tightened the handle's set screw or lubricated the valve.

During the preheating (priming) steps, if the cook is not able to see the almost transparent flame, he or she may think it has gone out and will open the valve, only to have liquid fuel surge out into the flame.

The valve is opened prematurely and a lighted match is applied before the jet has been sufficiently heated for proper vaporization, so liquid fuel is ignited.

The jet or burner is clogged and liquid fuel dribbles out. If this is the case, clear the obstruction with a pin or fine brush. If that does not work, do not use the burner; cover it and the valve handle with tape to alert your shipmates.

How to Use Calor Gas

Most British yachts use liquefied petroleum gas (LPG) as the fuel for the galley stove, and sometimes for other purposes such as water heating. In Britain LPG is marketed by Calor Gas Limited as butane (blue cylinders) or propane (red cylinders). Both are heavier than air, so any leak in the system is likely to result in an accumulation of gas in the bilges with the consequent serious risk of explosion. This danger can be minimised if the system and its appliances are properly installed and are used sensibly and carefully. It is a most necessary precaution to turn off the gas supply at the cylinder whenever gas is not being used. Modern gas appliances are fitted with flame failure cut-offs and atmospheric sensors, so that if the flame is extinguished or if the carbon dioxide in the compartment rises above a certain level, the supply is turned off. Where gas appliances are in use there must be adequate ventilation, although this is seldom a problem in a boat. It is also a wise precaution to fit an electronic gas detector called a sniffer, which sounds an alarm if the concentration of gas in the bilge approaches a dangerous level. The gas cylinder should be stowed in a gas-tight compartment outside the cabin (typically in a special cockpit locker) with a drain which runs overboard above the waterline.

The advantage of LPG is that it can be conveniently stored under pressure as a liquid, which takes up only about two per cent of the space needed to store it as gas. Butane and propane are similar, but propane turns into gas at a lower temperature and requires to be stored at a higher pressure, so it needs a different pressure regulator. Always use a cylinder upright, and never subject it to heat.

LPG used in the United Kingdom, France and the Mediterranean is nearly always butane, but propane is used in Scandinavia. As a general rule there is no inter-changeability of cylinders in these countries, but it is sometimes possible to arrange for Calor cylinders to be refilled abroad. All Calor cylinders, whether intended for butane or propane, are made to meet the higher pressure specification for propane.

The common 4.5kg Calor butane cylinder has a ⅝inch BSP male left-hand thread, on to which a hexagonal union nut screws. The larger 7kg and 15kg butane cylinders are quite different, with a 21mm Compact connector.

Sooner or later it will be necessary to exchange a full gas cylinder for an empty one, and the following instructions apply to the 4.5kg butane cylinder with a handwheel type control valve.

1. Turn the cylinder valve off, by turning clockwise. (Never remove the regulator or the connecting nut with the cylinder valve open).

2. Remove the regulator or connecting nut with the spanner provided (left-hand thread).

3. Replace the plug or cap onto the empty cylinder.

4. Remove the plug or cap from the full cylinder and retain it for later use.

5. Inspect the black washer and the mating surfaces to ensure they are clean and undamaged.

6. Fit the connecting nut to the cylinder (left-hand thread). Butane cylinders should not be over-tightened.

7. When gas is required, turn the handwheel valve anti-clockwise. Check the connection with soapy water to detect any leak.

A gas burner is lit much like one on a home stove without a pilot light. First open the valve at the cylinder and any valves in the line, then open the burner valve and apply a match. There may be flare-ups; if the flame seems to be surging, turn the burner off, shut the cylinder valve, and inspect the jets for obstructions (which may be cleaned out with a fine brush or pin) and the valves for air leaks. Do not use a doubtful burner.

The best way to make sure that gas does not find its way into the bilge is to clear the line of unburned fuel. When you have finished cooking, before turning off the burner valve, shut off the valve at the cylinder. Allow the fire to burn itself out, and then close the burner valve. This way, an accidental opening of a burner valve—say, when the cook bumps against it in rough weather—will release air, not a gaseous time-bomb.

'Never Fry Bacon in Your Birthday Suit' and Other Galley Safety Hints

Working on an unstable platform in a very tight area with plenty of distractions, a sea cook is exposed to more hazards than a chef working at home. Certain procedures and equipment, carefully and alertly followed and used, will cut most of the risk down to tolerable levels.

The combination of rocking boat, cramped quarters, hot food, and skimpy summer clothing has led to all too many accidents in the galley. Most stoves are gimballed to keep the top surface level when the boat is heeling up to about 40 degrees. However, her motion may be so quick that the gimballing is always a second or two behind, or off-centre heavy pots or casseroles may throw the balancing system off, so the chef should be alert to surprising lurches and spills even when cooking in a calm harbour, where a motor boat's wake may roll the boat. In rough conditions, then, be careful. Do not fill pots so far that they will spill over, and avoid using grease or oil (which may be out of the question anyway, since greasy food tends to stimulate seasickness). Fiddles (support rails) will keep pots from sliding about and capsizing, and a strong protective bar across the front of the stove will prevent the cook from falling directly on the burners. Experienced offshore cooks keep the floor beneath their feet absolutely clear of grease and oil, and also rig restraining straps or harnesses around their hips. Still, there will be spills, and the cook must dress appropriately. Mimi and Dan Dyer proclaim this valuable rule of thumb: 'Never fry bacon in your birthday suit.' One female chef never cooks in a bikini, and she keeps a tube of Acriflex in the galley to treat small burns.

If anybody on board is likely to get seasick, it is the cook in the cramped, airless, hot galley. Seasickness pills should be taken long before coming on board, and the diet a day or two before the start of the cruise should be grease- and liquor-free. If the misery does attack, the best thing to do is go on deck, get some fresh air, look at the horizon, and shed the malaise through activity. If you are not totally incapacitated, a stint at the helm will meet all three requirements.

Stove Fires

As our long discussion on stove-lighting procedures has probably made clear, the main safety worry in a boat is a galley fire. Half of our guest experts have experienced fires and flare-ups, and one suffered arm and hand burns due to a propane flare-up. Anybody using the stove *must* be competent (read *sober*) and observe these rules:

Light the stove with great care and never leave it unattended (except perhaps when heating water in a kettle in a calm sea).

Keep the stove and pans free of grease.

Have a pot or kettle of water at hand.

Know the location of fire-fighting devices such as an asbestos blanket (for smothering flames) and fire extinguishers.

Know where the fuel shut-off valve is and how to operate it.

Common sense requires that at least one fire extinguisher should be located within arm's length of the cook, but not in a place where the cook must reach through flames to get at it.

Fighting a Fire

With a minor flare-up or fire, your first step is to cut off the fuel supply by closing the valve on the supply pipe from the tank or cylinder. This will allow a minor fire to burn itself out in the burner, or at least prevent it from becoming a major one while you fight it in other ways. If shutting off the fuel supply is not sufficient and the fire threatens to burn flammable objects, douse it with the water in the pot, smother it with a wet or asbestos blanket, or put it out with the fire extinguisher, which will choke off its supply of air. A fire in a large puddle of alcohol may well spread if doused with water. This kind of fire should be smothered with a blanket or put out with the extinguisher.

Energy and Water Conservation

Few boats run out of water and cooking fuel, but since both may be hard to find and bring aboard and since fuel is expensive, conservation is a good practice. Most of us are much more aware of natural resource and energy conservation than we were ten years ago, and the same OPEC-stimulated common-sense procedures that we follow at home work on the boat.

Boiling water requires more energy than heating almost anything else. Many years of nervous pot-watching have taught me that one full kettle of water boils more slowly than two half-filled kettles. One of our informants advises, 'avoid heating too much water, use any leftover hot water for cleanup or face-washing, keep hot water in a Thermos, and avoid using food that has to be cooked in a large amount of water.' Marcia Wiley, executive editor of *Yachting* magazine, suggests always steaming, rather than boiling, vegetables.

Our experts had several suggestions for water conservation while washing dishes. Dishes should first be scraped very thoroughly and given a hard rub with a brush or paper towel, then washed in cold water using a liquid soap. Uncontaminated left-over cooking water can be saved for washing up. One cook we surveyed even uses leftover egg-boiling water for making tea and instant coffee (but another reported a superstition that reused egg water causes warts!). Clean sea water is an excellent resource on boats, especially on offshore passages. To conserve fresh water in the boat's tanks, dishes are often scraped and rinsed in salt water the boat is sitting in, drawn either by a foot-operated galley pump or with a bucket. Since salt deposits absorb moisture, do the last rinse in fresh water, or at least wipe the dishes with a sponge or towel damp with fresh water. Salt water may be used in small quantities for cooking eggs or potatoes. While research and the experience of abandoned sailors in life rafts strongly suggest that salt water should not be drunk, perhaps it may be used in small doses to save fresh water. During the 1972 Trans-Atlantic Race, as we sat becalmed and worrying about our water supply in a huge stagnant high-pressure system west of the Azores, our cook (an MD) made powdered lemonade with a mix of fresh and salt water.

With that foundation laid, let us now look at how some experienced seafaring cooks prepare for and cook their meals, while leaving themselves enough time to enjoy the sailing, too.

CHAPTER 13

Eating
Simply and
Well

―――――

While few people go to sea to eat gourmet meals—
most are escaping from hot kitchens and complicated cooking—everybody in a boat still must eat, preferably in a way that
complements the pleasures of living under sail. Just how you provide sustenance depends to a great extent on your original goals. If
you have set out to get away from a frantic shore life, you will probably choose to live and eat with relative simplicity and flexibility,
relying on frozen precooked casseroles and sauceless two-course
meals, frequently cooking while under way, changing your menus
to fit the day's weather and your itinerary, and inserting small,
special frills here and there. On the other hand, if you like to carry
your luxury with you like a turtle's shell, you may well fit your sailing activities around your culinary tastes and demands, staying
under way for relatively short distances and anchoring frequently to
allow the chef to spin out elaborate meals on a level platform.

The first of these lifestyles is the one that most people who
enjoy sailing and the footloose freedom of the sailing life usually
end up choosing, even if they originally wanted the second. Unless
they are willing to go ashore in search of three-star restaurants,
those who like luxury and who sail quickly discover that culinary
compromises must be made, starting with the sea cook's tools,
which, as we saw in the last chapter, simply are not up to a shore

kitchen's standards. Most boat stoves are small, stowage lockers tiny, refrigerators and ice chests none too efficient. On the human side, even the most ambitious sailing gastronomes usually realize within a day or two that they are, after all, on a vacation. Given a choice between the joys of relaxing on deck on a warm sunny afternoon in a beautiful and isolated bay, on the one hand, and stopping daily for fresh provisions so that they can slave away in a tiny, steaming galley over a four-course meal, on the other, most sailing chefs soon find themselves moving radically in the direction of simplicity.

This does not mean, however, that sailors have to live like Boy Scouts camping in the woods, scooping half-warm beef stew out of cans. Tasty, nutritious meals made from fresh meat and vegetables are within the realm of possibility of any cook whose boat has an ice chest and a two-burner stove. Add an oven and a well-filled spice rack and you can cook almost as successfully as you do at home—more so, in fact, since cooking afloat always improves the smell and taste of good, simple food. Neither does simplicity require dispensing entirely with formality. As we will see in the next chapter, seasoned cruising sailors strive to create an atmosphere of gracious living by observing two or three fairly impractical but highly pleasurable customs, much the way English explorers used to dress for dinner no matter what swamp they were slogging through.

Where and How to Stow the Food

The most important limits on the type and amount of food to be carried are storage space and refrigeration. Non-perishables can be crammed in just about anywhere. The primary stowage area is the set of lockers and bins in the galley, but most crews soon find themselves sticking food in places ostensibly set aside for other purposes. One of the experienced cooks that I surveyed reports that her biggest problem with stowage was competing with the crew's clothes.

Most boats have deep, relatively inaccessible bins under bunks and in the heads that are perfect for stowing non-perishables. Use caution, however; an excess of heavy items, such as canned goods, stowed away up forward will weigh down the bow and throw the boat out of balance. Given a choice, stow light stuff—cereals, bread, paper goods—forward, and put the cans aft, where there is more buoyancy. One boat I know well has a huge storage bin under the cockpit that is reached by crawling way aft in a quarter berth. Because it is deep and square, this space soon came to be called the 'lobster pound'. Besides its size, it has the advantages of being low in the boat and far from traffic; unlike goods stored on high shelves, the cans there cannot fly about and risk injuring people in rough seas. Stowing cans in the bilge under the cabin sole (or floor) offers the same benefit but with two disadvantages: when water gets into the bilge (which is inevitable) the paper wrappers will peel off and the cans may rust. A solution is to tear off the wrapper, label the contents on the can top with an indelible pen, and put the cans in plastic bags.

Food stowage should follow a logical plan. Many people organize by meals, putting all the ingredients for an individual dinner together. Others group by type—for example, stowing all the canned fruits in one place and all the canned vegetables in another. As a disaster back-up, it is a good idea to set aside two days' worth of emergency canned or dried rations and fresh water in plastic containers in an especially secure, dry place. With so many items scattered in so many places, the cook should make a written record of their whereabouts. A simple list might do, but it may be better to draw a map using the boat's accommodation plan, available from the builder or designer.

Perishables

Several members of our cooks' survey stress that the best way to keep perishable food from rotting is to buy only as much as you need, stow it so you will not forget about it, and eat it quickly. Even then, certain foods require special attention. Vegetables and fruits should be purchased as fresh as possible and stowed in a dark, cool, well-ventilated place. Many cooks hang them in string bags that must be secured so they cannot swing against the hull or a bulkhead and bruise the produce. Bread will mildew extremely rapidly in the marine atmosphere; stowing it in two tightly secured plastic bags usually keeps it dry.

Eggs present a challenging stowage problem. They should be as fresh as possible when purchased, and their life will be longer if they have never been refrigerated or washed. Before a long cruise, one cook I questioned likes to buy the eggs right at the farm, and when under way turn them every few days to keep the yolks from settling. To delay spoilage, many cooks coat eggs with vaseline or melted wax. Eggs may be put away in special plastic egg boxes in the icebox or refrigerator, or stowed with and cushioned by towels and paper goods in a dry locker in the heads.

Ice and Iceboxes

The standard way to preserve perishables is to keep them cold. On most boats I know, there are two cold places: a portable ice chest reserved solely for soft drinks, beer, and bottles of cold water; and the main icebox or refrigerator, where milk, eggs, meat, butter, and other perishable foods are stored. This way, the cool items most in demand on hot summer days are accessible without having to open the main cold storage, letting cold air escape. (In cool climates, water and canned drinks may be stored in the bilge). Many cruising boats today have refrigerators that run, one way or another, off the engine and the ship's batteries, and if the boat you are sailing in is so blessed you may skip the next three paragraphs and simply worry about whether the damn thing will break down and how you are going to fix it.

Loading ice is an art. Assuming that there is no old ice, start by emptying the icebox and thoroughly cleaning it out with a scrubbing brush, sponge, and liquid cleanser. Then dry it with paper towels before leaving the top off so the box can air for at least an hour. The spoiled milk and rotting food left over from the last cruise may be appalling in both quantity and smell. Be especially

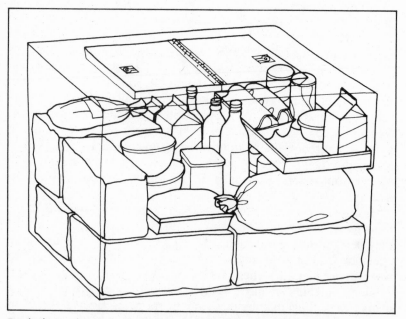

Pack the icebox as efficiently as possible, using block ice shaped with an ice pick, so that the blocks brick the bottom and sides. Wrap perishables carefully with one or two layers of plastic, and store milk, snacks and drinks so that they can be reached quickly with minimum loss of cold air. Sealable plastic containers are worth their weight in gold.

attentive to the drains, the sump where the run-off settles, and the various corners and dividers. Wash the cans and containers that you plan to put back, and do not forget to clean and air the lid, where many spills and crumbs accumulate.

Once the icebox is washed and aired out, load the ice. It must be block ice—not fast-melting cubes—brought aboard with old-fashioned ice tongs or, more frequently these days, in plastic bags. Do not skimp, especially if the weather is warm and your cruise is long; you will probably need to load at least sixty pounds at the beginning. Shape the blocks with an ice pick until they brick the box's floor with no wasted space either underneath or between, then build walls of ice up the sides. Water will run off through a drain into a sump or the bilge, which should be periodically pumped dry and scrubbed clean to keep it free of spilled milk and mouldy food. If there is no drain use a small hand pump, or water will eventually seep into food storage bags. It is a good idea to leave some blocks in their plastic delivery bag so that you will have several quarts of clean ice water when the ice melts.

Just how long the ice will last depends on the thickness of insulation in the box's walls, the quantity of food that must be cooled, the air and water temperature, and the amount of use the box receives. In hot weather, or in warm weather when it is opened frequently, a fully loaded icebox may remain cold enough with its original load of ice to preserve milk and meat for four days. But do not count on it; as the ice melts, replace it with another twenty or thirty pounds every two or three days. One way to increase efficiency is to bring all your food, and even frozen drinking water in milk jugs, aboard directly from your home refrigerator or freezer. Camping stores and some chandleries sell freeze packs to freeze at home and take aboard to lengthen the life of the ice.

Plastics, Plastics, Plastics

Because the icebox's temperature is relatively high as well as variable, all perishables should be protected in plastic wrap, bags, boxes, or bottles. *Avoid using glass containers whenever possible.* No matter how secure it seems, glass will eventually break, causing a mess and probably cutting somebody's foot or hand. If you must use a glass jar or bottle, stow it in a secure locker low in the boat or wrap it with tape or a towel.

Dairy products are the biggest worries. If milk spills, the icebox and, possibly, the bilge will begin to smell like a sewer. Some people have had such bad experiences with liquid milk that they will not allow it on board and use the powdered or canned variety instead. But if you cannot live without fresh milk, stow it with great care—not in cardboard containers, which will almost certainly leak, but in plastic containers with secure lids. The very best way to stow milk is the system recommended by Betty Noyes: pour it into plastic bottles with wide, screw-on tops that allow the entire bottle to be washed in hot water later. Sticks of butter and margarine can easily get lost between the cracks of ice blocks, will inevitably melt, and are difficult to slice one-handed; instead, take plastic tubs of margarine or other spreads, which preserve well and are easy to use. Empty tubs are handy storage containers for leftovers as well as for loose change and nuts and bolts.

Plastic bottles should also be used for other liquids, like orange juice, but because the consequences of a juice spill are less disastrous than with milk, a cardboard container may do for short passages as long as the top is kept closed with tape or a paper clip.

Judging from their responses to questions about preservation, the cooks I surveyed have obviously learned the hard way about keeping solid perishables. Several stressed that plastic is a much more secure and permanent wrap than aluminium foil. 'Put *everything* in plastic bags,' one insisted, and another uses two layers— first a plastic wrap and then a left-over bread bag or some other plastic bag. If you do use open plastic bags, secure them with rubber bands instead of metal twist ties, which will rust when they get wet.

Finding the container you want in a dark, crowded icebox will be difficult unless the food is stowed systematically. You may, for instance, put vegetables on one side, meat on the other, cans on the bottom, and dairy products on top. Whichever way you pack the food, do it as simply and logically as possible. No system is good if it cannot be explained in common English or if basic items are not easy to find. You will know that there is something wrong if every time a crew member wants a drink or a jam sandwich, the cook has to be asked to go below to hunt for the ingredients.

Meal-Planning Hints

While one of the joys of cooking on a vacation is that you can shrug off the burden of culinary conventions accumulated over a lifetime and eat what you want when you want it, good cooks feel that they have not done their jobs if they have not anticipated and provisioned for their shipmates' tastes, needs, and appetites. Some sailors stick to a breakfast-lunch-dinner schedule but take on more and larger helpings than they would ashore. Others eat about the same amount at meals but gorge on snacks. A well-provisioned boat with a crew that includes both types of eater will carry plenty of both types of food—meals and snacks—plus a varied supply of drinks.

Since space is limited and there is no store around the corner, everything depends on good planning. Before provisioning for a cruise, sit down and write out the menus, keeping everybody's preferences in mind. Before setting out to cook for people whose tastes are unfamiliar to you, it may be a good idea to send out a questionnaire like the one suggested below:

Crew Food Preferences

I.   BREAKFAST

Tick one:

  ( ) Orange juice
  ( ) Pineapple juice
  ( ) Grapefruit juice
  ( ) Apple juice
  ( ) Tomato juice

Tick one:

  ( ) Cereal, bread/toast, butter and marmalade/jam
  ( ) Eggs, bread/toast, butter and marmalade/jam
  ( ) Cereal, eggs, bread/toast, butter and marmalade/jam

Tick one:

  ( ) Marmalade
  ( ) Jam
  ( ) Honey

Tick one:

  ( ) Tea
  ( ) Coffee
  ( ) Milk

II.   LUNCH

Tick one:

  ( ) White bread
  ( ) Wholemeal bread

Number three sandwich preferences in order:

  ( ) Ham
  ( ) Cheese
  ( ) Cheese and pickle

( ) Cheese and tomato
( ) Egg
( ) Egg and tomato
( ) Beef
( ) Chicken
( ) Turkey
( ) Corned beef
( ) Tuna
( ) Salami

III. DINNER
Number three soup preferences in order:
( ) Tomato
( ) Mushroom
( ) Chicken
( ) Mulligatawny
( ) Mock Turtle
( ) Lentil
( ) Consomme
Number three meat dish preferences in order:
( ) Beef stew
( ) Roast beef
( ) Roast lamb
( ) Roast pork
( ) Turkey
( ) Chicken
( ) Cottage pie
( ) Steak and kidney pie
( ) Sweet and sour pork
Number two tinned dish preferences in order:
( ) Luncheon meat
( ) Corned beef
( ) Ham
( ) Ravioli
( ) Corned beef hash
( ) Spaghetti and meat balls
( ) Pilchards
( ) Herrings in tomato sauce

IV. ALLERGIES
Are there any foods (eg shell fish) to which you are
allergic? Please specify. . . . .

As at home, food is usually a compromise between convenience and taste, but it does not always have to be that way. There is no reason why you cannot visit your favourite take-away and carry the goodies aboard in the ice chest to be reheated for dinner on the first or second night. On a week's cruise, in fact, you may find yourself eating as many pre-cooked meals as you do freshly made ones, alternating them with an occasional cook's-night-off at a cheerful local restaurant. (Dinner ashore is a good time for the guests to thank their hosts by picking up the bill; that is why it is traditionally called a 'crew dinner'.)

Although some cooks shy away from them because of their grease and smoke, many American boats carry charcoal-fired barbecue grills. For obvious reasons, grills should always be used either ashore or hanging over the water, suspended from a sturdy clamp on the after pulpit. The same common-sense rules that apply for shoreside grilling should be followed on board, with the added provisos that you be alert to sparks or smoke blowing onto your neighbour's boat downwind, and that, after cooking, you carefully stow the leftover charcoal and dirty, greasy grill. Two heavy-duty plastic garbage bags and a cardboard box should suffice to isolate them from your sails, fenders, and sheets.

Depending on your tolerance for preservatives, you may even eat meals out of tins. I do, very occasionally. Tins are the best long-term packages for sauces, fruits, and vegetables, while tinned butter and bacon keep longer without refrigeration than the fresh kind. There is no reason why tinned meat stews have to remain as tasteless as the manufacturer made them. Even the blandest soup or stew can be enlivened by some spices and a cup of wine. Over several years of cruising my sons have gradually been initiated into the opinion that the best breakfast afloat is corned beef hash mixed with a dash of Worcestershire sauce and capped by a fried egg. Now that I think of it, their enthusiasm for—or at least acceptance of—this delicacy may be due to the fact that we never eat it ashore. If you too, can convince your crew that heaven is a tin of hash or stew, well, your cooking problems may be over. *Digestive* problems, no.

'Tasty simplicity' is the best description of a good meal afloat, and recipes should be chosen (or invented) with that objective in mind. This approach is neatly summarized by Sheila McCurdy, who has cooked across oceans and into tiny Caribbean harbours on many cruises, races, and yacht delivery trips:

> My philosophy of the galley is to keep matters as simple as possible. Good cooking enhances a cruise, but it is still secondary to the sailing. Those

who wish to indulge epicurean desires do not seek out sailing boats. The best sea cooks I know are not valued for their exotic dishes but for their flexibility, creativity, and persistence under dreadful conditions. It helps to have a sense of humour. One reassuring fact that a cook should keep in mind is that, in a boat, people will eat just about anything and be happy. With imagination and a little effort, a meal becomes a special occasion.

I learned to cook at sea and so, unlike most people, had to adapt to land cooking. For me the same rules apply wherever I cook. I tend toward simple, nutritious, well-seasoned meals. I try to minimize mess and avoid recipes with critical requirements such as timing, oven temperature, or rare ingredients, like fresh coconut milk in Maine or maple syrup in Portugal. Quantities can be difficult to guess when one does not know the crew. No one should go away hungry, yet a nightly feast is uncalled for. Common sense prevails. I have never known anybody to starve on a cruise.

Plan meals around other activities. One should never cut short snorkeling over a coral reef to peel potatoes.

Like most good cooks, Sheila is an improviser. 'I have rarely, if ever, followed a recipe from beginning to end,' she adds. 'I freely change ingredients and proportions based on whim and availability.' Once, during a transatlantic passage on a boat lacking yeast and baking soda, she found a way to bake bread using Alka-Seltzer as the riser.

Wine and Beer

As we will see in the next chapter, a bottle of wine or two can be a valuable asset to gracious living in a boat (but only if—like all alcohol on board—it is sampled judiciously when under way). There are certain built-in limitations to provisioning wine. One, of course, is its fragile glass container. Some wine is available in boxes, or you may always decant your own favourites into a plastic bottle. If you must use glass wine or liquor bottles, wrap them with towels or, better yet, stuff them in thick wool socks or shoe bags. Another problem is that while the quality of packaged foods does not suffer in a boat's bouncy, warm interior, that of many wines does. Older

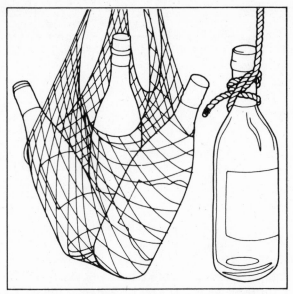

To cool wine, hang it overboard in a string bag
or at the end of a line.

wines, which have sediment, suffer more than younger ones, so if
you cannot live without vintage wine, carry along a strainer. Wine
may be chilled overboard, several feet deep into cool water, at the
end of a line—use a clove hitch locked by a half-hitch—or in a string
bag. When you use a bottle, try to finish it off in one sitting so that
you will not have to worry about leakage around the loosened cork.

Champagne anyone? It will take the abuse. One evening in
September 1979, in Newport, Rhode Island, a gang of cheerful
English sailors were distributing some good bubbly that they had
carried with them a month earlier on the very rough Fastnet Race
in Britain, then in the same boat across to America. It tasted just
fine.

As to beer—well, beer drinkers know what they like, and now
that some premium beers are available in cans, you may be able to
give it to them. The only caveat is that anybody who normally
downs a couple of brews on a quiet Saturday afternoon at home will
easily put away twice that many on a busy Saturday afternoon in an
active boat, not so much for the taste of it but to quench a raging
thirst. Therefore, low-calorie 'light' beers and the new low-alcohol
brands may be healthier than their weightier and more potent
cousins. Many years ago Sir Francis Chichester survived a one-stop
circumnavigation with the help of several kegs of beer wedged into
the cabin of *Gipsy Moth IV*.

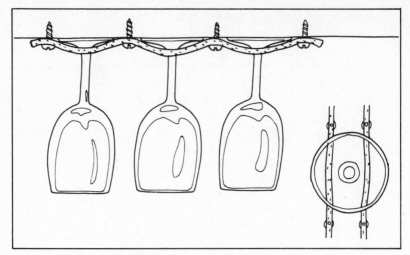

Some attractive plastic wineglasses are now available for gracious
nautical sipping, if you can figure out how to stow them. On board
Revelation, Carol Nicklaus and Eric Camiel hang their glasses
upside down, with the bases slipped under two lengths of
shockcord screwed to the underside of the galley cabinet.

Other Drinks

Cold liquids used on board vary with the crew's tastes. Tinned
—*never* bottled—soft drinks are of course popular, and everybody
has a favourite. Colas may be in special demand because they help
settle queasy stomachs. Powdered drinks mixed with cold water in
plastic bottles are convenient but can be messy. As ashore, the best
way to quench thirst is to take a drink of cool water; add a slice of
lemon or a teaspoon of powdered lemonade to override the faint
glass fibre taste of the water tank. Better still, at home fill some
clean milk jugs or plastic bottles most of the way with tap water and
freeze them. On board, the jugs of frozen water will help lower
temperatures in iceboxes and ice chests and, when they melt, will
provide chilled drinking water without depleting the boat's tanks.

Popular hot drinks include the usual coffee and tea. Worrying
about spills and coffee grounds, some skippers will not allow fresh
coffee on board. Obviously, they either are tea drinkers or could not
care less how bland their morning caffeine fix tastes, yet their concern about safety is legitimate. Coffee pots, whose high centre of
gravity invites capsize, must be used with great care when the boat
is under sail. Hot cocoa is a wonderful treat on a cold day. Many
people like Bovril, perhaps with a drop or two of sherry stirred in

('Shovril'). Tinned soup can be a meal in itself, but is more awk-ward to make than instant powdered soup, which, to me, tastes like salted dishwater.

The worst part of hot drinks is heating the water and juggling to pour them. Instead of boiling a pot of water for each cup, wasting both time and fuel, at the start of the day fill a large Thermos bottle with boiling water and leave it in a secure, visible place, say in the sink. Anybody who needs a hot drink may then make it at his or her convenience without lighting the stove. When under way, always pour hot liquids with the cup sitting in the bottom of the sink. One boat I sail on has a cup rack, undoubtedly borrowed from an air-craft's galley, that fits securely in the sink, thereby allowing several cups to be filled quickly without scalding the pourer. If there is any risk of spills, wear your foul-weather gear and rubber gloves.

Snacks

Snacks and treats should be easy to assemble, nutritious, filling, relatively unmessy, and not too dry (otherwise the crew will rapidly depelete the ship's water and drink supply). Among the energy-producing snacks and treats that our survey of cooks recommended are: plain biscuits (greasy ones will leave their imprint on sails, decks, clothes, and cushions), cheese, raisins, biscuits, chocolate, Mars bars, barley sugar, boiled sweets, chopped vegetables, nuts, and fresh fruit (especially grapes, apples, and oranges; bananas rot quickly).

Fruits and nuts are especially valuable snacks because they function as natural laxatives to help cure one of the sailor's biggest problems—constipation brought on by hours and hours of sitting. A bran breakfast cereal is another cure for this malaise. So is taking a long row or daily walk or jog ashore, which has the added benefit of providing a release from the tensions that inevitably accumulate when several people live almost on top of each other.

CHAPTER 14

Fun and Gracious Living

Y ou have probably noticed that the words *cautious, should,* and *must* have appeared more frequently up to now than *fun, may,* and *if you please.* Sailing, after all, is always challenging, can be difficult, and is sometimes even dangerous. Still, many of the most relaxed and enjoyable moments of my own life have been spent on the decks and in the cabins of racing and cruising yachts, bathing in the warm and joking camaraderie of my shipmates, including children.

The foundation of these pleasures is the joy of living in an active community of other people with nature. From that base spring the handful of simple habits and rituals that make up gracious living; the little and not-so-little things that add to enjoyment, comfort, and civilized life aboard a conveyance that quite frequently is uncomfortable and wet. Some of these customs are touches of formality that would seem inconsequential in our homes ashore but that add a gratifying sense of ritual and gentility to our moments afloat. Others are seafaring versions of those rules of decent behaviour that we all learn as we grow up and that we intuitively fall back on in order to get through life's crises. From a distance, sailing may not seem to need such conventions, but like any activity that crams people together in tight quarters in a difficult environment, it demands civility, a sense of humour, and tolerance.

Here, then, are some suggestions for improving and enjoying the quality of life on board a boat.

The Evening Rituals

We have made and quoted many praises of simplicity afloat—simple food, simple galleys, simple sail-handling rules, simple clothing. So often have we repeated this advice that we run the risk of being considered simple-minded. This emphasis is important because sailing can sometimes seem a complicated, variable-ridden pastime that most full-time sailors (much less weekenders) are not able to master completely even in a long lifetime. If we are to have any chance of making sense of the pastime's complexities, they must be sorted out, organized, and reduced to easily remembered rules of thumb; some of these complexities, in fact, must be eliminated.

Although simplicity is clearly a benefit on board a boat, we should not become so obsessed with it that all the fun is taken from a sport, that like life itself, overflows with unpredictability, humour, contradictions, and irony. In life ashore, we need rituals and ceremonies to keep chaos at bay. So, too in a boat.

Most of the sea cooks surveyed report that when afloat, usually

'Gracious dining is only limited if one is under sail and not at anchor'. This Trintella cruiser-racer is obviously at anchor.

before and during dinner, they follow one or two formal routines. Whether or not they also adhere to these rituals in their houses, they choose to make these embellishments an important part of their lives on board. A few hard-nosed types might think some of these little luxuries irrelevant, superficial, and in some cases, unsafe. There was a time when I felt that way, too, but incipient middle age has finally convinced me that a hair shirt is not only uncomfortable and unbecoming, but unnecessary.

If cruising sailors, a contentious lot, can agree about anything, they agree about in-harbour evening routines. In the afternoon, once the anchor is set or the mooring lines are secure and the boat is cleaned up, most people feel ready for a nap, a row, a swim, a walk or a shower ashore—whatever allows them a moment of privacy and reflection. They need that psychological 'one hand for yourself' to get them through the day.

Cocktail hour

Later, when the sun is sinking—about 1800—many crews gather in the cockpit under the shade of an awning (or, in miserable weather, around the cabin table) for a cocktail hour consisting of simple hors d'oeuvres, good conversation, and a drink or two. (Beware: a tiring day in the fresh air or hot sun may leave you weak and helpless before the onslaught of strong alcohol.) With the skipper's permission, an invitation to join in may be shouted, waved, radioed, or rowed across to a nearby boat containing friends or attractive-looking strangers. While acquaintances are made easily on the water, privacy is important, too; do not feel slighted if your invitation is turned down. Using the largest boat's biggest anchor, several boats may be rafted-up side by side, their masts and shrouds carefully kept apart through the judicious use of springs. The raft should be broken up immediately if the weather worsens. For their own relief—and that of adults who would enjoy some purely grown-up company—this is a good time for children to play card games way up on the foredeck or to get away from the old folks for a swim or a short row.

Wine, Wildflowers, and Candlelight

Although most cooks do not allow obsessive food preparation to get in the way of this informal party, the smart ones time dinner so that it is served before everybody is too drunk to eat. The time of sunset has nothing to do with it, as I learned the hard way while cruising one July down the Caledonian Canal in the Scottish Highlands, where the summer sun finally goes down at around 2300. Used to 8-ish New England sunsets, we kept sip-sip-sipping away on splen-

A kerosene lamp (shown here next to a
barometer and ship's clock) makes a cheerful,
warm light that suffuses the entire cabin.
However, because it has a glass dome and
flammable fuel, it should be watched with care.

did single-malt whisky, waiting for darkness to settle over Loch
Ness and herald dinnertime. By the time the sun finally sank, the
only crew member competent to handle the stove was the single
abstainer, my then thirteen-year-old sister, Kate.

How fancy can dinner be? Susie Page, who has cruised for
many years, tells us, 'Gracious dining is only limited if one is under
sail and not at anchor.' Amenities have a lot to do with it. In
Pageant, the Pages set a vase of freshly picked wildflowers on the
table, and they and most of the other cooks I surveyed report that
dinner at anchor is usually eaten under candlelight and served with
wine. Many boats have neat brackets for wine glasses and wine and
liquor bottles, but you can make do by wrapping glassware in
towels or by using wine boxes. Sometimes a change in the usual
amenities is an important ritual. When they sailed around the world
in *Rabbit*, Mimi and Dan Dyer celebrated every arrival in a new
port by using crystal glasses and special 'harbour' coffee cups,
which they carefully put back in storage when they weighed anchor.
Of course, what you eat makes a difference, too. Once again, the
little things are important. Adra and Chuck Kober drink only
regular coffee ('we never use instant') when they cruise in *Shibui* off
Southern California; other cooks take along special items like herbs,
spices, loose tea, a pepper grinder, and after-dinner mints.

Lighted candles, wine glasses, a coffee pot, and mints all demand a certain amount of special preparation and concentrated attention if they are to be used in a jumpy, damp sailing boat. The sacrifice is well worth making if any one of them contributes to the crew's happiness. The clear lesson here is that while some of these items may be utterly impractical some of the time—for example, it is not a good idea to light candles when the boat is rolling wildly in rough seas—every sailor will have a short list of 'nice-to-haves' that may be treated as essentials.

Order and Neatness Count

A cruising boat's interior is roughly the size of one small room, her galley about the size of a large cupboard. It does not take much thought to realize that the ingenious arrangement of floor space, lockers, shelves, bins, and bunks will not work at all—in fact may be counterproductive—if things are not kept organized and neat. Good housekeeping is important. So is a commonsense approach to using what little room is available.

First of all, the galley should not be cluttered with willing, eager, but unnecessary bodies. Let the cook do the job the way he or she wants to do it, which often means doing it alone because the space is so tiny and the tools so few. 'Offer the cook help,' one experienced chef recommends to potential cutters, choppers, and stirrers, 'but if not helping, stay out of the way.' Eager shipmates should avoid making the cook worry about hurt feelings if, of necessity, he or she spurns their requests to assist. The dishes, stove, sink, and cutting boards should be washed as soon as possible after each meal not only to free space and materials for the next one but also to avoid attracting insects. Every boat has her own dish-washing system. For reasons we outlined in Chapter 5, a cleaning routine that depends on volunteers may be the worst, since it often leads to unconscious misunderstandings and hurt feelings. Sometimes the cook assumes responsibility in a defensive manoeuvre to keep other people from taking over 'my' galley. That is the cook's prerogative, and the others can work off their sense of responsibility by enjoying their after-dinner mints and liqueurs while he or she washes up. Usually, however, the job rotates among the crew members from meal to meal, day to day, according to an announced schedule.

Nuisances at home, cockroaches and other bugs are horrible creatures to be forced to live with in a boat since the galley, where they generally congregate, overlaps the sleeping and eating areas. Keeping the galley clean is one way to deal with them, and you can always fumigate, but the best protection is not to let them on board in the first place. Cockroaches are most likely to arrive uninvited in the corners and recesses of cardboard boxes and paper bags; many experienced cooks always transfer their food to tote bags before carrying it aboard, leaving the paper containers ashore.

Never let the rubbish take over the galley or cabin. Rotten or unwanted leftover food may be heaved overboard to feed the fish and birds (throw it to *leeward*, thank you), but dump everything else into a garbage can lined with a sturdy plastic bag—or perhaps two bags, one inside the other, if you are worried about sharp edges poking through. Most people prefer to put the rubbish bin under a step in the companionway ladder, where it is automatically ventilated as well as visible and accessible to everybody who has a piece of gash in hand. When the bag is about two-thirds full, pull it out and tie up its neck so that the contents are loose (otherwise it might explode). If you cannot take the bag ashore right away, stow it in a big locker, the forepeak, or—better still—the dinghy towed astern. In some ports, the harbour master (a paid official who supervises moorings, aids to navigation, and other essential services) sends a boat around to pick up rubbish, or there will be a designated place to deposit it ashore.

The cabin as a whole must be kept tidy. Because the cook

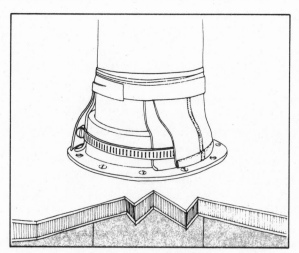

A major source of leaks is the partners, where the mast passes through the deck. It should be sealed by a mast coat, a rubber gasket held in place by a large hose clip, and covered by a well-shaped canvas gaiter.

spends more time below than most other crew members, she or he is frequently the best judge of cabin neatness and serves as a combination housemother and inspector general. Locker doors and drawers must be shut. Everybody should keep clothes in lockers, bunks, or seabags and foul-weather gear in the assigned locker or bin. The heads should receive a daily cleaning; the toilet must be scrubbed out and its lid left shut. In the interest of keeping the toilet's immediate surroundings from smelling bad, when the weather is rough men should not try to urinate below while standing up. 'Gentlemen always sit,' as old-timers say.

Finally, do everything you can to keep the cabin dry. Pump the bilge to prevent messy, oily water from slopping over onto the cabin sole. The moment spray begins to fly or rain begins to fall, shut the ports and hatches. If you notice water drops on the mast below the partners (where the mast passes through the deck), tighten the rubber mast coat on deck. Sponge up puddles of water as soon as they form, and wipe any interior surface exposed to salt water with a paper towel damp with fresh water. Once clothes get wet (and they will), be sure to isolate them. If the weather permits, peg wet clothes on the guardrails to dry in the sun after a fierce shaking to get rid of much of the superficial moisture. Later, shake the salt crystals off dry clothes, too. In rainy or overcast weather, store wet clothes in plastic bags until you can get to a laundry.

Be Sensitive to Smells

The cook has to be alert to the indirect ways in which cooking affects living aboard the boat. The most obvious concern is that food preparation and cooking should not overflow from the galley. But of almost equal importance is keeping the cabin smelling nice. One of the most gratifying aspects of cruising is that while almost all food tastes good on a boat, it smells even better in the fresh air away from land. Several days at sea will rest and revive a sailor's olfactory nerves to pick up even the meekest odours that, ashore, would be lost in the swirl of civilization. For example, one of the many pleasures of sailing to Bermuda is that the landfall is usually made not by sighting the archipelago's low coral outgrowths but by sniffing the moist perfume of its oleander shrubs. If odours in the atmosphere around the boat are more distinguishable, so too are smells on board. Spices are sharper, fruits are juicier, rum drinks are more tropical. Consciously or unconsciouly, good cooks combine foods for their pungency as well as for their tastes, much the way Oriental cooks design a stir-fried meal around its appearance. This does not take much work in the morning, for while its light grease may make frying risky, the meld of bacon's sharp tang with the rich stream of good brewed coffee is the most pleasant alarm clock that I know.

It is easy to go too far in this direction and create or permit overpowering, lingering smells. Keep the cabin well ventilated; open the hatches and ports, and if you have one, rig an air scoop through the forward hatch. Yet even on warm, windy days, when you would think there is plenty of ventilation, the smell of thick grease, over-fried onions, or rotten bananas will find its way into every locker and bunk—even every sleeping bag—and nauseate shipmates to the point of seasickness.

Keep Your Sense of Humour

Like any other part of life, sailing can fall into a deadly routine unless the crew works hard to do something about it. Long hours of sitting and gazing at the same shoreline, the same ocean, and the same faces can produce a malaise much worse than cabin fever. Call it cockpit fever or boat fever, it usually responds to a mix of laughter, song, variety, and privacy.

The evening cocktail hour is a great time for a group pick-me-up, and with the forbearance of neighbouring crews it can go on late into the night. An extroverted shipmate with a good voice and repertory of cheerful songs is a wonderful addition. Some of my fondest sailing memories include late-night concerts by Bob and Harvey Loomis, who are members of an amateur Gilbert and Sullivan troupe. W S Gilbert's patter-song lyrics never sound more silly nor Arthur Sullivan's ballads so sweet as when sung in a boat's cockpit. Of course, there is the possibility of too much of a good thing, but the Loomises—like most other good singers I know—are careful not to spread their talents too thin with overuse.

A good way to add some spice to a cruise is to break it with a celebration of some kind—a birthday party, say, or a national holiday—when most rules are forgotten and everybody's hair is let down. On the other hand, spontaneity is an important part of good fun. In early July 1982, before we went off on the Trans-Atlantic Race from Bermuda to Spain in Clayton Ewing's 55-foot yawl *Dyna*, I asked my watch leader, Steve Colgate (proprietor of a well-known sailing school), if and when we might be served a cocktail. Steve said that if the skipper followed his normal, cautious policy we might be favoured with a single glass of sherry on Bastille Day. However, after ten days of painfully slow sailing, during which we fell way behind schedule and everybody's enthusiasm for sailing quietly faded into bare tolerance, Clayt emphatically changed his policy. One evening, as the off-going watch sat down to eat, he reached into the drink locker under his bunk and pulled out the first bottle he touched, a half-litre of scotch. He then asked the cook to grab the first tin his fingers brushed in the refrigerator. It was a Coke, but that was good enough for Clayt, and we all had a small, harmless scotch and Coke. It tasted terrible, but the inspired foolishness did wonders for our morale. The next night, the same stab-in-the-dark selection process came up with bourbon and lemonade. This nonsense went on every night until, in late July, after an agonizing three weeks of sailing, we finally crawled to the finish. A couple of times we chanced upon a conventional combination of drinks, but in light of our absurd circumstances—eleven men drifting around in the middle of an ocean for no other reason than to try to beat some other people doing the same thing—it was much more fun to break the rules.

When Sailing Gets Gloomy

There are times when no amount of joyful song and good cheer will make up for sustained bad weather or a poor mix of personalities, and somebody (or everybody) becomes unhappy. The first to notice and try to do something about it may be the cook. Sheila McCurdy offers some wise words:

> An additional duty the cook often takes on is that of morale officer, probably because the galley is the primary source of diversion when weather or some other conditions have turned sour. Some special treat at teatime, or a few gentle, joking words, can keep close living spaces more tolerable.

A sympathetic cook—usually, but not necessarily, a female one —can do wonders with someone's burgeoning depression. So, too, can a cook who plays the Fool to an overserious skipper's Lear. But often the greatest help is for unhappy crew members to find some diversion and privacy ashore or, if shore is inaccessible, to enjoy a few hours to themselves on board, often in their bunk with a book. Couples especially may find it hard to adjust to the exuberant chaos of a crowded boat. While they may have a cabin to themselves, they sometimes find that the kind of privacy they need for their normal intimate life (for which read *sex*) is totally lacking. One solution is for the various couples to go their separate ways every now and then in order to allow each pair a private evening either on board or ashore.

Keep Your Priorities Straight

Cheering-up aside, the cook's primary concern is to see that everybody gets enough tasty food to survive a cruise without both malnutrition and boredom. The cook should aim to provide properly for him- or herself, and then multiply that serving by the number of people on board. After all, cooks like cruising, too, as I found when I asked sea cooks about what they enjoy most about sailing. Most say nothing about cooking, little about actual sailing, and a lot about activities once the boat reaches her destination and drops anchor. Several cooks say their greatest pleasure is 'a quiet anchorage'. Others mention exploring harbours or rivers in dinghies or going ashore to paint and draw. One skipper who also cooks describes his rewards as 'the challenge of the navigation, the finding of new places, the remote and quite anchorage, and self-reliance, with no umbilical cords to the rest of society.' Yet others say that they enjoy meeting new people, just as long as the anchorage is not crowded. The closest anybody comes to the galley is 'picnic lunches or early dinners on a deserted beach or rock'—perhaps with some lobster bought from a passing fisherman and boiled over a wood fire.

Gracious living on board a boat, then, requires that cooking be kept in perspective. Flexibility and a sense of humour are important if the cook is going to have a good time, and if the cook's having fun, so probably is the rest of the crew.

CHAPTER 15

Sailing
with
Children

The world consists of two kinds of people: those who can get along with and understand children and those who cannot. Parents are not necessarily in one group or the other, and neither are non-parents; that makes taking children in a boat somewhat problematical. Having sailed with my sons, Will and Dana, for many years, I am not about to romanticize the experience any more than I would single parenthood (or parenthood itself, for that matter). At worst, it is like the normal, harried, noisy, somewhat thankless experience of living with children, but one compressed geographically into a tiny arena from which there is almost no escape. At best, it overflows with joyous surprises and offers a complete change from the usual daily routine. It can be one of the most satisfying experiences that a parent and child can share.

If you want to find out how your children take to sailing, why, take them sailing. You will soon get a sense of their interest in and aptitude for the pastime as you expose them to the sailing life, with all its pleasures and challenges, and some of its fears. Like adults, children learn how to sail faster in small boats than in large ones. A capsizable dinghy works best partly because her small gear can be managed by small bodies, but primarily because it rewards good technique and punishes bad with decisive quickness. If you do it wrong you get very wet; if you do it right you stay dry. After many years of teaching sailing in relatively large three-person boats, instructors have begun to use singlehanders such as Lasers (with cut-down rigs) in order to leave youngsters on their own and maximize the amount of time they spend at the helm—an excellent idea that is turning out new generations of better and more independent sailors. Sailboards work well for the same reason (and also because they are a great platform for showing off, which every child needs to do from time to time).

Perhaps an outline of one youngster's sailing life will suggest some possibilities. Until I was ten my family lived in Ohio, and I first sailed with my father on holidays at his boyhood home on Long Island, New York. He gave me the run of the boat on short day-sails, wisely allowing me to discover if I liked it before imposing detailed instruction and complicated terminology. I liked it. That settled, my first sailing lessons came at a summer camp on Maine's Kennebec River. A year or so later, we moved to Long Island and I and my brothers were given two 13½-foot Blue Jay sloops, boxy and roomy and made of plywood. My boat was bright red and was called *Lucivee,* which I was told means 'baby lynx' and which was inspired by a family tradition of boats named *Lynx.*

That was where I began to sail in earnest, at first knocking around the harbour under the watchful eye of a couple of college-student sailing instructors, later venturing out onto Long Island Sound for races, in which I did creditably enough to inspire a child's dreams of glory. Like all adolescents I was hungry for success in whichever arena worked best for me. Some find it in football, others in gymnastics, still others in academics. Sailing and learning about its history and traditions—that was my scene. (Many years later, when I worked with America's Cup winner Dennis Conner on his autobiography, *No Excuse to Lose,* I was fascinated to discover that he had made the same discovery in much the same way in San Diego, although his interest was more competitive than mine.)

As often happens, the rewards of early success stimulated harder work and greater ambitions, all fertilized by a library of sailing instructional and history books given to me by my father (and to him by his). An annual, week-long family cruise aboard a chartered boat in Maine or Massachusetts opened another door of the pastime. Like many teenagers before and since, I became captivated by the never-ending complexity of navigation and rigging, the relaxed camaraderie of a crew, and the almost spiritual satisfaction that comes when a sailor helps a boat to sail well. The energy and knowledge accumulated during those years eventually led to wider-ranging boating experiences. In 1964, when I was nineteen, I was fortunate to be invited to join a four-month voyage in a 77-foot ketch from San Diego to Sicily, and eight years later—after college, graduate school, and army duty—I sailed in a race from Bermuda to Spain. My writing about that transatlantic race led to a position on the staff of *Yachting* magazine, where sailing was a part of the job, and five years later I set out on my own to write books about the pastime that had been such an important part of my life for so many years.

I was lucky: my father, who knew and loved sailing, encouraged me in many ways, and my family moved in circles that involved yacht clubs, which, until the early 1970s, were almost the only places where a child could receive thorough sailing instruction and go out on the water every day of the summer. Fortunately, alternatives to that expensive exclusivity have long since made sailing available to many more people. After several summers of off-and-on sailing with me to find out if they liked it, my boys were enrolled in a local sailing school to learn sailing theory, terminology, and boat handling. At first, when they were nine and ten, the boys mastered the basic skills in a boat called a Puffer, which is a lighter, faster version of a Blue Jay. The next summer, they moved on to the much racier and tippier Laser, and Dana (when he was ten) earned his beginner's certificate on a Windsurfer—a type of boat that did not even exist until 1969, three years before he was born. Although I do not own a cruising boat, both boys have enjoyed the side benefits of having a father who is a sailor. By the time they were in their teens, they had been on a few short cruises, and we often sail together on annual boat delivery trips from Maine, usually with my father in a delightful three-generational crew whose cumulative experience stretches from the 1920s to the 1980s.

Along the way, I—like all sailing parents of sailing children— have been forced to cope with a variety of problems, including allowing the children to learn at their own speed and even leaving them ashore if that is their pleasure. Among the other concerns were (and continue to be) clothing, safety, enjoyment, and living together on a boat in relative harmony. Other parents may benefit from my experiences.

What to Wear

The same questions concerning adult clothing apply to children's gear. Theoretically, the amount and quality of gear that *you* purchase will depend on the amount and type of sailing that *they* do— and, especially, on how cold and wet they will get. In fine weather, a T-shirt and bathing suit will work well, along with gym shoes for

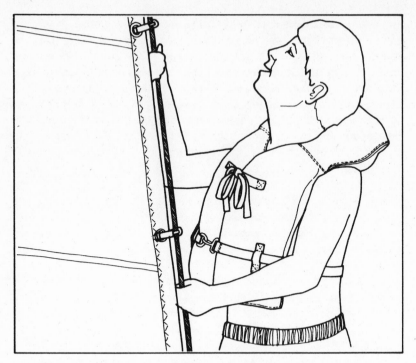

The main worry about sailing with children is that they may fall overboard. Less than expert swimmers must be required to wear lifejackets like this horseshoe type, which is less confining than a vest. Most cruising families have very definite rules about when and where children may go on deck in rough weather.

any sailing on boats with deck fittings. Be alert to sunburn; make sure the child wears a long-sleeved cotton shirt most of the time until he or she is well tanned. Like time and distance, the wind-chill factor is an abstraction ungraspable by the average twelve-year-old mind. Dressing a child properly for cool weather, therefore, is a herculean chore that often meets with protests along the lines of 'But I'll look like a polar bear!' A diplomatic solution is to pack—*you* pack—a seabag with another, skimpier outfit that the child may exchange for the bulky clothes that he or she finds so distasteful, or (more likely) put on over or under them upon discovering that you were correct from the beginning. If your children are like mine, you will also take along plenty of extra socks; Dana, who once 'accidentally' fell into the reflecting pool in front of the Lincoln Memorial in Washington, DC, takes pleasure in dangling from anchor rodes and mooring warps with his toes in the water.

Since Dana is not the only child who enjoys getting wet, any special protective gear you provide may never be used. Normal, zip-up, knee-length raincoats worked fine on board whenever I was able to cram my sons into them. Now they have, and sometimes even wear, more expensive PVC foul-weather jackets bought at a local chandlery. Normal rubber boots serve in place of seaboots. Every child who goes out on the water regularly must have his own proper life jacket, and be made to wear it when required.

Safety Worries

Most mothers and (secretly) most fathers, too, worry deeply about their children's safety on board a boat. The same rough guidelines that careful, loving parents follow at home apply on board, but there are some special rules that apply uniquely to a sailing environment. The ones that I find most important are:

Always know where your children are on the boat, especially when they are on deck. It may help to have them wear a shirt or sweater with a distinctive colour.

Make sure that children know who on deck is in charge, and that the person's commands must be obeyed implicitly. Since children like and need limits in their lives, observing this guideline will be as reassuring to them as it is to their parents.

Develop a tone of voice that means and is understood as *'Listen to me! This is important!'*

As soon as a child old enough to follow instructions comes aboard for the first time, demonstrate the safety equipment and any potential hazards. If you do not feel qualified to do it, ask somebody who knows the boat well to give the child a careful tour. You should accompany them to translate warnings into the child's language.

With all that understood, let your child roam anywhere within the confines of the guardrails.

Drown-Proofing
Your worst fear, obviously, is drowning. Teaching the child to swim early and well is the first step toward dealing with this problem, and swimming lessons at the local pool or at school are a good investment. But any young child and all children (or, for that matter, adults) whose swimming ability is unproven should follow

these rules, from the most elementary for normal weather to the most restrictive for rough weather:

> Wear a lifejacket whenever on deck or in the cockpit.

> Stay below or in the cockpit.

> Wear a safety harness and hook it to an object near the middle of the boat whenever on deck or in the cockpit.

In easy conditions, older children who can prove they are good swimmers by, say, swimming twice around the boat need not observe these rules, but the skipper's word is law when the weather gets rough. Toddlers present the most serious safety problems. Infants are rarely mobile enough to get out of the cockpit, and older children, if they have been lovingly disciplined, respect and are proud to observe the rules. But children from about one to four are too mobile, unbalanced, and vague about instructions to be trusted to stay where their parents leave them. For that reason, the decks of many toddler-crewed cruising boats are fenced in by mesh strung along the guardrails.

Falling, Cold and Strains

Two health hazards endemic to adults rarely affect children because of their small size and relatively large fat content. One of these is an injury caused by a fall; a fall that is serious for a tall adult is usually shaken off quickly by a four-footer. The other hazard is hypothermia, or drastic loss of body heat. A scrawny kid may get cold quickly and a distracted parent may not notice the usual symptoms—shivering, vagueness, passivity—but most children probably resist hypothermia better than most adults. On the other hand, children may be injured because they become unrealistically confident of their ability to perform chores best left to larger, stronger people—chores like trimming heavily strained sheets, handling warps, and lugging anchors. It is a good idea, once the boat is under way, to give the children an idea of the forces involved by getting them to trim a sheet or pull on a halyard. It looks easy until they try to do it. Once children realize how large the strains are, they usually stay well (and safely) away from big loads.

But do not be *too* protective, especially of near- and actual adolescents. That is the age when children are constantly taking new risks, and when a good parent, at the price of many grey hairs, is encouraging the taking of those risks. Until about the age of eleven or twelve, the children's world is often so benign that they cannot imagine getting hurt, but beginning at this age they want to (and, for the sake of maturation, must) discover that possibility. If there is any way that a sailor this age or older can catch a small but healthy dose of reasonable fear without being scared so badly that he or she swears off boats for life, parents should take advantage of it. Sailing a dinghy or sailboard in windy weather is one of those experiences; so is rowing a dinghy into rough seas.

Jobs for Children

What jobs can children perform? Quite a few are available, but, remembering that they are only children, an adult should not demand either total dedication or absolute perfection in the performance of the vast majority of them. Certainly children should be requested and expected to clear up after themselves and, observing a written schedule, to help with communal chores such as washing dishes and swabbing the deck with a mop or scrub brush. But when it comes to sailing and navigating the boat, there will be much less contention and disappointment if adults put themselves in a frame of mind where they are gratified and surprised if the kids volunteer to help.

One place where most children will be more than happy to serve is at the helm, and that is also where they make their greatest contribution to the vessel's welfare while larger people are exercising their bigger muscles on sheets, halyards, sails, and anchors. Some awful day, in an emergency, a grown-up swimming after a rapidly disappearing boat may wish that he had taught his child how to steer. For those reasons—and also because steering is a lot of fun—any child who shows an interest in handling the tiller or wheel should be given it once the boat is clear of land and traffic. Let the child steer just as long as desired so that he or she may learn by making mistakes. While the child is working at it, gradually show the novice something about the points of sailing, which way to shove the helm to alter course, and how to trim sails, steer by the compass, and tack and gybe. Other jobs that children may enjoy performing are taking bearings, spotting aids to navigation, watching the read-out on the depth sounder, listening to radio weather forecasts, making log entries, and clearing tangled halyards. Many children are fascinated by navigational skills, perhaps because so much of their own energy is dedicated to pinpointing their own positions on the great chart of life. Kids who are computer buffs frequently master the intricacies of a Decca receiver or other electronic device more quickly than computer-illiterate adults. Whatever the job, tell them how important a contribution they are making and reward them by taking them seriously.

Besides the immediate, utilitarian benefits, plenty of rewards fall out from a child's sailing accomplishments, whether or not he or she is sailing with his or her parents. Children who are good at something and see their skill properly recognized often develop a confidence that they carry fruitfully into other parts of their lives. As the child develops, so too does the parent. I was recently reminded of this during a cruise on a complicated and powerful 51-foot ocean racer. We had to lower a big genoa jib, and I handed the helm over to a shipmate and went forward. So that the jib would drop directly on deck and not fall overboard into the bow wave, I shouted aft, 'Bring her up a little.' The helmsman headed up to a forereach exactly as I would have done, we let go the halyard, and the sail collapsed on itself in neat folds on the foredeck as he professionally swung the bow off, bringing the bow back on course. As I walked aft after securing the sail, it finally sank in that this skilful helmsman was my ten-year-old son—the one who falls into reflecting pools, loses his baseball mitts, forgets his homework, and is surprised whenever he does something well. Right then, he looked like another Dennis Conner as his hands caressed the wheel with gentle strength. He was still a child, of course, and too much should not have been expected of him; but that, I reflected, would soon change.

Having Fun on the Big Gym

For a child, a sailing boat has all the advantages of both a big gymnasium and a small castle, and a normally eager, athletic, and individualistic boy or girl will find plenty to do all day. If the exercise is balanced by some private time spent alone and by plenty of rest, everybody on board regardless of age will enjoy the child's presence.

Most obvious when a child first comes aboard are all the things to swing on—the boom, halyards, sheets, bowlines, and mast. By the time they reach adolescence, kids become as obsessed about climbing the mast as mountaineers are about scaling Mt Everest. This urge may be satisfied at first by strapping the child securely into a bosun's chair and hauling him or her up to the top of the spar with a halyard. Be sure to tie a line to the chair so you can pull a light child down again. By the time he or she is hauled up about 20 feet, the child will know whether this is fun or not. Parents should be sure to praise the anxious child who sensibly calls a halt to the adventure as well as the daredevil who wants to keep going. As children get stronger and their hands tougher, they may try shinning up the mast on the halyards. It will be easier when the boat is

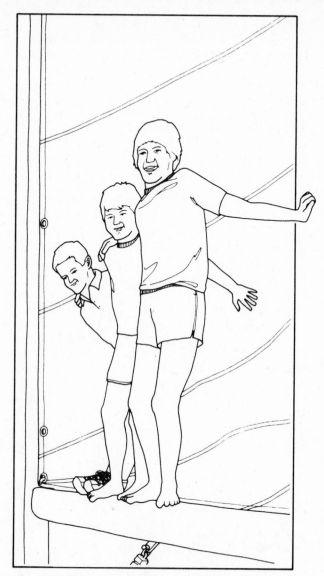

The boat herself is a huge, safe gymnasium. Just
keep your eyes on the young athletes.

heeled, when they can almost walk up the windward side. While I
have never known a kid (including myself at that age) fall off a mast,
if this activity makes a parent nervous to the point of acute dis-
traction, perhaps it should be left to school gyms (or postponed
until that parent is below taking a nap).

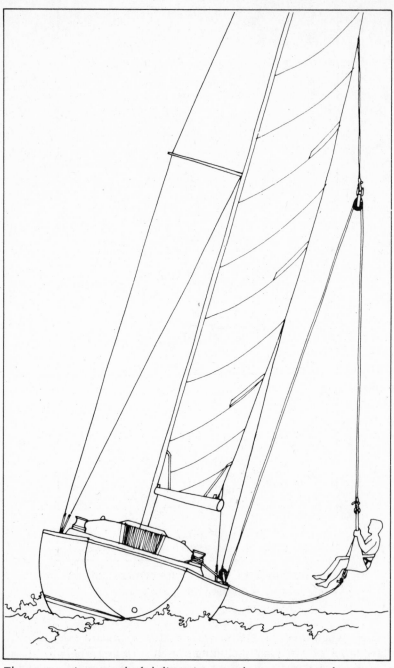

The trapeze is a wonderful diversion on a breezy, warm afternoon for adults as well as children. The fore and aft position of the deck block for the guy determines how far forward the rider swings.

The Rousmaniere Trapeze

A lot of fun can be had by swinging out from a sailing boat on a trapeze rigged from a halyard. I modestly take credit for refining this adventure to a science through many hours of experimenting with delighted children. It works only on a boat with powerful sheet winches and only when there is enough wind to heel her over at least 20 degrees, until her leeward rail is just kissing the water. This is how the trapeze is set up:

1. Working on the leeward side, snap a block into the shackle of the highest free halyard—usually a spare jib or spinnaker halyard—and lead a very long, relatively heavy line such as a spinnaker or jib sheet through the block.

2. Tying one end of the line to the guardrails, haul up the halyard as you feed out the line, until the block is about two-thirds of the way up the mast. Turn the halyard several times around its winch and cleat it. You now have a rope guy running through a block suspended from the mast.

3. Lead the guy through a block snapped to the rail about halfway between the leeward shrouds and the boat's beamiest point, and then back to the largest winch in the cockpit. You probably will have to lead the line through another block to make it lead up to the winch drum at an angle about 15 degrees below the horizontal; if the line comes in at or above the horizontal, there will be a riding turn, jamming it on the drum.

4. Now shackle or tie (with a bowline) the other end of the guy to the bosun's chair. To be doubly safe, wrap the pin of this and all other shackles in the system with a layer of tape.

5. Tie or shackle a retrieval line to the bottom of the bosun's chair and lead it through a block on the rail at the boat's beamiest point. If there is a boarding gate in the guardrails (a section that can be disconnected to facilitate boarding and unboarding), open it.

The trapeze is now ready. Wearing a bathing suit, the rider steps into the bosun's chair, a strong adult trims the guy (perhaps with the help of a winch handle grinder), and the rider rises from the deck and flies out to leeward through the boarding gate, directly abeam of the widest point. If he or she is forward of that point and threatening to swing into the leeward shrouds, move the lead block on the rail aft; if aft of the widest point, move the lead block forward.

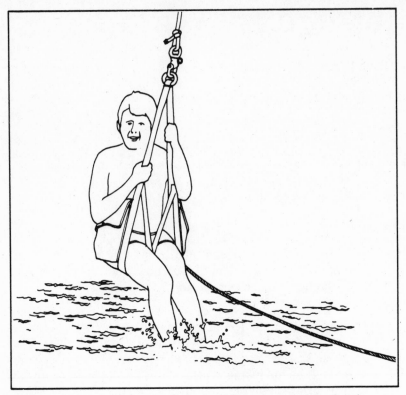

The diaper-type of bosun's chair provides great security for the swinger. Tape the pins of the shackles so that they do not open accidentally.

The person tending the guy controls the swinger's altitude, raising or dropping him or her into the water as whim allows. To pull the swinger back, haul on the retrieval line and have an adult sitting or standing on the leeward deck to make the grab.

Spinnaker Flying

A riskier type of trapeze artistry, spinnaker flying is done at anchor on boats larger than about 40 feet (12m). Because this exercise is controlled by the wind and can be wild, if not dangerous, I do not recommend it for use in gusting winds and by anybody younger than about sixteen.

1. Anchor the boat by her stern, with her bow pointed downwind. Set the smallest spinnaker with sheets but without a pole, and with a line about 1½ times the length of the foot tied

between the two clews. Hoist the spinnaker about two-thirds of the way so that when filled it flies *well* ahead of the bow.

2. Shackle the bosun's chair to the line—either to a knot in its middle or with a snatch block that can slide back and forth between the clews. The snatch block gives the wilder ride. Let one spinnaker sheet go, letting the sail flag out before the boat and the chair drop to the water.

3. The swinger jumps into the water and climbs into the chair, and the sheet is trimmed to fill the sail, which will lift high above the water and, as it oscillates, throw the rider around unpredictably. To drop the rider into the water, collapse the spinnaker by letting go a sheet *only* when he or she is well forward of the pulpit. Serious accidents have been caused by falls onto the pulpit and bow.

Quiet Fun

Crazy swinging is not the only fun a child can have on a sailing boat. A row in the boat's dinghy, a spin on her sailboard, a swim to a nearby island—all can provide both pleasure and the short daily vacation from adults that every child (and every parent) requires. On board, too, there are many ways children can enjoy themselves quietly. Some of these go with the nautical surroundings. Practising the basic knots—the bowline, double half-hitch, and rolling hitch —can be fun, especially if it is a group effort involving an adult expert. Tutored by an experienced grown-up or by a book like the classic *Ashley Book of Knots,* a boy or girl who enjoys detailed work may learn the basics of traditional marlinspike seamanship, including splicing and decorative rope work. On the other hand, the child who shows an interest in the history and technical aspects of sailing may, as I did, settle down with a specialized book for hours. One endlessly fascinating activity is to tow a model boat or wooden stick astern at the end of a long string (for some reason lost in time, we called those sticks 'weewogs' when I was a boy). After some practice, you can make the thing submarine and dance in the air. Bird-watching seems to interest more adults than children, but a well-illustrated natural history guide to the area you are cruising in may well attract a young reader or two.

When you pack for a cruise with children, include a tote bag or seabag full of the kinds of entertainment that they and you enjoy at home: their favourite books, a couple of decks of cards (and a guide to card games), a magnetized chess or Scrabble set (but keep it away from the compass!), some puzzle or word game books, crayons and

drawing paper, and on and on. You and they know what pleases
them. Cassette music and story tapes are wonderful to have aboard
for adults as well as children. Earphones, whether on a plain
recorder or a Walkman, are well worth their price, since they allow
a crew member to listen to what he or she likes without worrying
whether the music will offend shipmates' tastes. Another benefit of
earphones is that they provide the solitude that every child needs
for an hour or so each day. Even in a crowded boat, a little privacy
is essential to gracious living.

PART IV

When Sailing Gets Difficult

———

CHAPTER 16

Night Sailing, Getting Lost, Heavy Weather, and Five Other Problems

W̲e can talk all we want to about how well everything should go in normal conditions, but (like life ashore) sailing often consists of extended periods of relative ease puncutated by brief moments of legitimate fear. Someday you will have to sail in the dark or in fog, or the weather will get rough, or a sail will tear. These things and more may, in fact, happen all at once. We are concerned with problems here, not life-threatening emergencies (which we will discuss in the next chapter). This chapter describes eight hassles that cause discomfort and, if not dealt with quickly, can lead to an emergency. Alertness, calm, good leadership and followership, and good attention to detail are important when dealing with them, but you must also know some specific steps to take. If any of these eight problems turn into an emergency, it probably will be because the crew panics and allows common sense and their knowledge of basic mechanical and sailing skills to fly overboard.

When faced with potential danger, head, if possible, to a sheltered harbour and anchor. Sometimes, however, you cannot get to port. In that case, sail or motor away from crowded channels and threatening lee shores and stop or drastically slow the boat. In smooth water, you can stop her simply by turning off the engine or lowering the sails and letting her drift, but if there is very much sea (waves) you will have to steady her motion by leaving at least some sail up. Too many people panic in a situation like this because, being automobile-addicted modernists, they are used to relying on engines to get them out of trouble. But sails can do the job just as well. To stop the boat, heave-to: back the jib, trim the mainsail flat, and sail just above a close-hauled course, with the mainsail partially luffing. She will jog along comfortably at a speed of about one knot. Alternatively, get on a beam reach, let the main boom all the way out to the leeward shrouds, and hold it there with a line. With the jib lowered, she will slide very slowly to leeward while making about one knot ahead. In neither case are you really stopping the boat, but you are allowing her to ride at a low speed while you solve your problem.

Sailing at Night

Night sailing in good weather is one of the most pleasant things you can do in a boat. With phosphorus sparkling in the bow wave and wake, she seems to charge along at twice her normal speed in her own small, quiet world. Boats a mere fifty yards away appear like distant, skimpily decorated Christmas trees, and on board, your shipmates' features become shadowy in the red glow of the binnacle light as they lie back and silently gaze after stars and satellites. Yet, while it can be extremely pleasant, night sailing also involves some challenges to a sailor's eyesight and judgment that, if unmet, may lead to an emergency.

The main problem is finding your way around the boat without tripping over sheets, winches and fittings. First of all lines should be coiled and winch handles stowed so that decks are clear. A crew member should walk round the deck and examine all gear at least once every two hours. And at least one bright torch should be handy on deck for inspecting sails and rigging when night vision and the moon do not combine to provide enough illumination. Other torches should be of the rubber-covered waterproof type which, although more expensive, last much longer at sea than the ordinary shoreside torch. Their use should be restricted as much as possible, and white lights used sparingly both on deck and down below to protect the crew's night vision. The steering (binnacle) compass must have a red light. Ideally, a red bulb should be used over the chart table (if you cannot find a red one, simply rouge a white one with nail varnish or a red crayon). The colours on charts were chosen to show up clearly under red.

Any boat which is under way at night should carry a bright light for signalling other vessels. Larger boats carry exceptionally bright lights that run off the electrical system; smaller ones have

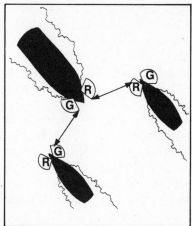

(Left) A collision is likely if you can see both the red and green sidelights of an approaching boat. Turn hard to starboard — 'show her your red'. (Right) But if you see only one sidelight, you may safely hold your course — unless it is a vessel crossing from your starboard side.

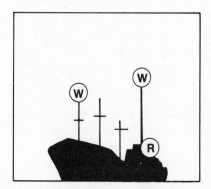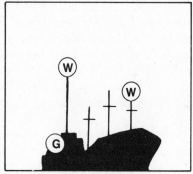

If the white masthead lights of a ship are aligned, a collision is imminent. But if they are not aligned, their relationship with a sidelight should indicate which way the ship is heading. Be careful: ships move a lot faster than may appear.

powerful torches carried within reach of the helmsman. With either type, the best way to make yourself visible to an approaching boat is *not* to shine your light in the other fellow's eyes; it will only blind and confuse him. Rather, shine it on your sails, which will reflect brightly over a considerable distance.

When another vessel does appear on the horizon (or closer), do your very best to identify her and her course and speed and to predict what your relative positions will be when you cross. This is easier said than done at night, when shore lights, poor visibility, and a crowded channel may make what is actually a very simple situation look very confusing. Lights on a big ship may be extremely misleading because they are set high in the air and far aft. Also, without a wake in sight, it is very difficult to judge the ship's speed. Remember the rule of thumb: she is heading at you if both her sidelights are visible. Whatever the situation, whatever kind of boat is approaching, if you have *any* worry that there may be a collision, assume the worst: the people on the other vessel are incompetents who have no awareness of your existence and no knowledge of the rule of the road. Turn away from them as fast and as far as you can, wait for them to pass, then resume your course. (See Chapter 10 for more on avoiding collisions.)

Steering at Night

When steering in the dark, try not to stare at the compass; your eyes and coordination will quickly blur and the spinning compass card and dim light will mesmerize you. Instead, keep your eyes moving from side to side and up and down, occasionally glancing at the compass. Best of all, steer by a lighted landmark (make sure it is not another boat's stern light!) or a relatively stationary star (heading north is always easy since the north star moves only 2½ degrees daily). In a steady wind, you can keep to a fairly reliable course by steering by the apparent wind direction, using either the old-timers' technique of feeling the wind on the back of your neck or a more modern device such as a lighted masthead wind indicator or a lighted apparent wind indicator in the cockpit.

Taking Bearings at Night

Because a lighted aid to navigation at night is more conspicuous from a greater distance than an unlighted one, navigation at night is often easier than during the day—assuming that you can find the aid in the first place. Still, taking accurate bearings at night is a major challenge, especially in rough weather when the boat's heading is never constant. Keep your eyes sweeping over the horizon, take at least two bearings each on at least two lights roughly at a right angle to each other, and if you have any doubts, take the bearings again. Near shore, navigation at night can be a full-time job, sometimes for two people—one to take the bearings and the other to plot them.

Do not make navigation by night any more complicated and dangerous than it has to be. Take advantage of the facts that white lights can be seen from farther away than green or red ones, and that lighthouses, being much higher in the air, have considerably greater ranges than lighted buoys. In unfamiliar waters or when you are not in a hurry, rather than sailing a straight-line course to your destination, plan a series of short doglegs toward the brightest aids to navigation on the chart. This way you will hop between good fixes and minimize error.

Getting Lost

In Chapter 9 we stressed the importance of systematic navigation; the rules of thumb we laid out there are important whether or not you know where you are. Even the most compulsively systematic navigator is sometimes unable to say what his position is. When you get lost, the vital first step is to *admit it*. Do not let false pride talk you into denying what is patently the situation; you could find yourself in even worse trouble. Second, do not get too emotional. Frustration, self-criticism, despair, guilt, and panic will only lead to worse errors. Approach the problem with all the calm and objectivity you can muster.

In good visibility, day or night, the quickest and simplest way to get away from a tight spot—a shoal area, a rapidly approaching shoreline, even a fog bank—is to turn round through 180 degrees and retrace your track to an aid to navigation where you can re-figure your position and course. Meanwhile, take as many bearings on charted objects as you can; even a single position line will help. If, on the other hand, you are out of sight of land and realize that you are lost, head towards where you think land is and look for a landmark or buoy.

But when the visibility is poor and you get lost on a moonless night or in fog or rain, you may not be able to trust a reciprocal course to get you away from nearby shoals. If that is the case, stop or drastically slow your forward progress; drop the anchor if you are very anxious. Pull out the chart and logbook, and using all available evidence calculate your present position and the course that got you to it. If your crew has any ideas or observations, listen to them; some people have an uncanny intuition for position-finding or a superb observational ability that functions independently of maps and charts. Avoid the temptation of taking some simple action that could get you into hotter (or rather shallower) water. This fresh examination usually turns up a stupid error that you committed several hours before, back when you calculated or plotted the course. Even very experienced navigators have been known to make one or more of the following gaffes:

Referring to the wrong day in the tide table, or failing to add an hour for daylight time.

Using the wrong mileage scale, or (my favourite mistake) carrying one chart's mileage scale on the dividers over to a chart with a different scale, say when moving from a small-scale chart to a large-scale one.

Over- or underestimating the boat's speed.

Plotting the course using the outer, true ring on the chart's compass rose rather than the inner, magnetic ring.

Using an old or uncorrected chart with outdated information on magnetic variation, navigation aids or depth of water.

Fog and Bad Visibility

Navigating in fog is like a blind person walking: it can be done just as long as you have a point of departure and a system for measuring your progress from it. In navigation the system is called running your distance. The departure point, for example, might be the last buoy you see before you enter the fog, when a log reading is taken. Then, knowing from the chart the course and distance to the next buoy, you can proceed from buoy to buoy, taking the log reading at each mark and setting a new compass course in order to arrive at the next. In this way you can work your way from buoy to buoy like a blind person counting steps between street corners.

An alternative method is to use a time base—running out your time. If you know your speed and the distance to the next buoy, you can figure out how long it is going to take either by using time/speed/distance tables provided for the purpose in almanacs, or from the formula:

$$\text{time} = \frac{60 \times \text{distance}}{\text{speed}}$$

where time is in minutes, distance in nautical miles, and speed in knots. Be sure to add favourable tidal stream or to subtract contrary stream from your speed.

If, for example, the distance from the departure buoy to the next buoy is 4.1 miles and the speed is 6.3 knots, it will take 39 minutes to make the leg. All the navigator has to do is press the stop watch when the boat passes the first buoy and set the compass

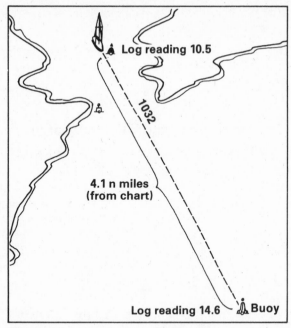

Log reading 10.5

1032

4.1 n miles
(from chart)

Log reading 14.6   Buoy

The more accurate way to navigate from one
buoy to another is by course steered and
distance run, using log readings. An alternative
method is to calculate (from the recorded or
estimated speed) how long it will take to get
from buoy to buoy, and use a stopwatch, but
this assumes that a steady speed is maintained.

course for the second buoy. Thirty-nine minutes later, alter course
to pass the second one; it is there even if it is invisible in the fog.

Used in conjunction with electronic aids such as the Decca
Navigator, this system of dead reckoning should get you safely to
your destination. Sometimes, however, the fog may be so thick that
any progress is unsafe, mainly due to the danger of colliding with
other vessels. If you are in a channel crowded with bigger ships, get
to the very edge of it, using the echo sounder if necessary, and stop
until the fog clears. Keep a watch on deck and sound the appropriate fog signal. Because clear hearing is important to detect other
vessels, eliminate or reduce all unnecessary noise—flapping sails,
chatter, clicking winches. It may be best to down sail, stop the
engine, and anchor. The appropriate signals are:

If under sail or unable to manoeuvre, long-short-short blasts
on the horn at least every two minutes.

If under power and making way, one long blast on the horn at least every two minutes.

If under power but stopped, two long blasts on the horn at least every two minutes.

If anchored, ring a bell forward for five seconds every minute.

Fresh Winds and Heavy Weather

When the wind is so strong and the waves are so large that you are fighting the helm, getting soaking wet, and beginning to wish for a quiet meal ashore, you are in heavy weather. It has more to do with comfort and the feel of the boat than with the actual strength of the wind in knots; small boats become difficult in wind conditions where many large ones are just beginning to come to life. Some people claim to enjoy sailing in heavy weather and a few of them actually mean it, but for most people, sailing on the edge of control and the edge of the boat is not pleasurable. It can, however, be manageable.

Handling rough stuff requires a slightly different attitude to sailing in light winds. Do not be passive; pull sheets, halyards, and the helm aggressively and forcefully. Hold on tight; use your safety harness. If you get seasick, go on deck and get active. Steer around large waves into relatively smooth water. Most important, be alert to the boat's angle of heel and balance. As the wind increases, reduce the heel angle and the speed (to keep the boat from pounding wildly in waves) in the following sequence:

Step 1: Depower the Sails

To reduce heel, weather helm, and speed, the first step is to moderate the side forces in the sails by depowering them. This is like putting a governor on a car engine to limit rpm and horsepower. The first stage in depowering is to trim the sails flat. To flatten the mainsail when sailing close-hauled, tighten the outhaul and cunningham, and pull the sheet down hard (leaving about 5 degrees of twist to leeward in the leech from clew to head). Trim the jib sheet in almost all the way, again leaving about 5 degrees of twist along the leech and a slight arc from leech to luff to provide some shape to redirect the wind; a board-flat sail is completely inefficient.

If there is still too much heel and weather helm, continue depowering by trimming the sails farther outboard (toward the rail). Let the mainsail traveller car down to leeward and trim the jib through a block to leeward of the normal lead—for example, a

Many boats will balance fairly well in heavy weather under a small jib or a deeply reefed mainsail alone, as this cruiser shows.

snatch block hooked to the rail. Upwind, moving the leads outboard decreases side forces while keeping forward forces about the same (it is standard procedure when reaching in all conditions).

If heel and weather helm remain a problem, try depowering the sails by letting them luff a little, trimming the sheets a couple of inches short of optimum. Or spill wind from the top of the sails, where the wind's heeling leverage is greatest, by twisting them off more than the usual 5 degrees. To increase twist, move the jib lead aft a few inches and ease up on the mainsheet or kicking strap (boom vang). In gusty winds, you may always feather or pinch up (turn into the wind) a few degrees to temporarily depower the sails until the blast has passed on. In any case, keep the boat moving so that you can steer over and around the waves.

Step 2: Shorten Sail

If depowering the sails does not work, you must shorten sail either by setting a smaller jib, reefing, or lowering a sail, and in this way decreasing the exposed area. Whichever method you use, it is always better to shorten sail before it is absolutely necessary rather than wait until the boat is badly overpowered, so stay alert to the wind strength and balance.

Changing jibs involves several steps and good coordination by the helmsman and crew. It can be quite slow with a small crew working on the foredeck in very rough weather. First, take the replacement, bagged sail on deck and tie it to the windward rail near the mast. When the waves are big or heavy spray is flying, do not open the forehatch unless you want to take water below; instead, shove the bag up through the main hatch into the cockpit, then take it forward.

With a small or inexperienced crew, or in very rough weather, lower the old sail and put it away before working with the new one. Have two or more people sit on the foredeck (with their safety harnesses hooked on) and pull the jib down by the foot as the sheet and halyard are eased. The helmsman can help by forereaching or by bearing off to a run so that the mainsail blankets the jib; the worst points of sail for lowering a jib are a beam and broad reach, when the foot of the jib is way to leeward of the bow and hard to grab. Once the sail is right down, the others hold it tightly while one sailor unsnaps the halyard and hooks it to the bow pulpit. The halyard is then tightened to keep it from tangling around the spreaders. The old sail is tied to the rail with nylon straps called sail ties. (Later, it may be dragged aft on the windward side, folded in big two- to three-foot flakes running from leech to luff, folded or rolled up, put in its own bag, and taken below.) Then the new sail is hooked onto the forestay—starting with the lower hanks (snap hooks) and working up toward the head—and its sheets are led properly.

I am assuming that the sail is attached to the forestay with hanks (metal snap hooks). However, on many cruiser-racers the boltrope on the luff of the jib is fed into one of two grooves in a device attached to the stay, so the old sail can still be up while the new one is hoisted. This arrangement works best when the old sail is lowered to windward, inside the newly hoisted sail, which keeps it from blowing overboard. Once the old sail is on deck, it is attached to the boat only at the corners—by the halyard at the head, the tack fitting at the tack, and the sheets at the clew. By all means get this kind of jib tied down on deck as soon as possible.

Sheets for small jibs are usually led farther forward than ones for large jibs; the proper lead location should be marked on deck. Double-check all leads and the bowline used to tie the sheet to the jib clew. The loop through the clew should be small and tight and the tail of the knot should be at least four inches long. Then hook on the halyard and immediately pull the sail up. Somebody must usually stand on the bow keeping tension on the luff so the halyard aloft does not get slack and tangle on a spreader. Again, the helmsman can take load off the sail by forereaching or running. Keep a little tension on the sheet as the sail goes up to prevent violent flogging, but do not trim it properly until the jib halyard is all the way up. Finally, take the empty sailbag below and leave it in some visible place—for example, tie it to the companionway ladder—and tell everybody on deck where it is (few frustrations are greater than that of losing a sailbag).

With larger or more experienced crews, and in better weather, you may get the new sail out of its bag and ready for hoisting before lowering the old one. Tie the new one to the leeward rail with bow

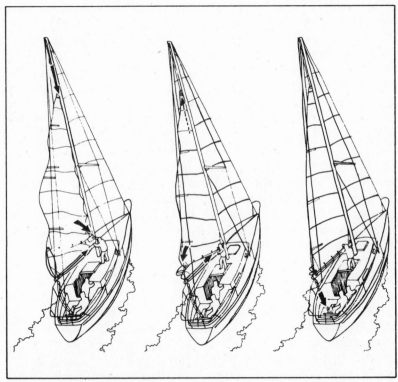

(Left) To tie in a reef, first ease the main sheet and tighten the main boom's topping lift. Then lower the halyard until the luff cringle (ring) is at the tack. (Centre) Hook on the cringle, tighten the halyard, and haul in on the leech reefing line to pull the leech cringle down to the boom. The leech line should pull the sail both out and down. (Right) Ease the topping lift, trim the main sheet, and tie up the loose sail with some light line. Finally, square off all the lines you have been adjusting.

knots in sail ties. After the first sail is lowered, tie it down then free and hoist the new one. While leaving a sail on deck may seem safe, prudence requires folding it in large flakes and stowing it below. All too often a wave may drag it overboard, ripping out stanchions and guardrails along the way.

Reefing (making a sail smaller) is most commonly done using the tie-in system in the mainsail. Before reefing, ease the mainsheet until the sail luffs and tighten the topping lift (a line running from the boom's end to the top of the mast). Then lower the halyard and, with the boom supported by the topping lift, pull down on the luff until an eye called a cringle can be inserted over a hook near the tack. (Sometimes the luff cringle is pulled down tight with a line). Next, pull in on a line already running from the boom up through a cringle on the leech until the cringle is lying on the bunched-up sail. Tighten the halyard, ease the topping lift, and trim the sheet again with the sail area reduced by about one-third. To keep the reefed part of the sail from flying about, lash it to the boom with light line led through small eyes in the cloth. It is a good idea to always keep the first reef line led through the lower leech cringle so that you are ready to tie it in. If you are anticipating very rough weather, rig the second reef line, too.

Some boats have roller-reefing systems for the mainsail either on the boom (which is rotated to wind up the foot of the mainsail) or on the luff (where a wire inside the mast is rotated to wind up the forward edge of the sail). More common is a roller reefing/furling arrangement for the headsail, where the luff of the sail is rolled up to reduce area. With the second system, keep some tension on the sheet so that the sail rolls up evenly.

Lowering one sail and not replacing it, while it may not work on all boats due to different balance requirements, can be the easiest and quickest way to shorten sail. Most boats can run or reach and some can sail close-hauled under mainsail alone, though traveller adjustments or reefs may be required to ease weather helm. The jib can sometimes be carried alone on a reach without too much lee helm. The closer the largest part of the sail is to the mast, the less effect it will have on balance, so in very heavy weather many boats sail quite nicely on any point of sail under a reefed mainsail or a small jib set just forward of the mast.

You may be tempted in heavy weather to lower all the sails and proceed under engine. Unfortunately, the rough seas that always accompany high winds almost inevitably make this inefficient: few boats' engines are sufficiently powerful to push them through rough seas, and with all the pitching, the propellers are out of the water as much as they are in it.

Lost Halyards

Sometimes the shackle end of a halyard will get loose and fly around just out of your grasp. One way to deal with this embarrassing problem is to shin up the mast, grab the halyard, and slide back down with it. Or at least it *seems* like a solution until you try it and get stuck halfway up. You will need tough hands, a pole-vaulter's shoulder muscles, and vicelike knees to climb more than ten feet.

Another solution is to pull somebody up the mast on another halyard using a bosun's chair. Lead the halyard to the biggest winch on board. One crew member turns the winch drum with the handle while the other tails, carefully watching that the person going aloft is not pulled into the spreaders or stays. Nobody should stand under the trapeze artist—he may drop any tools he takes up—and nobody but he and the tailer should issue any orders. On the way down, the line shoud be eased out in long, steady, milkmaid's motions so that the chair and its priceless contents drop smoothly. Never haul anybody aloft in rough seas; the end result will be bad bruises or fractures due to banging on the mast.

A less acrobatic way to retrieve a lost halyard blown out from the boat by the wind is to sail the boat under it. This requires making tight circles to try to get the halyard to swing directly into the waiting arms of a crew on the foredeck. Whether accidental or otherwise, the manoeuvre is guaranteed to stimulate a mood that, like the pendulum you are trying to create, will swing inexorably from fierce tension to genial hilarity. A helpful tool during this tricky exercise is a boat hook (a long rod with a hooked end), for grabbing the shackle as it flies around just out of arm's reach.

Torn and Flying Sails

Every now and then, you will hoist a jib only to see its clew fly way out to leeward unencumbered by a sheet. Or a hastily secured shackle or improperly tied bowline will come undone. Or a sail will tear. What to do? You can head up into the wind to bring the clew back over the deck and get one, two or more crew members (the number depending on the amount of wind) to grab and hold it while somebody tries to hook the sheet on. Inevitably, it takes so long to do this that the boat loses all steerageway and the bow swings off before the knot or shackle is fixed. The sail either pulls somebody into the water or flies out to leeward so that you are back where you started. Therefore, if your crew is eager to show off their strength this way, use the engine to keep her moving close into the wind. A less dramatic but much more effective way to retrieve a flying sail is to luff into the wind, drop the jib on deck, bear off to sail under mainsail alone until the sheets are put back on, and then hoist the sail again. Pulling a sail up and down a couple of times is a lot easier than dragging a shipmate out of the drink.

If it is the spinnaker that has lost a sheet, bear off to a run and, using the other sheet, pull the spinnaker right behind the mainsail so that it is blanketed. In light wind you should be able to hook the lost sheet back on; otherwise, drop the sail, rig it properly, and set it again in the mainsail's blanketing zone so that it does not fill until it is all the way up.

To prevent sheets from coming off in the first place, make sure they are put on correctly. Tie a bowline with a long tail to keep it from undoing itself while it tightens under first tension or shakes during a tack. Wrap a shackle with a turn of tape after clipping it to the sail.

Dragging Anchor

A lot was said about anchoring in Chapter 11, but since dragging anchor is not unusual, it is worth saying more about the problem here. Usually the anchor digs in and stays dug in all day, night, or week until you are ready to leave. Sometimes, though, the wind shifts in the middle of the night, the boat swings, and the hook lifts out and does not reset. A sound sleeper may not know all this until somebody on another boat yells *'You're dragging!'* at the top of his voice at two in the morning—or, worse, until the keel bangs on the rocks. If you are like me, however, you never sleep soundly aboard a boat under your command, at least not for the first two or three nights until your senses are attuned to the feel of the boat—to the firm bobbing of the bow that means that the hook is set firmly and the gurgling, wilder pitching and sluicing about that indicates she is dragging. When the motion changes, anybody below (and especially anybody sleeping far forward) will sense that something is amiss and probably wake up.

When you get the bad news, wake another competent person, rush on deck, and start the engine and leave it in neutral; you may need it at very short notice to help reset the anchor or move. Then evaluate the situation. If there is no immediate danger of running aground or ramming another boat, go up on the bow and inspect the anchor rode. Perhaps the rise of tide has pulled the hook out of the bottom, or a wind shift has spun the hook out. If that is a possibility, let go several feet of rode to increase the scope and narrow the angle between the rode and the water. Cleat the rode and go aft and go slow astern under power for about fifteen seconds (or tell somebody in the cockpit to do it). If the anchor sets, the boat should go almost straight astern and the bow will resume its reassuring bob-bob-bob. But if it keeps dragging, the bow will swing from side to side and continue pitching. As she drops astern, look around for an object ashore (such as a streetlamp or house light) or on the water (like a buoy or a mooring) to use as a marker after the engine is put back into neutral gear. If the object seems to move and the bow continues to rise and fall sharply, you are still dragging, so heave out more rode and go astern.

If the anchor does not reset itself after a couple of attempts, or if you are worried about running out of room astern, weigh anchor as we described in Chapter 11, move to another part of the harbour, and reanchor. But check the chart first; I once ran aground only five feet outside a channel in the Massachusetts harbour of Cuttyhunk while reanchoring in the middle of the night. Remember to switch on your navigation lights before getting under way (and to turn them off again when you reanchor). If you have an echo sounder, turn it on—or have one of the crew ready with the lead line. Before dropping the hook, make sure your new location has good holding ground, with a sandy or mud bottom, and is protected from wind and waves by a spit of land or a reef. Do not automatically assume that the weather will not change; after all, it probably was a big wind shift that caused you to drag in the first place.

If there is any chance of a storm building up, seriously consider dropping a second anchor, leaving one or two crew members on deck on anchor watch, or even stowing the hook and heading out away from land. You will lose some sleep, but otherwise you could lose your boat. In 1982 a gale surprised several dozen yachts in the Mexican harbour of Cabo San Lucas and drove them ashore before their crews could escape, while a handful of skippers who had heard the weather forecast safely rode out the storm in the Pacific.

A frequent cause of problems in crowded anchorages is the boat's dinghy. Left overnight at the end of a painter (bow line) astern, it may capsize or tangle in another boat's rode. (Granted, any harbour that packed is too crowded for a safe, quiet night's stay, but sometimes you have no choice). If the dinghy cannot be deflated or pulled on deck, shorten the painter as much as you can or tie her alongside, protecting the boat's topsides with fenders. In any case, remove all oars, floorboards, and other gear before leaving the dinghy for the night, for if she capsizes her equipment will be lost.

Running Aground

Every now and then, you will make a small steering or navigational

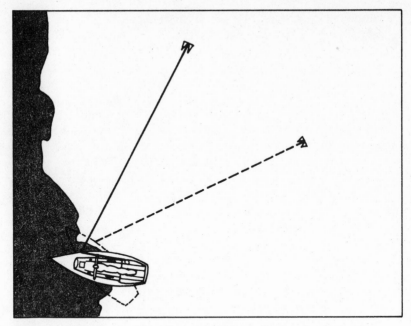

If you are aground and cannot get off by sailing or by using the engine, row out a light anchor and try to pull yourself off using your largest sheet winch. Be sure that the rode does not chafe on anything, and stay away from it; if the load is big and the rode breaks, its backlash will be dangerous.

mistake and run your boat's keel or hull up on the rocks, sand, or mud. Rarely is running aground very dangerous; in fact, in shallow waters like Chesapeake Bay or the East Coast rivers in England it is so common as to be unremarkable. If you are lucky, you can sail or motor her off; otherwise, you must pull her off one way or another. How long you stay 'on the bottom' is usually determined by how fast you ran ashore, how soft it is, and the state of the tide. Expect a long wait after running hard into soft mud when the tide is going out, a short one after slicing slowly into hard sand on a rising tide, and no wait at all after bouncing off some rocks (though your keel may be dented).

Even if they are not guarded by buoys, shoals can often be spotted from a near distance. One piece of evidence is the number and shape of the waves, which are more and steeper over shallow areas than over deep ones. The water colour changes as the bottom nears the surface, getting darker over mud, weed, and rocks and lighter over sand. Fishermen almost always set lobster pots, oyster stakes, and fish weirs in shoal areas, following the cue of gulls and other birds, which usually hunt their prey in shallow water.

Getting off on Your Own

To get off on your own, you must decrease the boats' draft while aiming her away from the shoal area. Turn the helm to steer her back to deep water, then put the engine ahead and trim the sails to spin her on her keel, trimming the jib and easing the mainsail to spin to leeward and vice versa to spin to windward. Increase the angle of heel by moving all the crew to the leeward side, even hanging them off the boom if possible. If she remains stuck, put the engine into neutral, ease the sheets, and have the crew run back and forth across the deck to rock her and break the suction of the bottom on the keel, then try sailing and motoring off once again.

If sailing and motoring off do not work, or if the tide is ebbing and there is little time, spin the bow by *kedging off*. Take the anchor out into deep water in a dinghy and lead the warp through a large block shackled on the bow (it provides a better lead than a fairlead) and back to a big winch. With the help of the sails and engine, trimming the warp while the boat is heeled should swing the bow around. The warp will be heavily loaded and can whiplash dangerously if it snaps, so have everybody stand clear.

Towing Off

When you cannot get off by your own efforts it is usually a question of waiting until the tide refloats the boat, unless you are able to get a tow from some passing craft. In the worst situation, if the yacht is in serious and immediate danger—due perhaps to worsening weather and an ebb tide, or to dangerous rocks—you are justified in making a distress signal, as described in the next chapter.

Most tows are given between fellow yachtsmen with good grace, although some small token of appreciation for the inconvenience caused would not come amiss. When dealing with commercial craft or fishing boats it is best to settle on terms in advance before passing over your tow line, which should be your heaviest warp secured to the strongest fitting up forward—the anchor winch, a through-bolted cleat, or the mast (using a bowline)—and carefully protected from chafe with rags or pieces of split hose. The tow should be kept short and the pull moderate as the bow is gradually swung towards deep water. Heel the boat to decrease her draft, and to reduce the resistance between the keel and the bottom.

If you need a tow home later on, lengthen the line considerably so that your boat rides comfortably in the trough of the third wave behind the tow boat, and steer to prevent the line from chafing on the forestay.

A Stalled Engine

Just like every other mechanical device, a boat's petrol or diesel engine is a blessing when it works and a curse when it does not. While your best guide for getting a recalcitrant engine started is the owner's manual, several problems recur so frequently that we would like to discuss them and their solutions here, with the obvious caveat that if you cannot get the machinery working again you should not panic. Your boat, after all, does have sails that will take her just about everywhere there is open water and wind. Alternatively, you can anchor, call for a tow, or change your plans. But you should not give up just because the engine will not start. One capsize that resulted in a sinking and three deaths was due at least partially to the crew becoming discouraged when the engine packed up; they turned in just when their boat needed careful handling in a gale. Do not allow that to happen to you and your crew.

With petrol engines, found most often on outboard-powered boats, the sparking plugs are the source of most malfunctions. If the engine will not start or if it runs rough, unscrew the sparking plugs and clean off the accumulated carbon deposits with a fine abrasive like sand paper. If the points are badly worn or widely spread, replace the plugs. You should use a special plug spanner to replace the plugs about one-quarter turn harder than hand-tight.

With inboard engines—which in modern sailing boats means diesels—voltage losses and shorts are the main electrical problem. This is not surprising considering the humidity of the marine environment and the typically circuitous, hidden wiring systems that are so hard to inspect. Carry some rags to wipe off moisture, a can of silicone spray (which displaces moisture), and some plastic-coated tape to cover exposed wires. If the starter does not work, spray silicone into the key hole and over all the terminals. Then try running the rag the entire length of the wires between the key and the block and clean off the terminals, using emery paper on corrosion. Tape over any worn spots. Look especially carefully around the engine, whose heat can play tricks with the wiring. I once spent half a day trying to trace down the cause of a starter failure, calling every manufacturer's representative listed in the owner's manual, before one of my shipmates noticed that the insulation on a wire had melted from contact with the hot engine block. She quickly cut away the damaged wire, spliced in a replacement, and secured the wire away from the engine. We were soon on our way.

If all you get is silence when you turn the key, the solenoid may be stuck or malfunctioning. A device that makes the connection between the engine and starter, the solenoid is located in a small tube or box, usually near the starter motor. First try freeing it with a sharp blow with a light tool. If that does not work, you can bypass it. Run a large-gauge wire around the solenoid from the terminal for the wire from the ignition switch to the terminal for the wire to the starter. Or hold a pair of pliers or a screwdriver so that there is metal contact on those two terminals (making sure that there is insulation between your hand and the metal) while somebody turns the ignition key.

Perhaps the battery is low. In some boats you can charge the batteries by plugging into an electrical outlet at a marina; otherwise, you must take them to a garage. While you are lugging the things ashore, try to figure out why they drained to begin with. Modern electronic devices like speedometers and navigational instruments draw a small current, but the main culprits are electric lights, refrigerators and hot and cold water systems—frequently those within reach of children. During the day and between meals, turn of the master switches to lights, pressure water, and other unneeded accessories. Most cruising boats larger than about 30 feet have two batteries that can be used either in parallel or separately and are both charged by the engine. One battery should be reserved solely for starting the engine; use the other for lights and accessories when under sail or at anchor. Keep an eye on the ammeter and charge up when necessary by starting the engine and running it at fairly high rpm for an hour or so. (Regular use at moderate speeds also keeps lubrication oil properly circulated).

A common cause of engine problems is blockage in the fuel line, which is announced by a stall like the one that happens when the tank is dry. Fuel may be contaminated with water or dirt when it comes aboard, or it may pick up sediment stirred up from the bottom of the tank by the boat's motion. Modern fuel filters will separate dirt and water, but they are not effective at clearing air locks caused by bubbles in a near-empty tank. To clear air locks in a diesel engine you must bleed the fuel line and pump, opening vent plugs and turning over the engine until unadulterated fuel spurts through. Instructions for this should be found in the engine handbook, and it is advisable to know where the venting points are situated in your own installation.

So much for relatively minor problems. Now, in the final two chapters, we will look at what you should do if you are ever caught in a downright emergency.

CHAPTER 17

Seamanship
and Health
Emergencies

Compared with such challenges as skiing and driving a car in a big city, sailing is marvellously safe. It is so safe, in fact, that when HM Coastguard warns about boating dangers, many people become embarrassed, as though somebody has made a social *faux pas*, and try to change the subject to a more cheerful topic. In response, the authorities and their few followers who are concerned about boating safety become increasingly strident, which only stimulates more yawns. That is a shame. Sometime, somewhere, just about every sailor is going to face the possibility of getting into serious trouble, which means that the studied indifference that many sailors show to boating safety is potentially very dangerous. It also denies the normal, instinctive fear of the wind and water that sheer human cussedness will not allow most of us to admit, even to ourselves. The first step toward avoiding a catastrophe on the water is to confess that the sea is not the warm, embracing creature that bad poets (who have never left land) believe we can shape to our own ends. To quote Lord Byron, a great poet who did go to sea,

Roll on, thou deep and dark blue ocean—roll!
Ten thousand fleets sweep over thee in vain;
Man marks the earth with ruin—his control
Stops with the shore.

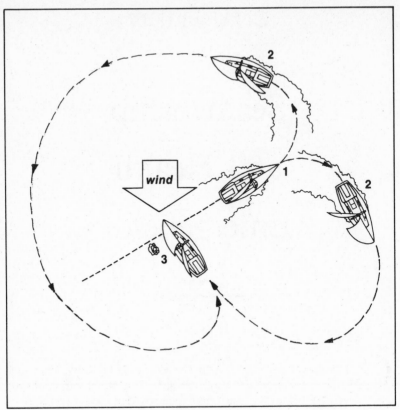

If somebody falls overboard, immediately stop the boat's forward progress, turn back, and make the approach on a close reach. Pick up the swimmer on the leeward side unless the water is very rough and there is a danger of the boat sliding into and over the victim.

While we cannot eliminate the insolent pride of the macho sailor, perhaps we can more firmly ground expectations in reality by describing ways to handle the most common emergencies that occur in boats. In this chapter we will first tell how to deal with five serious seamanship and health problems—man overboard, hypothermia, seasickness, sunburn, and capsize. Then we will describe how to call for help. And in Chapter 18 we will analyse some yachting catastrophes to identify seven ways that sailing boats typically get into life-threatening situations.

When Someone Falls Overboard

In Chapter 8 we showed ways to avoid falling overboard by moving around on deck carefully and hooking on with a safety harness, but if somebody does take a tumble, the following procedure should lead to a prompt recovery. During the pre-cruise safety briefing (described in Chapter 5), talk this routine over step by step with your shipmates. You might even practice it using a lifebuoy or a buoyant cushion as the victim.

1.   **Stop the boat's progress away from the swimmer.** This is the most important step to take. Some Decca sets have a 'man overboard' facility to help you return to the scene of the accident: if fitted, this should be operated at once. Luff the sails, head up into the wind, turn 90 degrees to either side and proceed slowly—do whatever must be done to stay near the swimmer. You can make a drastic, sudden course alteration even with a spinnaker up in fresh wind—granted, with a little chaos, but considering that a life may be at stake some confusion can be tolerated. It is, however, important to keep the boat under control.

2.   **Assign one person to look and point at the swimmer.** This should be that crew member's only job. In poor visibility, take a compass bearing on the victim and throw buoyant objects (special man overboard poles, cushions, or paper towels).

3.   **Turn on the engine.** But do not put it in gear unless you must use it to get back to the swimmer (say, in a calm) and until you are sure that no lines are dangling near the propeller. However, do not plan on depending entirely on the engine to get you back to the swimmer in rough seas and when the boat is heeling, when an outboard engine's propeller will rarely be in the water and even an inboard's propeller will not be much help.

4.   **Swing back toward the swimmer, aiming just upwind of him or her.** Under sail, make your approach on a close reach, on which you can quickly increase speed by bearing off slightly or slow down by heading up. As you approach, luff the sails until you just have steerage way. To keep the speed low and improve visibility of the swimmer, you may have to lower the jib. Under power, make the final approach dead into the wind, but if the waves stop your forward progress, approach across the wind and seas.

5.   **Retrieve the victim over the downhill, leeward rail.** Trim the sails to heel the boat. Haul the victim onto the leeward deck. It may be necessary to rig the boarding ladder or some form of scrambling net. Nobody should dive in after the

swimmer unless the swimmer is unable to help him- or herself and the rescuer is connected to the boat with a line. Playing hero here may well kill two people instead of saving one. If you are unable to sail or motor to within grabbing distance, get upwind of the swimmer, throw a line with a buoyant object on the end, and retrieve him or her by hauling in the line. If necessary, launch the dinghy—or even the liferaft.

When Your Fingers Get Numb and
Your Mind Gets Vague

If a normally alert crew member suddenly complains of numbness, becomes disoriented, and begins to move and work clumsily, the chances are that he or she is hypothermic. *Hypothermia* is severe loss of body heat, and it can happen even on warm summer days if you are drenched. As the body is chilled, it automatically cuts off blood circulation in the extremities—the hands, head, and feet—in order to protect the vital organs. The circulatory deficiency may lead to poor dexterity and bad judgment; this is a serious business for sailors, who must be agile and clear-thinking if they are to perform jobs like steering, sail trimming, and navigation. As he or she becomes colder, the victim becomes less and less competent— physically and mentally—until, at the worst, body temperature drops to about 85 degrees and the victim dies.

The only sure, safe cure for hypothermia is for the victim to be warmed *gradually* in a sleeping bag or blankets or with the affectionate help of another body, meanwhile drinking warm, sugar, non-caffeinated liquids. *Do not* try to induce rapid warming and blood circulation by rubbing the numb extremities, exercising, drinking hot drinks, or taking stimulants such as liquor or caffeinated drinks. Any or all of these may have been prescribed by your grandmother, the old-time navy, and various other sources of common wisdom; even grandmothers can be wrong, as the following documented story suggests. A few years ago off the British coast, ten men were picked out of a lifeboat after their ship sank in a winter storm. All ten were issued the traditional English medicine of a couple of glasses of brandy, which stimulated their circulatory systems so efficiently that the cold blood in their extremities raced into and stopped their hearts. If the body temperatures had been brought back to normal through gradual warming, they probably would have survived.

When You Get Seasick

Before ever stepping on board a boat, most people know whether they are susceptible to motion sickness. If they are, they should have thought about and looked into the different types of available medication, most of which need to be taken at least a couple of hours before going aboard. The problem with most older pills has been that they induce drowsiness, which is conducive neither to pleasure nor to good seamanship. Non-sedating treatments include a two-pill combination originally designed for use by astronauts (one pill eases motion sickness and the other keeps you alert), a medication that is absorbed through the skin from a patch adhered behind the ear, and ginger pills. Some people who have used all three report success; others report none. Frankly, I would not know which medication works best. The closest I have ever been to contracting the messy malaise was when a shipmate lit a cigar in the poorly ventilated cabin of a boat rolling like a log in a flat calm and long swell. The ship's cigars were of such high quality that their supplier, the captain, insisted that they should not be smoked out in the wind. This reasoning made good sense one way and lousy sense another.

Cooks are most liable to seasickness because they spend more time below than most sailors and their systems are assaulted by a wide variety of smells and motions as well as by confinement. Some cooks in our survey say they do not get sick at all, but others not blessed with cast-iron stomachs and built-in gyroscopes make several helpful recommendations, among them, 'If the feeling comes on me suddenly in the galley, I try to go up topsides for a while and take the helm or busy myself up in the fresh air. That helps more than anything.' Perhaps steering serves as a remedy because it makes you focus on the horizon, the only immovable object in a boat's galaxy. Other advice included abstaining from liquor for a night or two prior to sailing, avoiding greasy and spicy foods before and during rough weather, and munching on something simple (like dry biscuits) to keep food in your stomach when you are too queasy to eat a real meal. During a rough reach across the Caribbean, my shipmate Donald Starr kept himself going by periodically downing a raw egg flavoured with Worcestershire sauce—perhaps not your idea of a tasty meal, but nutritious all the same.

When the Sun Is Hot

Sunburn is an occupational hazard for anybody who spends time outdoors when the sun is high. For many years a dark tan was

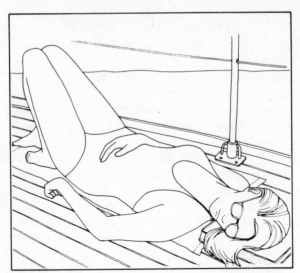

Sunglasses and a good sun lotion are essential if
you want to enjoy the sun while avoiding its bad
effects.

honoured as a badge of the good life, but too many people have paid
the price with skin cancer. I know one former winner of the
America's Cup who is not allowed outdoors without full-length
clothing and a huge sun bonnet. Pharmaceutical companies market
whole lines of sun lotions for different skin sensitivities. Use a
reliable brand such as Uvistat.

If you are blond and prone to burning, consider using zinc
oxide as a sunscreen. While it is greasier than normal sun lotions,
and while its white colour is not very stylish, zinc oxide is inexpen-
sive and has the added benefit of being an effective first-aid cream to
use on cuts, scrapes, mosquito bites, and other open wounds. Its
colour has one advantage: you will know that it is time to smear on
some more cream when the white has rubbed off.

To work right, sun lotions must be applied assiduously whenever the sun is out. Burning is probably more likely on hazy days
than on bright, clear ones. Apply the lotion freely to all exposed
areas of skin, and do it early, before you are distracted by the
mechanics of sailing the boat; later, add layers as you perspire and
rub up against gear, and always after swimming. Be especially
attentive to the extremities that are so vulnerable as you look up at
sails—the nose, ears, and forehead. Do not forget the back of the
neck or the inch or two of tender skin that may seem to be protected
by shirt sleeves or trouser legs, but which will be exposed when you

stretch your arms and legs to steer or trim sheets. The lower lip is another spot which often suffers from the sun; protect it with Uvistat-L, or Lypsyl.

While modern lotions are efficient when used in a timely manner, the most reliable sunscreen is a layer of long, loose, light-coloured cotton clothing pulled on when the sun is high, between brief tanning sessions. A sweatshirt and a pair of the now-fashionable drawstring trousers will cover the body without stifling it; a big sun hat or a peaked cap will protect the forehead.

Besides sunburn, the hot sun can cause severe eyestrain—a bad problem on sailing boats, where the sheen off the slick water, white sails, and bright deck can be torturing. Eyestrain can lead to fierce headaches and accompanying depression and bad judgment. Many boatowners equip their boats with cockpit awnings and low-glare brown sails, but the simplest protection is a good pair of sunglasses. Polarized lenses are especially worthwhile because they pick up and highlight the colour differences on the water between shallow and deep areas, and between wind puffs and lulls.

When Your Boat Capsizes

Although large keel boats can tip over or swamp (fill with water) or even sink in extreme, hurricane conditions, these words on capsizing are directed mainly to people who sail dinghies and small keel day-sailers, whose flotation tanks or blocks of foam will keep them buoyant.

The worst that can happen—and too many times has happened —is that the crew becomes separated from the swamped boat and drown. Therefore the most important guideline is to *stay with the boat*—even if you cannot right her, even if there is an inviting beach only a half mile away. A half mile can quickly turn into a very long swim in rough seas and a strong current. Most modern, high-performance (fast and tippy) dinghies capsize easily and are righted just as readily. They are also self-bailing; their small, shallow cockpits capture little water, and that is easily drained (when the boat is sailing fast) through retractable sluices in the bottom called self-bailers. To right a dinghy, stand on the fully lowered centreboard, grab the gunwale, and lean back. You may have to lower the sails to decrease the water's resistance to your leveraging action. If somebody on a passing motor boat offers to help, ask him to pull up on the top of the mast as you bounce on the centreboard. The mast must be pointed downwind during a righting; otherwise she will flip right over again when she is upright.

Once the boat is upright, climb aboard, collect any objects floating around, trim the sails, open the bailers, and head off on a fast reach. The cockpit should be dry in a couple of minutes. Some older boats have large, deep cockpits that do not self-bail; the crew must bail the water out with buckets or have a motor boat tow her slowly back to shore.

When You May Call for Help

There are various ways by which you may call for help: with visual signals, sound signals and radio transmissions. Not surprisingly there are international rules about the form these signals take and the circumstances which justify their use—only when the boat is in serious and immediate danger, and help is urgently required. The

If you are in real distress, the simplest form of official distress signal is to repeatedly raise and lower your outstretched arms, above and below the horizontal.

distress signals most appropriate for use in a yacht include the following:

The continuous sounding of fog-signalling apparatus. To avoid any doubts this is best done as a succession of the letters SOS in Morse (see below).

Rockets with red stars fired singly at short intervals.

The letters SOS in Morse (three dots, three dashes, three dots) made by any signalling method (for example by flashing light or on the foghorn).

The spoken word 'Mayday' by radiotelephone, described in more detail below.

The International Code signal 'NC' (made by flags, for example, where N is a blue and white chequered flag and C has blue, white, red, white, blue horizontal stripes).

A square flag with a round object either above or below it, fairly easily displayed by a flag with a round fender or anchor shape.

A rocket parachute flare showing a red light—probably the most effective visual signal, particularly at night. The use of flares is described below, and should be covered in the pre-cruise safety briefing.

An orange smoke signal, for daytime use.

Slowly and repeatedly raising and lowering the arms outstretched from the body, above and below the horizontal.

Distress Flares

Distress flares serve two purposes, first to raise the alarm, and second to pinpoint the boat's position when help is on the way. When close inshore a red hand flare will do both jobs, but when more than about three miles from land a parachute rocket which projects a red flare to a height of more than 1000ft (300m) is required to alert the rescue services: once rescuers are within visual range a red hand flare (or orange smoke by day) can be used to identify the position of the casualty.

Flares should be stowed where they are protected from damp but accessible when required. White flares are used to indicate a boat's position, as a warning to larger vessels, and one or two should always be stowed within easy reach of the cockpit. Flares have a life of three years if carefully stowed; they should be inspected regularly and be replaced by the expiry date shown on them. All the crew should know where the flares are stowed and how to fire them. Hand flares should be held firmly downwind, to avoid burning particles dropping onto clothing or into a liferaft. Rockets turn into the wind, and should be aimed vertically or slightly downwind in strong conditions: if aimed into the wind they will not gain altitude. When the cloud is low, a rocket should be fired at 45 degrees downwind, so that the flare burns under the cloud. Suggested scales of allowance are given in the appendix.

Radiotelephone distress messages

Most cruising boats are equipped with Very High Frequency/ Frequency Modulated (VHF/FM) radio that can transmit and receive signals within about 30–40 miles (depending on the heights of the aerials concerned), utilising 57 frequencies between 156.00MHz and 174.00MHz. Each frequency, or channel, is allocated for one or more of the following functions: distress/safety and calling, intership, public correspondence, port operations, ship movement, and yacht safety.

Channel 16 (156.8MHz) is the Distress Safety and Calling Frequency, on which all vessels are encouraged to keep watch at sea. Ashore, all the Coast Radio Stations operated by British Telecom and all major stations of HM Coastguard listen on Ch 16. So, in coastal waters, any distress call on Ch 16 will almost certainly be heard and acted upon. It is very important that Ch 16 is kept clear for this purpose, and not used for traffic which should be passed on a working frequency.

As for any other distress signal, a Mayday call (which has priority over all other transmissions) must only be made when the vessel is in serious and imminent danger (or on behalf of another vessel unable to make a call). A distress message must be cancelled if assistance is no longer needed. If you are sure that a Mayday call is justified, this is the correct procedure:

1. Switch the set on, and select Ch 16, on high power.

2. Operate the set's alarm signal generator for 30 seconds to one minute (if time allows and the set is so equipped).

3. Press the 'transmit' button and say slowly and distinctly: MAYDAY MAYDAY MAYDAY, THIS IS (name of yacht, spoken three times).

4. Then continue speaking: MAYDAY ... (name of yacht, spoken once) MY POSITION IS LATITUDE ... LONGITUDE ... (or true bearing and distance from a

charted geographical point). Then give the nature of distress and the type of assistance required. A brief indication should be given of the type/size of boat, and the number of persons on board.

5. If time permits, repeat your position. Conclude the transmission with the spoken word OVER, and release the 'transmit' button. Remain tuned to Ch 16.

6. You should expect an immediate acknowledgement from a ship or shore station. If this is not forthcoming, check that the set is correctly switched on, with Ch 16 selected, and repeat 3–5 above. If no answer is still received, the message should be repeated on any other channel which might attract attention.

If you should hear a Mayday call, write down all the important details—particularly the name of the vessel and her position. Should no other station acknowledge the distress call, you must do so—and take whatever other action is possible in the circumstances, such as trying to pass the distress call to a shore station.

The Urgency Signal Pan-Pan may be used when a distress signal is not fully justified, and indicates a very urgent message concerning the safety of a ship or person. The prefix Pan-Pan gives priority over all other traffic except distress messages. The procedure is similar to a Mayday call, but commencing PAN-PAN PAN-PAN PAN-PAN. In the event of a medical emergency, use the prefix PAN-PAN-MEDICO PAN-PAN-MEDICO PAN-PAN-MEDICO, and the message will be dealt with by the nearest Coast Radio Station: communication with the doctor or hospital concerned should be on a working channel, to clear Ch 16.

I hope that you will never have to use any of these emergency procedures, but you should know them just in case. In the next and last chapter we will examine seven factors that can turn emergency into disaster.

CHAPTER 18

Seven Ways
Boats Get into
Trouble

For several years, in the course of my career as a yachting journalist, I have studied and described several catastrophes involving pleasure sailors and pleasure boats. Not a pleasant task, you may think, but in its own way a valuable one, for while examining the tragedies of, for example, the 1979 Fastnet Race and a storm that killed several people off America's southeast coast three years later, I assembled enough grim detail to isolate some factors—seven in all—that often come into play when boats get into deadly trouble.

The sad story of a boat called *The Sting* summarizes many of these factors. In the New Orleans Lightship Race of March 1983, Gulf of Mexico, this 29-foot (9-metre) sloop was knocked over on her side. Two men on deck, who were either not wearing harnesses or not hooked on (accounts are unclear) were washed overboard. One man grabbed some trailing lines and was recovered. The other drowned in the 59-degree water as his shipmates tried unsuccessfully to get man overboard gear to him and then, after finally turning the boat, to motor and sail back to him through ten-foot (three-metre) seas.

Later, an official inquiry by the Gulf Yachting Association found that, while *The Sting* was both seaworthy and properly equipped with safety gear, the crew was not prepared. Among the words that figured prominently in the inquiry committee's report were 'panic', 'confusion,' and indecision.' Though exceptionally talented racing sailors, the six young men of *The Sting* were, to quote the committee, 'inexperienced in ocean racing in extended heavy weather conditions.' By the time of the accident, 'the crew had experienced severe seasickness and were extremely fatigued after twenty hours at sea in deteriorating gale force weather conditions.' Yet at no time during those twenty hours did the skipper discuss man overboard procedures or issue a direct order requiring the wearing of life jackets and safety harnesses. The inquiry also determined that, except for the absence of a life jacket, the drowned man had been dressed as if for dinghy racing, in a one-piece foul-weather suit whose trouser legs were taped around his sea-boots—an outfit guaranteed to retain water and pull a swimming body down and under with the efficiency of an anchor.

After reading such a tragic account and before engaging in a rage of sanctimonious finger-pointing we should remember how frequently *all* boats get into trouble—usually much less serious, to be sure, but trouble all the same. A boat's crew is human, hence prone to making mistakes. Her environment is natural, hence surprising and sometimes startling in its variability. And a boat's own nature and driving forces are complex, hence unpredictable to everybody except a few gifted, widely experienced seamen. For most of us, then, sailing mistakes are inevitable. Sooner or later, anyone can dress poorly and become hypothermic; miscalculate the boat's position by a few hundred yards or metres by using the wrong chart scale; steer the wrong course because the right one was garbled in transmission from the navigator; let out too little rode and drag anchor; carry on too long in rough weather without shortening sail; wrongly identify a buoy or harbour in a hurried sighting; and so on. In normal conditions these errors are often quickly discovered and their consequences usually are trivial. Fortunately, most sailing boats are so slow that if their crews are reasonably alert and follow a cautious routine of double-checking, none of these (and hundreds of other small errors) will have dangerous consequences. Every now and then, however, serious problems if not disasters result from a combination of errors or accidents—generally, but not always, in heavy weather.

My study of more than a dozen capsizes, sinkings, and abandonments indicates that it is human error rather than breakdowns in the boat and her rigging that usually leads to fatal disasters. Some of the accidents I have analyzed involve only two or three of the seven key factors, but most involve at least four. For more about these catastrophes, see my book *Fastnet, Force 10* (London: Nautical Books, 1980).

A Rushed, Ill-Considered Departure

An important factor in many accidents is that the crew is pressured to meet a schedule imposed by somebody else. As a result, they are forced to start out in threatening weather, with unfinished repairs, or with shortages of storm equipment, food, water, fuel, tools, and other necessities.

Races obviously impose this kind of pressure. Not many of the 300 boats entered in the 1979 Fastnet Race would have headed out into England's western approaches under the prevailing forecast for a mild gale if the race had not started when it did. But they came to race, and as it turned out, a storm of near-hurricane proportions swept them all, drowned fifteen sailors, and sank four boats. Cruises may also begin prematurely because the crew is sailing during an all too short vacation imposed by a boss or some other obligation. Flight schedules, or ferry, train and tide tables may also force a crew to time their departure to the chronological clock rather than wait for decent conditions.

Lesson 1: The only timetable that ultimately counts is the one imposed by the weather.

The Route Is Potentially Dangerous

Some sailing areas in some seasons are predictably risky. The vernal and autumnal equinoxes in late March and September always seem to be surrounded by a month or so of sudden storms. The autumn is most dangerous in the western Atlantic, the Gulf of Mexico, and the Caribbean because that is the hurricane season; even boats hugging the shore to stay close to ports can get in terrible trouble when they are surprised by gales. In an Atlantic gale in October 1982, a 58-foot (18-metre) ketch, *Trashman,* fell on her side off a huge wave and sank about sixty miles off the Carolina coast (later, three people died in her liferaft) and a 42-foot (13-metre) yawl, *Scrimmage,* was rolled over and almost sunk within sight of a Maryland resort town (fortunately with no loss of life). It takes a big gale indeed to cause so much trouble for such large boats.

Even at other times and in other places, before setting out on a cruise keep track of weather changes by obtaining the shipping and coastal forecasts which are available from various sources, as listed in your nautical almanac. Listen to the routine radio forecasts whenever you are at sea.

Lesson 2: Choose routes that take you through areas of predictably decent weather.

The Route Has No Alternatives

Survival in rough conditions often depends on the ability to choose an alternate course away from bad weather or shoal water. The seaman's traditional fear of a lee, or downwind, shore is based as much on the 'no exit' sign that the land sticks high in the air as it is on the wretched prospect of being dashed onto the beach. The main problem that *Scrimmage* faced in the October 1982 gale was that she was pinned against the coast by a strong northeasterly wind. She could not beat out into the Atlantic against the storm, and with huge seas breaking at channel entrances, she was unable to sail into a protective harbour. *Scrimmage* was eventually blown over a shoal area where breakers capsized her. A crew member was lost overboard when his safety harness lifeline snapped, and only through extraordinary seamanship and courage (plus a bit of luck) was the boat saved and the man recovered.

Lesson 3: Whenever possible, put yourself in a position where you may choose alternate courses.

The Crew Is Unprepared

A crew that is too small, untalented, untrained, or unhealthy is frequently involved in bad sailing accidents. Let us go through those adjectives one by one.

An excessively small and untalented crew is one that is not prepared to handle the boat safely in the worst conditions expected for a cruise, race, or passage. As a rule of thumb, there should be enough good sailors on board so that at all times the boat is adequately steered and navigated, the sails are safely handled, and everybody gets enough rest and food. For a day's sail, it may be sufficient to have only a competent skipper and at least one crew member who can steer a compass course and handle sails. For an overnight sail during which everyone will need a few hours' sleep—and they will if their good judgment is to stay intact—you will need at least two people who are competent skippers plus at least two good helmsmen and sail handlers.

An untrained crew may be talented and large, but because the skipper has not alerted its members to the boat's emergency equipment and routines, they may not be prepared to handle life-threatening situations. Besides training expert sailors to work together in emergency procedures, a skipper should also train beginners in one or two basic skills, like steering in good weather and (if they are good with electronics) radio navigation. Too often, a novice's intelligence, eagerness to learn, and skills go underused.

An unhealthy crew is one not physically or psychologically prepared to take the rigours of the worst possible weather that can be met on a cruise or voyage. Here we are concerned with endurance, not knowledge. In *Grimalkin,* one of the boats hit hardest by the 1979 Fastnet Race storm, the two most talented sailors had per-

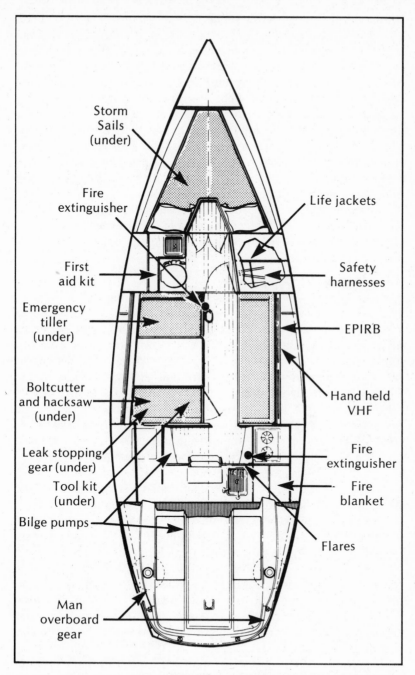

Storm
Sails
(under)

Fire
extinguisher

First
aid kit

Emergency
tiller
(under)

Boltcutter
and hacksaw
(under)

Leak stopping
gear (under)

Tool kit
(under)

Bilge pumps

Man
overboard
gear

Life jackets

Safety
harnesses

EPIRB

Hand held
VHF

Fire
extinguisher

Fire
blanket

Flares

An emergency equipment chart like this one will save you and your
shipmates a lot of time should you ever get into trouble. This is
also a good system for keeping track of food supplies.

manent physical problems which, while not affecting strength or performance in normal conditions, were so debilitating in the cold gale that both men collapsed and were left for dead by their shipmates. One of these men, the first mate, was badly arthritic and did in fact die of exposure soon after his shipmates abandoned the boat in a liferaft. The other who was mildly epileptic, eventually regained consciousness to find himself alone on board with the corpse of the first mate. Interspersing periods of work with periods of rest, he determinedly pumped the boat out, and signalled for help until rescued by a helicopter. Serious illness, sleep deprivation, hypothermia, hunger, and nicotine, alcohol, or drug abuse can be harmful to good judgment and endurance.

Lesson 4: The crew must be large and talented enough to handle the boat under the worst possible conditions; they must be trained in the boat's routines; and they must be in sound health—and stay that way.

The Boat Is Unprepared

Boats frequently get into trouble not because a major piece of gear, like the mast or the steering gear, breaks down, but because relatively small damage or a seemingly minor oversight creates a chain effect that leads one link at a time to catastrophe. For example, *Trashman* was an extremely strong boat with an Achilles heel— large glass windows, for which the builder had provided thick, Plexiglass protective shutters. When she was caught in the October 1982 gale, her crew installed the shutters only on the windward side because that was the side the waves were coming from. However, she fell sideways off a wave onto the unprotected leeward windows, which were smashed open. She went down five minutes later.

In the 1979 Fastnet gale, there was no way that some crews could get in out of the extremely cold, harsh weather since storage batteries, tools, and other heavy objects broke loose during knockdowns and capsizes, shattered furniture, and made cabins dangerously inhospitable. A few sailors suffered serious head injuries; one man was hit by the stove, which fell out of its gimbals during a rollover. Forced out into the cockpit, the sailors were worn down to the point where many could see no alternative to abandoning ship in liferafts—a decision fatal to six of them.

Lesson 5: Try out all emergency and storm equipment well before you have to use it, and keep a 'worst case' state of mind when you install gear.

The Crew Panics After an Injury

Often a crew handles bad weather well and confidently until somebody is injured. Then panic sets in, storm tactics are changed, and instead of actively engaging with the boat and the storm, the crew becomes passive and even gives up. Well before her windows were stove in, *Trashman* was surviving reasonably well by running before the waves. Then a crew member (whose safety harness lifeline was attached to the binnacle in the middle of the cockpit) was thrown entirely across the boat and badly injured. Fearing for her, the skipper immediately ordered the engine turned on and *Trashman* headed toward the Carolina shore. After a couple of hours, the engine's cooling system failed. The exhausted, discouraged crew took to their bunks, leaving the boat to fend for herself, lying beam-to breaking seas. Soon after, she was fatally damaged. Perhaps if the skipper had focused more on the larger issue of survival, he would have held his course.

In the Fastnet storm, a few sailors suffered serious and frightening injuries; again, in most cases, the focus of the crew's concern and energy shifted from the boat's seaworthiness to the injured person's welfare. As morale plummetted, mistakes began to be made. In some boats, within an hour or two there was a capsize, a rollover, or a hasty decision to inflate the liferaft and abandon ship in order to get the injured person away.

Lesson 6: Do not allow a crew injury to distract you from the job immediately at hand, which is to get the boat and the whole crew safely through the storm.

The Command Structure Is Unclear

For most of us, pleasure sailing is a voluntary activity which is meant to be fun. Much of the time, a good crew can function well in a relatively informal way with commands coming in the form of suggestions and with many crew members taking part in decision making. If the pastime were otherwise, it would lose half its adherents. But when emergencies threaten, strong leadership and a well-defined command structure are required. People lacking experience and confidence will feel and perform better if they can trust the skipper and his lieutenants to exercise decisive judgment. This is where laid-back attitudes about discipline and organization may very well be counter-productive, regardless of their contributions to the happiness of normal life.

Bad weather is no time for leadership by committee or for a skipper who is not respected by his crew. The most competent and experienced people on board—those women and men who have seen a gale or two and can handle responsibility—must be placed in charge, even if they are not the titular skipper and watch leaders. Orders about essential safety procedures and gear must be firm, clear, and frequently repeated both in anticipation of an emergency and during a rescue operation. Leaders must not simply retire to the helm and shout commands. They will be much more effective if they mix with the crew and set an example—by wearing and using safety harnesses, by sharing (even taking the initiative in) the toughest jobs, and by resting and eating when they can.

A backup chain of command must also be established. In the Fastnet Race gale at least two boats were needlessly abandoned, with resulting loss of life, after the skippers were lost overboard and frightened crews impulsively inflated the liferafts. In both cases, if a clearly designated, well-respected second-in-command had immediately asserted leadership and reduced the level of panic, the rafts might have remained in their canisters and the men would have remained in the yachts—which, though damaged, succeeded in surviving the storm.

Lesson 7: The command structure must be firm, competent, and clear in dangerous conditions.

In Summary

Most of what we have discussed makes common sense, but some of it goes against human nature; ignoring an injury to a friend does not come easily even to soldiers in combat. The problems that we have described are so terrible and occur so rarely that most skippers and crews are tempted not to discuss them at all out of fear of frightening each other or causing bad luck. Yet these issues are substantial, and while we do not recommend preparing for them with such perfectionist vigour that sailing becomes more a chore than a pleasure, no crew should head out into open water without talking them over, inspecting vulnerable gear, and preparing for emergencies.

The sailing lifestyle that we have described in these pages is in turn pleasurable and challenging, romantic and trying, soothing and thrilling. This is as it should be with a pastime so fulfilling, so rich in its encounter with nature, and so overflowing with tradition. For sailing to be all these things, and for you to get the greatest reward from them, you the sailor must go about it consciously and thoughtfully, with due respect for the forces involved. Whether you are buying foul-weather gear, or navigating into a Brittany harbour, or reefing the mainsail, or cooking a three-course banquet to eat in the cockpit, or anticipating bad weather—whatever you do in or concerning a boat, do it with regard to the consequences and do it well. Of all the hundreds of rules and hints and skills covered here, this one is always the most important.

APPENDIX 1

Things You Must, Should, and Want to Have When You Set off on a Cruise

---

International regulations, the requirements of your insurance company, recommended scales of safety equipment, common sense, and personal taste dictate what equipment must and should be on board any boat going off to sea. A checklist will make preparations a little easier; here are lists of required and 'should have' safety equipment, plus a list of suggested 'nice to haves' that can make life aboard more pleasurable.

Once aboard, all this equipment can easily be lost in the boat's rabbit warren of lockers, bins, nooks, and crannies unless there is some kind of guide. You can keep things straight by making a list of items in alphabetical order. For example:

> Fire Extinguishers—in galley and on mast
> First-aid Kit—in heads locker
> Flares—in red box under companionway stairs
> Games—in green canvas bag, forward cabin
> Life Jackets—in forward starboard hanging locker

Better still, use a clearly labelled diagram. Yacht designers and builders produce drawings called accommodation plans to show how the bunks, lockers, tables, and other furniture are arranged in the cabins. Photocopy this plan, mark the location of all important equipment on the copy, and photocopy *that* document. Prominently post one copy of this treasure map or your alphabetical list over the chart table and store another one in the chart table in the same waterproof folder where the ship's registration papers and other valuable documents are stowed.

Recommended Safety Equipment

First, in Britain there are just a few items which any yacht is required to carry by law—adequate navigation lights and the means of making sound signals, to comply with the *International Regulations for Preventing Collisions at Sea,* while all yachts with an overall length of 45ft (13.7m) or more must have lifesaving and firefighting equipment which conforms to government rules obtainable from Her Majesty's Stationery Office.

Second, racing yachts are required to carry such equipment as may be specified by their class association or club. For example, ocean racers are required to comply with the regulations of the Offshore Racing Council, obtainable from the Royal Ocean Racing Club, Seahorse Building, Bath Road, Lymington, Hants, SO4 9SE.

Having said the above, in this country there are no legal or specified requirements for the average cruising yacht to carry certain items of equipment. Many of the items or attributes which satisfy safety afloat should have been provided by the boatbuilder. Apart from navigation lights, already mentioned, they include bilge pumps which will suck water from every part of the hull, seacocks on all hull openings (where pipes from heads, cockpit drains, galley sink etc pass through the hull), proper installation of the engine fuel system and the gas supply to the galley stove, guardrails around the deck edge, and emergency steering arrangements. It should go without saying that all matters concerning the construction of the boat and her rig, and the quality of her many fittings, must conform to recognized marine standards, such as are required for a Lloyd's Register Building Certificate.

Ultimately however the safety of a boat and her crew is the responsibility of her skipper, and he must ensure that they are equipped and prepared for any eventuality. To assist, an approved scale of recommended safety gear has been compiled and is summarised below, while further advice and information can be obtained from HM Coastguard stations. These notes apply to yachts of 18ft (5.5m) to 45ft (13.7m) in overall length which are intended for sea-going cruises, remembering that such boats must be equipped for the worst conditions that may be encountered.

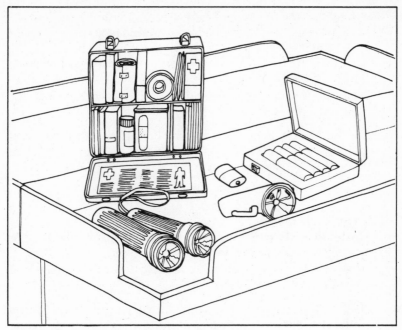

All cruising boats should carry a complete first-aid kit, a variety of torches in waterproof cases, and suitable flares, shown here in a waterproof box.

Lesser standards can be accepted for day-sailers operating in inshore waters.

Personal Safety Equipment

A lifejacket for every person on board. These should conform to BS 3595 or a similar standard. They must be stowed in a safe place, where they are easily accessible, and should be checked periodically. The straps should be adjusted to suit individual crew members, particularly young persons: special lifejackets are available for children. Lifejackets must be worn whenever the weather deteriorates, and always by non-swimmers. They can also save lives when proceeding to or from shore in a small tender.

A safety harness for every person on board a sailing yacht. These should conform to BS 4224 (BS 4474 for children), or a similar standard which requires adequate strength for all the components. A harness must be properly adjusted, and should be worn when on deck in bad weather or at night. A harness is of course useless if its safety line is not clipped to a secure fitting or to a jackstay provided for that purpose.

Man Overboard Rescue Gear

Lifebuoys. There should be least two lifebuoys (normally one port, and one starboard) within easy reach of the helmsman, so that they can be dropped overboard quickly should somebody go over the side. They should certainly be fitted with an automatic light, and preferably with a dan buoy and flag, a whistle and a drogue to reduce drift.

Buoyant line. A buoyant heaving line, 100ft (30m) long with a minimum breaking strain of 250lbs (115kg), should be stowed near the helmsman.

Flotation Equipment

Inflatable life raft. A life raft to carry all on board should be stowed on deck or in a locker opening directly to the deck. It should be serviced annually, and the crew should understand how to inflate and enter it.

or   **Rigid dinghy.** A rigid dinghy fitted with permanent (not inflatable) buoyancy, with oars and rowlocks secured, should be stowed on deck.

or   **Inflatable dinghy.** An inflatable dinghy intended for life-saving should either have two air compartments, one of which is kept inflated, or if only with one air compartment kept fully inflated. It should be stowed on deck, with oars and rowlocks secured.

Firefighting equipment

Fire extinguishers. The average cruising yacht, up to 30ft (9m) in length, should carry at least two dry powder extinguishers, or the equivalent, of not less than 3lb (1.4kg) capacity. Larger craft should carry in addition at least one such extinguisher of not less than 5lb (2.3kg) capacity. Dry powder extinguishers are good for general firefighting tasks, but carbon dioxide (CO_2) or foam are alternatives. If BCF or BTM extinguishers are carried the crew should be warned that they give off toxic fumes.

Fire blanket. A fire blanket should be stowed near (but not behind) the galley stove, for dealing with flare ups.

Bucket with lanyard. Water is excellent for cooling down a fire, and for preventing re-ignition.

General Safety Equipment

Distress signals. The merits and use of hand held flares and parachute rockets have been discussed in Chapter 17. For coastal cruising a boat should carry at least two red hand flares, two red parachute rockets, and two hand held orange smoke signals. If proceeding more than seven miles offshore she should have at least four red hand flares, four red parachute rockets, and two buoyant orange smoke canisters. An outfit of four white hand flares, to indicate the boat's presence, is suggested.

Radar reflector. This should be as large as possible, and mounted at least 10ft (3m) above sea level. The Firdell type of reflector is more efficient than the conventional octahedron.

Barometer. An aneroid barometer, or better still a barograph, should be carried, correctly set to the prevailing atmospheric pressure in harbour.

Radio receiver. A radio is essential for the reception of shipping forecasts on BBC Radio 4 (200kHz or 1500m), forecasts for coastal waters, and gale warnings.

First aid kit. In terms of time a cruising yacht can be a long way from medical attention, and it is important to carry a good first aid kit—and know how to use it. Seasickness is the most common affliction, and crew members should be encouraged to use their own remedies with the minimum side effects.

Bilge pumps. A seagoing boat should be fitted with two bilge pumps, with good strainers in the bilge, easily accessible for cleaning. Each pump should be sited so that it is easy to use, perhaps for a prolonged time, and so that it can be conveniently dismantled for cleaning and inspections. Pumps should be operable without having to open cockpit lockers etc. Limber holes in the bilges must be kept clear in order to allow water to reach the pump suctions.

Anchors. Two anchors should be carried, each with warp or chain of appropriate size and length.

Towing warp. In addition to normal mooring lines, one long and heavy warp should be carried for towing and general use.

Tool kit and spares. Sufficient tools and spares should be carried to rectify the more common faults in the engine and in other mechanical items. Tools should include heavy wire cutters for severing the standing rigging in the event of dismasting.

Name. The boat's name should be painted in letters at least 9in (220mm) high on the superstructure or on dodgers.

Electric torches. At least one powerful torch which can be used as a miniature searchlight and for signalling should be available. This, like other torches for general use, must be of the waterproof variety.

Navigational Equipment

Whatever electronic aids to navigation may be fitted, it is essential to carry certain fundamental items for navigation, and the following is a suggested list:

Steering compass. This must be installed where it is easily visible to the helmsman, and other equipment must be fitted a safe magnetic distance from it. It must have been swung and corrected for deviation, with a deviation card supplied. It must be fitted with a dimming light for use at night.

Hand bearing compass. This is used for taking bearings of shore objects or other vessels, and in emergency can be used as a steering compass.

Charts. A sufficient outfit of charts must be carried to cover the intended cruising ground, and adjacent waters including possible harbours of refuge. Charts must be kept corrected from *Notices to Mariners*.

Almanac. An up-to-date almanac should be carried, containing such information as: tide tables, tidal stream atlas, radio navigation aids, communications, times and details of weather forecasts, lights and fog signals, harbour details etc.

Chart table instruments. Plotter or parallel rules, dividers, pencils, indiarubber.

Clock or watch. At least one reliable timepiece must be carried.

Binoculars. A pair of marine-type binoculars, say 7×50, should be available.

Stopwatch. A stopwatch is needed for timing the characteristics of lights, and for navigational problems.

Pilot books. Excellent cruising guides are available to supplement the information from charts or other sources, in all the popular cruising areas.

Echo sounder. An echo sounder is the one electronic instrument which is really good value in a cruising yacht.

Lead line. A lead line should be carried as stand-by, and is also sometimes useful when anchoring.

Log book. A log book, which can be a ruled notebook with columns completed in pencil to suit, is essential for recording navigational information and as a diary of events.

Documentation

For coastal cruising round the British Isles the documentation required by a yacht is minimal—although radio sets need to be licensed and any boat should be fully insured against loss, damage or third party risks. If however you intend to cruise abroad, rather more is required.

Registration. There are two distinct methods of registering a British yacht. The first, which applies to all vessels over 79ft (24m) in length, and to all vessels which are company owned or subject to a marine mortgage, is the Part 1 registry run by the Registrar of Ships at various Registry ports around the coast. The Registrar is a Customs and Excise official, and can normally be located at the Custom House. This method is complicated and expensive, but it does have the advantage of establishing title or ownership. The second method of registration, which is perfectly satisfactory for the purposes of occasional cruises abroad, is by the Small Ships Register, details of which are available from the Royal Yachting Association, Victoria Way, Woking, Surrey, GU21 1EQ.

Certificate of Competence. In foreign countries there is an increasing demand for yacht skippers to produce some form of document to substantiate their ability to handle their craft. This applies particularly when chartering a boat overseas. If a skipper or owner does not already hold an appropriate RYA certificate (eg Coastal Skipper or Yachtmaster Offshore) it is possible to obtain a Helmsman's (Overseas) Certificate of Competence from the RYA—provided of course that the necesary skills are held.

Customs. Any yacht coming to or leaving the United Kingdom must conform to Customs regulations, which are summarised in nautical almanacs or available as Customs Notice No 8 from any Custom House. Notice of departure must be given by completing form C1328, and depositing Part

1 at the nearest Customs office before departure. On return, Flag 'Q' must be flown until formalities are completed. The skipper is required to notify the nearest Customs office by telephone or in person, within two hours of arrival. Abroad the procedure varies from country to country.

Passports. In most countries a passport is needed for one reason or another. When cruising abroad it is useful to carry duplicated lists of the names of the crew and their passport numbers. For a few places vaccination certificates are needed for endemic diseases.

'Should Have' Gear

Apart from equipment to cover safety and emergency needs, or the documentation required in certain circumstances, there are many other items which justify a place on board a cruising yacht. At the end of Chapter 3 there is a check list for personal gear to take aboard. Below is one for the minimum equipment that is suggested before setting off on a cruise that will last a week or longer.

1. General

a waterproof suit and sea boots for each of the crew
a sleeping bag for each person
full fuel and water tanks (if the tanks are small, carry a jerry can of each, too, but petrol must never be stowed below deck)
several canvas (or plastic) and string bags for stowage and shopping
two buckets, scrubber, sponge and leathercloth
a dozen clothes pegs
warps and fenders
a swimming/boarding ladder
a snorkel and swimming mask
a bosun's chair
ensign and club burgee
Flag 'Q' and courtesy flag(s) if bound foreign

2. Tools and Spares

the need for essential repair gear has already been mentioned. The tool kit should include: a sharp knife with a spike, large and small adjustable spanners, a selection of open-jaw spanners for sizes up to 1in (25mm), 'Mole' grips, a selection of screwdrivers, pliers, hammer and chisel, punches, hacksaw and blades, a hand drill and drill set, files, 'Allen' keys, and a

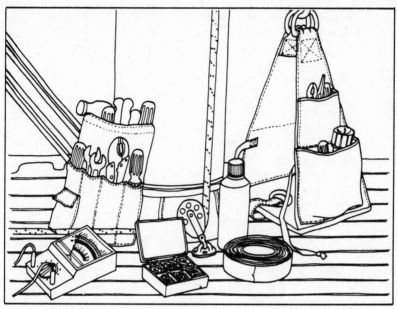

Tools, fastenings, lubricants, a voltmeter, and a bosun's chair for going aloft may all come in handy some day.

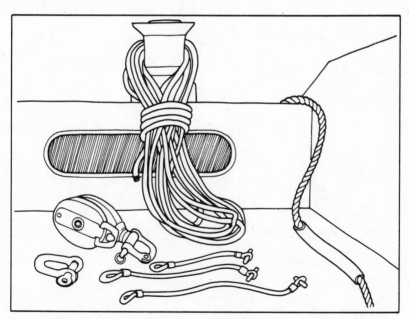

Spare line, shackles, and blocks are needed, as are some lengths of shockcord for furling sails, and chafing gear to slip over the anchor rode where it passes over the bow roller.

variety of cotter pins, stainless steel bolts, nuts, washers and screws
a sealed can of engine oil
a small can of light oil (3 in 1)
an aerosol of WD40 or equivalent
a small can of solvent for cleaning oil off warps, fenders, shoes, etc
waterproof grease and grease gun
two rolls of heavy waterproof tape
epoxy glue (Araldite)
hydrometer and distilled water for the battery
spare hose and 'Jubilee' hose clips
gasket material
sail repair kit (including light tape)
twenty feet of marline or other light line
light shockcord
a spare main/jib halyard
spare jib sheets
spare mainsail battens
two spare blocks
four spare shackles
a spare or emergency tiller, in case the tiller or wheel breaks

3. The Galley
full cooking fuel tanks or gas cylinders
large garbage bags
food storage bags
plastic wrap
freezer tape
five rolls of paper towels
three emergency meals in tins
pots and pans: at least a frying pan, a large pot, a small pot, and a kettle
implements: at least a spatula, a serving spoon, and a fork and spoon for all
matches or gas lighter
liquid dish soap
a dish scrubber
a corkscrew

4. The Heads
five rolls of toilet paper
three bars of soap
air-freshener spray

a large first-aid kit and manual; *The Yachtsman's Doctor* (Nautical Books, 1986) is handy and comprehensive.
non-prescription seasick pills
several tubes of sun lotion

5. The Chart Table

coast and harbour charts covering the largest possible area that you will cruise in
a plotter or parallel rules
dividers
a large notebook (or log)
a box of 2B pencils and a small sharpener
a chart magnifier
a nautical almanac providing tide tables and information on radio navigation aids, communications, weather forecasts, lights and fog signals, harbour details etc.
an accurate watch with stopwatch function
a local cruising guide
a radio to receive weather broadcasts
binoculars
a hand bearing compass

6. Lights

a battery-powered, 360-degree, white anchor light to hang from the forestay when anchored
four torches (with waterproof rubber or plastic casings) with spare batteries and bulbs
an extremely powerful battery-operated signal/searchlight
spare bulbs for all navigation and cabin lights
a voltmeter to test wiring circuits
spare fuses

'Nice to Have' Gear

Here are a few take-aboard options which, while not making sailing any safer or easier, certainly make living aboard more interesting and fun.

a field guide to local wildlife; escapist reading material; a tape player with earphones and a wide variety of cassette tapes; a sketch pad and drawing pencils; two decks of playing cards with the same backs (some cards will inevitably fall into the bilge); a game, such as magnetized chess or Scrabble set; a guitar, harmonica, or recorder—and a musician who can play; a Frisbee, football, tennis ball, or soccer ball for shore exercise.

Glossary of

500 Important

Sailing Terms

(with a Sample
of Curious Derivations)

―――――

One of the most complicated and challenging aspects of sailing is its complex terminology. It drives some people mad: why not say *left, right,* and *front,* instead of *port, starboard,* and *bow?* One reason is that if you use landlubber terms in a boating context, your shipmates who already know *port,* etc, will not have the slightest idea what you are talking about. The language is already in place, so just try to do your best to master it. Experience, reading, and patient shipmates will be your best teachers.

Here are the definitions of some 500 common sailing terms in general use today. The entire sailor's language has a much larger vocabulary—one special dictionary, René de Kerchove's classic *International Maritime Dictionary,* is a thousand pages long—but this is all you will need on the decks and in the cabins of today's pleasure boats. For trivia and crossword puzzle buffs, after the main glossary we will look more closely at the thirty terms that make up the hard core of the sailor's language.

A

Aback. With sails backed, or trimmed to windward.

Abaft. Behind.

Abeam. At right angles to a boat.

Aboard. In a boat.

Adrift. Unsecured.

Afloat. Floating.

Aft. Toward the stern.

After. A prefix denoting location toward the stern.

Aground. Stuck on the bottom in shallow water.

Aid to navigation. A buoy, lighthouse, or other channel marker.

Air. Wind.

Alee. To leeward, away from the wind. 'Hard alee' (or 'lee-oh') is a command for tacking.

Aloft. In the rigging above the deck.

Alongside. Beside.

Amidship(s). In the middle of the boat, where she is widest.

Angle of attack. The angle between the sail and the apparent wind or the rudder or centreline and the water flow.

Apparent wind. The wind felt on the moving boat.

Appendage. A rudder, keel, centreboard, or skeg.

Astern. Behind the stern.

Athwartships. Across the boat.

Auxiliary. A sailing boat that has an engine.

Aweigh. Describes an anchor unhooked from the bottom.

B

Babystay. See **Jackstay.**

Back. (1) to trim a sail to windward; (2) counterclockwise shift in the wind direction.

Backstay. A stay running aft from the upper part of the mast, either permanent or running (adjustable).

Backwind. Wind flowing from a forward sail into the leeward side of an after sail.

Bail. To remove water with a bucket or bailer.

Balance. The degree to which all the forces on a boat are symmetrical so she sails with slight weather helm.

Ballast. Weight in the keel or on the windward side that restrains the boat from heeling too far.

Ballast-displacement ratio. The numerical ratio between the ballast and displacement.

Barber hauler. A sail control for changing the athwartships lead of the jib sheet.

Barometer. An instrument that shows atmospheric pressure in millibars.

Batten. A wooden or plastic

slat inserted in the leech of a sail.

Beam. A boat's greatest width.

Beamy. Wide.

Bear away. To head off, away from the wind.

Bearing. The angle to an object in relative or compass degrees.

Beat. A course sailed as close to the wind as is efficiently possible, or a close-hauled course.

Below. Beneath the deck.

Bend on sails. To install sails on the boom and forestay.

Berth. (1) A boat's position at a jetty or pontoon; (2) a 'wide berth' is a large margin of safety; (3) a bed in a boat.

Bight. Any part of a line between the ends.

Bilge. The lowest part of the boat's hull.

Binnacle. A support or pedestal into which a compass is secured.

Bitter end. The end of a line.

Blanket. To come between the wind and a sail so the sail is not full.

Block. A nautical pulley made up of a sheave that rotates on a sheave pin (or centre pin) or on ball bearings and hung from metal or plastic sides called cheeks.

Board. (1) Abbreviation for centreboard; (2) to go on a boat; (3) a leg or part of a course.

Boat hook. A pole with a hook on its end.

Boat speed. Speed through the water.

Boltrope. The line along the luff and foot of a mainsail and the luff of a jib.

Boom. The spar that extends and supports the foot of a mainsail.

Boom vang. A tackle or hydraulic system that restrains the boom from lifting. Also called a 'kicking strap'.

Boot top. The painted band on the boat's topsides just at the waterline.

Bottom. (1) The submerged land; (2) the boat's hull under the water, or underbody.

Bow. The most foward part of the boat.

Bow roller. Stemhead roller for the anchor cable or rode.

Braided line. Line or rope made up of a hard core inside a soft woven cover.

Breeze. Wind or air.

Broach. To get out of control and head up sharply, usually when sailing off the wind.

Broad on. About 45° (the bow or stern); sometimes 'broad off'.

Bulkhead. A wall separating a boat's cabins that provides athwartships support for the hull.

Bunk. A bed in a boat; sometimes 'berth'.

Buoy. A floating object marking a channel or a mooring.

Buoyancy. The upward force that keeps a boat floating.

By the lee. Sailing on a run with the wind coming over the quarter on the same side that the boom is trimmed, making a sudden gybe likely.

C

Cabin. A room in a boat.

Calm. Little or no wind. A 'flat calm' is totally devoid of wind.

Canvas. Sails or sail area.

Capsize. To turn over.

Cardinal points. North, east, south, and west. The inter-cardinal points are northeast, southeast, southwest and northwest.

Carry away. To break.

Cast off. To let a line go.

Catamaran. A multihull with two hulls separated by a deck or crossbeams from which a trampoline is suspended; abbreviated 'cat'.

Cat boat. A wide, shallow boat with a large mainsail and no jib.

Cat rig. A single- or two-masted boat with no jib.

Caught back. With the sails backed, or trimmed to windward.

Centreboard. A retractable appendage that increases or reduces the draft and the lateral area of the underbody.

Centre of effort. The point in the sail plan that is the balance point for all the aerodynamic forces.

Centre of lateral resistance. The point in the hull's underbody that is the balance point for all the hydrodynamic forces.

Centreline. An imaginary line that runs down the middle of the boat from bow to stern.

Chafe. Abrasion or wear.

Chain plates. Straps on or inside the hull to which shrouds are secured.

Chandlery. A marine hardware store.

Channel. Water sufficiently deep to sail in.

Chart. A nautical map.

Charter. To rent a boat.

Chine. The intersection between the topsides and the boat's bottom in some forms of construction.

Chop. Short, steep waves.

Chord. An imaginary line drawn between the luff and leech of a sail. The chord depth is an imaginary line drawn to the deepest part of the sail from the chord. The ratio of chord depth to chord length represents the sail's draft—a high ratio indicates a flat sail; a low ratio, a full sail.

Circumnavigation. A voyage around the world.

Cleat. A wooden, plastic, or metal object to which halyards, sheets etc can be secured without taking a hitch. There are two kinds of cleats, horn and self-jamming.

Clevis pin. A cylindrical pin with head and split pin that secures one fitting to another.

Clew. The after lower corner of a mainsail, jib, or mizzen, and either lower corner of a spinnaker.

Close-hauled. Sailing as close to the wind as is efficient; also 'beating' and 'on the wind.'

Coaming. A low wall around a cockpit.

Cockpit. A recessed area in the deck containing the tiller or wheel.

Coil. To arrange line in easily manageable loops so it can be stowed.

Companionway. Opening leading down from the deck to the cabin.

Compass. A magnetized card in a glass dome that indicates the direction of magnetic north.

Compass rose. A circle on a chart that shows the direction of north.

Cotter pin. A small pin used to secure a clevis pin and to keep turnbuckles from

unwinding. Also called a 'split pin'.

Course. (1) The compass direction that is steered; (2) the sequence of buoys rounded in a race.

Cradle. A frame that supports a boat when she is hauled out of the water onto shore.

Crew. Everybody who helps sail a boat.

Cringle. A large reinforced eye in a sail.

Cruise. Two or more days spent continuously in a boat that is underway.

Cruiser-racer. A boat comfortable enough for cruising and fast enough for racing.

Cruising boat. A boat used only for cruising.

Cunningham. A line controlling tension along a sail's luff, invented by Briggs Cunningham.

Current. Horizontal movement of the water caused by the wind (not the tide).

Custom boat. A boat built specifically for one client, as against a stock boat.

Cut. The shape or design of a sail.

Cutter. A single-masted boat that sets two headsails at a time.

D

Daggerboard. A centreboard that is retracted vertically rather than hinged.

Dampen. To cause to moderate.

Danger sector. The sector of a lighthouse's light which marks shoals or other dangers.

Day-sailer. A boat without a cabin that is used for short sails or racing.

Dead. Exactly.

Dead-end. To secure an end of a line to an object.

Dead Reckoning (DR). The calculation of a boat's position based on course and distance run.

Deck. The top of a hull.

Depower. To lessen heeling forces by making sails less full or allowing them to luff.

Deviation. A compass error caused by metal objects on board.

Dinghy. A small, light sailing or rowing boat.

Displacement. A boat's weight—more accurately, the weight of the water she displaces. A 'light-displacement' boat is relatively light for her length.

Displacement boat. A relatively heavy boat that cannot plane.

Distance run. The mileage covered during a given time period.

Dock. (1) The water next to a float or pier; (2) to bring a boat alongside a jetty or pontoon.

Docking line. See **Mooring warp.**

Dodger. A fold-up spray hood at the forward end of the cockpit.

Doghouse. A small deckhouse, above the cabin top or coachroof.

Double-bottom. A watertight compartment between the bottom and the sole, or floor.

Douse. To lower.

Downhaul. A line that holds an object down.

Downwind. Away from the direction from which the wind blows.

Draft (or draught). (1) The distance between the waterline and the lowest part of the keel; (2) the amount and position of fullness in a sail.

Drag. (1) Resistance; (2) when an anchor breaks out and skips along the bottom.

Drift. Distance covered due to tidal stream or current.

Drifting. In a calm, to be carried by the tidal stream or current.

E

Earing. A reefing line led through a leech cringle.

Ease. (1) To let out (a sheet); (2) to reduce pull on (the helm).

Easy. Without undue strain, smooth.

Ebb. The dropping, outgoing tide.

Eddy. A circular current.

End-for-end. A reversal of a line.

EPIRB. A small radio beacon for transmitting an emergency, position-indicating signal.

Estimated Position (EP). A best estimate of a boat's position based on dead reckoning but with an estimation for leeway and for the effect of tidal stream.

Eye. A loop.

Eye of the wind. The precise wind direction.

F

Fairlead. A fitting through which a line passes so chafe is avoided.

Fairway. The middle of a channel.

Fair wind. A reach or run.

Fake. To make large loops on deck with a line or cable in order to eliminate kinks.

Fast. Secure.

Fastenings. The screws and bolts that hold a boat together.

Feather. To spill wind from the sails in a gust by heading up from close-hauled to a forereach.

Feel. The helmsman's sense of how well the boat is sailing.

Fender. A rubber bumper hung between the boat and a jetty or pontoon.

Fend off. To push off.

Fetch. (1) To sail a course that will clear a buoy or shoal, also 'lay'; (2) the distance between an object and the windward shore.

Fish. To repair with turns of light line.

Fitting. A piece of a boat's gear.

Fix. A position based on two or more position lines.

Float. See **Pontoon.**

Flood. The rising, incoming tide.

Flotation. Foam blocks or air tanks that keep a swamped boat afloat.

Fluky. Unpredictable and weak.

Following sea. Waves from astern.

Foot. (1) The bottom edge of a sail; (2) to steer slightly lower than close-hauled in order to increase boat speed.

Force. A measurement of wind strength in the Beaufort scale.

Fore. Prefix indicating location toward the bow.

Fore and aft. Everywhere on the boat.

Forepeak. A stowage compartment in the bow.

Forereach. To carry way while heading almost into the wind.

Foresail. A jib.

Forestay. A stay running from the foredeck to the mast, on which a jib is set.

Foretriangle. The area bounded by the mast, foredeck, and forestay.

Forward. Toward the bow.

Foul. (1) To tangle; (2) to violate a racing rule.

Foul-weather gear. Water-resistant clothing and boots.

Founder. To swamp or sink.

Fractional rig. A rig whose forestay goes partway up the mast.

Free. (1) On a broad reach or run; (2) a freeing wind is a lift, or a shift aft.

Freeboard. The distance from the deck to the water, or the height of the topsides.

Fresh air. Wind of about 17–21 knots (Force 5).

Front. The boundary between cold and warm air masses.

Full. (1) Not luffing; (2) with deep draft.

Full and by. Sailing close-hauled with sails full.

Full sail. All sails set.

Furl. To roll up and secure a sail to a boom.

G

Gadget. A specialized piece of gear.

Gaff-rigged. With a four-sided mainsail, whose top edge is supported by a spar called a gaff.

Galley. A boat's kitchen.

Gangway. Any form of passage or access.

Gear. Generic term for all equipment in a boat.

Genoa. A large jib whose clew overlaps the mast and mainsail.

Gimbals. Supports that allow a compass, table, or stove to remain level as the boat heels.

Give. Stretch.

Give-way vessel. Under the rules of the road, the vessel that must take action to avoid the stand-on vessel.

Gooseneck. The fitting securing the forward end of the boom to the mast.

Goosewinged. With the jib and mainsail set on opposite sides, when running before the wind.

Gradient. The relative proximity and barometric pressure of adjoining isobars on a weather map.

Grommet. A small metal ring set into a sail.

Ground tackle. The anchor and anchor rode.

Guardrail. A wire, supported by posts, called stanchions, that encircles the deck to restrain the crew from falling overboard.

Gunwale. A boat's rail at the edge of the deck, pronounced 'gun'l'.

Gust. A strong puff of wind.

Guy. A line controlling the position of a spinnaker pole; the after guy pulls the pole back and eases it forward; the fore guy restrains it from lifting.

Gybe. To change tacks by bearing away until the sails swing across the boat.

H

Halyard. A line or wire rope that hoists a sail and keeps it up.

Hand. (1) To lower. (2) a crew member.

Hank. A small snap hook that secures the jib luff to the headstay.

Harden up. To head up.

Hard over. As far as possible in one direction.

Hatch. An opening in a deck, covered by a hatch cover.

Haul in. To trim.

Haul out. To pull out of the water.

Head. The top corner of a sail.

Heads. A boat's lavatory.

Headboard. The reinforcement in the head of a sail.

Header. A wind shift requiring the helmsman to alter course to leeward or the crew to trim sheets.

Heading. The course.

Head off. To alter course to leeward away from the wind; also 'bear off,' 'bear away'.

Headroom. A cabin's height.

Headsail. A jib.

Head sea. Waves from ahead.

Head to wind. With the bow heading dead into the wind.

Head up. To alter course to windward, toward the wind; also 'harden up,' 'come up,' and 'luff up.'

Headway. Forward motion.

Heave. To throw.

Heave-to. To sail along slowly with the jib backed.

Heavy weather. Rough seas and gale-force winds.

Heel. The amount a boat leans over.

Helm. (1) The tiller or steering wheel; (2) the boat's tendency to head off course: with weather helm, she tends to head up, with lee helm, to bear away.

Helmsman. The person who is steering.

High. (1) Several degrees to windward of the required course; (2) pinching, or sailing too close to the wind.

High cut. With the clew high off the deck.

High performance. Very fast.

Holding ground. The bottom in a harbour. Good holding ground, such as mud, grabs an anchor securely.

Hounds. The location on the mast of the shrouds and lower rigging.

House. To stow or make secure.

Hull. A boat's shell, exclusive of appendages, deck, rig, and cabin.

Hull speed. A boat's theoretical maximum speed determined by multiplying the square root of her waterline length in feet by 1.34.

I

Inboard. In from the rail.

In irons. Head to wind with no headway or sternway.

Isobar. A line on a weather map marking points of equal barometric pressure.

J

Jackstay. A stay, usually wire, running between two points, eg for lifelines of safety harnesses.

Jib. A sail carried on the forestay.

Jiffy reef. A reef that is tied in. Also called a 'slab reef'.

Jumper strut. A strut sticking out from the mast near the jib halyard block of a fractional rig; over the strut passes the jumper stay, which when tensioned helps keep the top of the mast straight.

Jury rig. An improvised replacement for damaged gear.

K

Kedge off. To use an anchor to pull a grounded boat back into deep water.

Keel. A deep appendage, or fin, under the hull whose lateral area counteracts leeway forces and whose weight counteracts heeling forces— usually permanent but sometimes retractable.

Ketch. A two-masted boat whose after mast, the mizzenmast, is shorter than the forward mast, the mainmast, and is also located forward of the rudder post.

Kicking strap. See **Boom vang.**

Knockdown. A drastic increase in the angle of heel.

Knot. One nautical mile per hour.

L

Laid line. Line of rope made up of large strands (usually three of them) twisted around each other.

Land breeze. A wind blowing from the shore to the water.

Landmark. An object on the shore that can be helpful when navigating.

Lanyard. A short line.

Lash. To tie.

Launch. (1)To move a boat into the water from land; (2) a powerboat used as a ferry between land and a moored boat.

Lay. To sail a course that will clear a buoy or shoal; also 'fetch'.

Layout. The arrangement of gear on deck or of furniture in the cabin.

Lazy. Not in use.

Lead. (1)A block for a jib sheet; (2) to pass a line through a block.

Lee. Short for 'leeward.'

Lee bow. To have the tidal stream pushing the boat to windward.

Leech. The after edge of a mainsail, jib, or mizzen, and both side edges of a spinnaker.

Lee helm. A boat's tendency to head off, away from the wind, unless checked by the tiller or wheel.

'Lee-oh'. Command for tacking.

Lee shore. Land onto which the wind is blowing and which is to leeward of the boat.

Leeward. Downwind.

Leeway. Side-slippage to leeward.

Leg. A part of a passage or race sailed between two buoys or aids to navigation.

Length. Length overall (LOA) is the distance between the tip of the bow and the end of the stern. Waterline length (LWL) is the distance between the most forward and most aft points touching the water when the boat is at rest.

Liferaft. An inflatable boat for use in emergencies.

Lift. A wind shift allowing the helmsman to head up, or alter course to windward, or the crew to ease sheets.

Light. (1) Describes a sail that is luffing; (2) an illuminated aid to navigation or boat's navigation light.

Light breeze. Wind of 4–6 knots (Force 2).

Light line. Line smaller than 6mm in diameter.

Line. Any length of rope that has a specified use.

Loose. To let go.

Low cut. With the clew near the deck.

Lubber's line. A vertical mark inside the compass, aligned with the vessel's bow.

Luff. (1) The forward edge of a mainsail, jib, or mizzen, and the windward edge of a spinnaker; (2) fluttering or flapping in a sail when it is not trimmed far enough or is being backwinded by another sail, or when the course is too close to the wind.

Luff curve. A convex (in a mainsail) or concave (in a jib) curve in a sail's luff to account for mast bend or forestay sag.

Lull. A relatively calm period between wind gusts.

M

Magnetic. Relative to magnetic north, as against true.

Mainmast. The mast, or the taller of two masts.

Mainsail. The sail hoisted on the after side of the mainmast, pronounced 'mains'l'.

Mark. A buoy used in a race course.

Marline. A general-purpose tarred light line.

Marlinspike. A pointed tool on a sailor's knife used for splicing, to pry open knots, start holes in wood, and accomplish other odd jobs.

Mast. A wooden or aluminum pole supported by standing rigging from which sails are set.

Masthead; The top of the mast.

Masthead fly. A wind direction indicator at the mast-head.

Masthead light. A white light illuminated when under power at night, located *not* at the top of the mast but about two-thirds of the way up the mast.

Mast step. The support for the bottom (heel or butt) of the mast.

Millibar(mb). A unit of atmospheric pressure, with 1 mb equal to 0.03 inches (0.75mm) of mercury.

Mizzen. The small, aftermost sail on a ketch or yawl, set on the mizzenmast.

Moderate breeze. Wind of about 11–16 knots (Force 4).

Mooring. A permanently emplaced anchor with a pendant and buoy to which a boat may be secured.

Mooring warp. A line which secures a boat to a jetty, quay or pontoon.

Motion. The degree of instability of a boat's deck while she sails in waves.

Motor sailer. An auxiliary sailing boat with an especially large engine and spacious accommodation.

Mousing. A length of light line or wire that secures a pin in a shackle.

Multihull. A boat with two hulls (a catamaran) or three hulls (a trimaran), or one hull and an outrigger.

N

Nautical mile. The unit of distance used at sea, 6076 feet (1852 metres), or approximately one minute of latitude at the place concerned. One knot = 1 nautical mile per hour.

O

Obstruction. A buoy, vessel shoal, or other object requiring a major course alteration to pass to one side.

Ocean racer. A boat with minimal accommodation used for racing overnight or long distances.

Offshore. (1) Out of sight of land; (2) from the land toward the water.

Off the wind. Reaching or running.

On board. In a boat.

On even keel. Not heeling.

Onshore. From the water toward the land.

On the beam. Abeam.

On the bow (stern). To one side of the bow (stern); also 'off the bow (stern).'

One-design. A racing boat, usually a day-sailer, designed and built to the same specifications as all other boats in her class.

Open boat. A boat without a deck.

Outboard. (1) Out toward and beyond the rail; (2) a portable engine on the stern.

Outhaul. A sail control that secures the clew of a boomed sail, and adjusts tension along its foot.

Overcanvassed. Having too much sail.

Overhang. The distance the bow and stern extend beyond the waterline.

Overhaul. (1) To tighten a lazy (unused) line or the tail of a line in use in order to check that the lead is fair and that there is no chafe; (2) to overtake.

Overlaping. Alongside of; an overlapping jib extends aft of the luff of the mainsail, and an overlapping boat has her bow or stern alongside another boat's stern or bow.

Overnight. For two or three days.

Overpowered. Heeling too far and difficult to steer.

Overstand. To lay or fetch a buoy or shoal with room to spare.

Overtaking. Coming up from astern and about to pass.

P

Padeye. A metal loop to which blocks and shackles are secured.

Painter. A bow line on a dinghy.

Part. (1) to break; (2) one of the sections of line in a tackle.

Partners. The deck opening for the mast.

Passage. More than 6 hours spent under way.

Pay out. To ease.

Pendant. A short length of wire or line used as an extender on a sail, halyard, or anchor rode, pronounced 'pennant.'

Pier. A platform on posts that sticks out from the shore.

Pinch. To sail too close to the wind when close-hauled.

Pitchpole. To somersault.

Plane. To skip up and across the bow wave at high speed.

Planing boat. A light boat that planes in fresh winds at speeds exceeding her theoretical hull speed.

Play. (1) To trim a sheet assiduously; (2) a loose fit.

Plot. To draw a boat's course and position on a chart.

Point. To sail close to the wind.

Points of sailing. Close-hauled, reaching, and running.

Pontoon. A floating platform to which boats may be secured.

Pooped. Smashed by a wave breaking over the stern.

Port. (1) The left side, facing forward; (2) a small round window; (3) a commercial harbour.

Porthole. A small round window; also 'port'.

Position line. A line along which the vessel lies. Two position lines provide a fix.

Pound. To smash down heavily on waves.

Preventer. A line that restrains the boom from gybing accidentally.

Puff. A quick, local increase in wind velocity.

Pulpit. A stainless-steel guardrail around the bow or stern.

Q

Quarter. The after sections of the rails and topsides.

R

Race. (1) An especially strong, turbulent stream; (2) an organized competition between boats.

Rail. The outer edge of the deck.

Rake. The tilt of a mast.

Range. (1) The difference in water level between high and low tides; (2) the full extent of a light's visibility.

Reach. (1) To sail across the wind; (2) a stretch of water or a channel (between the mainland and an island, for example).

Reef. (1) To decrease a sail's size; (2) a shoal composed of rocks or coral.

Reeve. To lead a line through a block or cringle.

Regatta. A series of races in which cumulative scores may be kept.

Render. To run easily through a block.

Rhumb Line. A line that cuts all the meridians at the same angle (approximately the most direct course between two points over short distances).

Rig. (1) The spars, standing rigging, and sails; (2) to get a boat ready for sailing or prepare a sail or piece of gear for use.

Rigging. The gear used to support and adjust the sails: standing rigging includes the spars, stays, shrouds and rigging screws; running rigging includes the sheets and halyards and their blocks, as well as sail controls such as the outhaul and kicking strap.

Rigging screw. A threaded fitting used to adjust the length of a shroud or stay.

Right-of-way. The authority, in normal circumstances, to stay on the present course.

Roach. The sail area aft of the imaginary straight line running between the head and the clew.

Rode. The anchor warp and/or cable.

Roller furling. A way to stow sails by rolling them up at their luff.

Roller reef. A reef secured by rolling the sail up on itself.

Rudder. An underwater flap that is adjusted by the helm to steer the boat. It pivots on the rudder post.

Rules of the road. Laws that, when observed, prevent collisions.

Run. (1) A course with the wind astern; (2) distance covered.

Running lights. The navigation lights illuminated at night on the starboard and port sides and on the stern, when under way.

RYA. Royal Yachting Association.

S

Safety harness. A web or rope harness worn on the upper body and attached to the deck with a lifeline to prevent a sailor falling overboard.

Sailboard. A surfboard rigged with a sail that the standing sailor holds up.

Sail controls. Lines, tackles, and other gear used to hold a sail in position and adjust its shape, such as the sheets, traveller, outhaul, cunningham, and kicking strap.

Sail cover. A protective cloth tied over a furled sail to protect it from ultra-violet rays and dirt.

Sail handling. The hoisting, trimming, and lowering of sails.

Sail ties. Straps used to secure a furled sail or to lash a lowered sail on deck so it does not blow away; also called 'stops' and 'gaskets.'

Schooner. A boat with two or more masts, the forwardmost of which, the foremast, is shorter than the aftermost, the mainmast.

Scope. The ratio between the amount of anchor rode let out and the depth of the water.

Scow. A fast, flat-bottomed day-sailer, as raced on lakes.

Scull. To propel a boat by swinging the helm and rudder back and forth.

Scupper. A deck or cockpit drain.

Sea. (1) A wave; (2) a body of salt water smaller than an ocean but larger than a sound or gulf.

Seaboot. A rubber boot with a nonslip sole.

Sea breeze. A wind blowing from the water to warmer land, filling the space left by rising heated air.

Sea cock. A valve opening and closing a pipe through the hull.

Sea condition. The size and shape of the waves.

Seakindly. Comfortable in rough seas.

Sea room. Enough distance from shore and shoals for safe sailing.

Seaway. Rough water.

Seaworthy. Able to survive heavy weather.

Secure. To fasten or cleat.

Self-bailers. Sluices in the bilge of a small boat to remove water when she is under way.

Self-bailing. Automatically draining.

Self-steering. Automatically steering without a helmsman.

Set. (1) To raise (a sail); (2) the direction in which the tidal stream and/or current flows.

Set up. To rig.

Shackle. A metal hook that secures a line to a fitting, a line to a sail, or a fitting to a fitting.

Sheave. The roller in a block.

Sheer. The curve of the rail as seen from alongside.

Sheet. (1) The primary sail-control line, which pulls the sail in and out; (2) to trim.

Shifty. Frequently changing direction.

Shoal. Dangerously shallow water.

Shock cord. Elastic line.

Shoot into the wind. To head directly into the wind.

Shorten down. To set a smaller sail.

Shorthanded. With a small crew.

Shroud.   Athwartships (lateral) support for a mast.

Sidelights. The navigation lights illuminated at night on the starboard side (green) and on the port side (red), when under way.

Singlehanded. Solitary.

Sisterships. Boats of the same design.

Skeg. A small, fixed fin attached to the underbody near the stern.

Skipper. The person in charge of a boat.

Slack. (1) Not moving; (2) loose; (3) to ease.

Slat. To roll in a calm with the sails slapping back and forth noisily.

Slip. (1) A dock between two pontoons in a marina. (2) Where a boat is hauled out of the water.

Sloop. A single-masted boat that sets one jib at a time.

Slop. A confused seaway.

Small boat. A day-sailer less than 30 feet (9 metres) long.

Snap hook. A spring-loaded hook used as a hank and for other small jobs.

Snub. To wrap a line once around a winch or cleat so most of its pull is ab-

sorbed.

Sole. A cabin or cockpit floor.

Sound. To measure depth.

Spar. Any mast, boom, or spinnaker pole.

Speed made good. A boat's speed as measured by her progress over the ground.

Spinnaker. A light, ballooning sail used when sailing off the wind.

Splice. To make an eye in the end of a line or link two line ends together by interweaving strands.

Spill wind. To allow a sail to luff.

Spreader. An athwartships strut holding shrouds out from the mast and providing lateral support.

Stanchions. Metal posts supporting guardrails.

Stand-on vessel. Under the rules of the road, the boat with right-of-way.

Starboard. The right side facing forward.

Stay. A wire which supports the mast fore-and-aft (eg forestay, bobstay, jumper stay, backstay).

Staysail. A small jib tacked down partway back from the forestay.

Steer by. Use as a guide when steering.

Steerage way. Enough speed through the water to allow efficient steering.

Stem. The forward edge of the bow.

Step. To install a mast in

a boat.

Stern. The aftermost part of the hull.

Sternlight. The white navigation light illuminated at night at the stern of a vessel under way.

Stern way. Motion astern.

Stiff. Resistant to heeling.

Stock boat. A boat with many sisterships built by the same manufacturer from the same design, as against a custom boat.

Stop. A sail tie.

Stow. To put in the proper place.

Strong breeze. Wind of about 22–27 knots (Force 6).

Surf. To slide down the face of a wave.

Swamp. To be filled with water.

Swell. Long waves created by prevailing winds or a distant storm; also 'ground-swell.'

T

Tack. (1) With the wind coming over one side or the other; (2) to change tacks by heading up until the sails swing across the boat; (3) the forward lower corner of a mainsail, jib, or mizzen, or the lower windward corner of the spinnaker.

Tack down. To secure the sail's tack.

Tackle. A mechanical system of line (parts) and blocks that increases hauling power, pronounced by some as 'taykle'.

Tail. (1) To pull on a sheet or halyard behind a winch; (2) the section of the sheet or halyard behind the winch and cleat.

Tang. A metal strap on the mast to which a stay or block is secured.

Telltale. A piece of yarn or ribbon either tied to the shrouds to help the crew determine wind direction or sewn to the sails to help them trim or steer.

Tender. Heels relatively quickly.

Thimble. A metal or plastic eye worked into an eye splice to protect the line or wire against chafe.

Three sheets in the wind. Drunk.

Tide. The rise and fall of water due to the moon's and sun's gravitational pull, as against tidal stream, which is the lateral motion of the water.

Tide rip. A line of rough water where a fast-moving tidal stream meets stationary or contrary-moving water.

Tied-in reef. A reef secured by tying cringles to the boom, as against roller reef; also called 'jiffy reef' and 'slab reef.'

Tight leech. A leech pulled down so hard that it forms a straight line between the head and the clew.

Toe strap. A strap in the cockpit to restrain the feet of the crew when sitting out to windward.

Toggle. A metal fitting inserted between a stay and the mast or rigging screw, or the rigging screw and the chain plate, to provide universal movement and prevent the rigging screw from bending.

Topping lift. A line or wire that holds up the boom or spinnaker pole.

Topsides. The outer sides of the hull.

Trailerable (or trailable). Capable of being towed behind a car on a trailer.

Transit. Two objects or lights which, when aligned, indicate a channel.

Transom. The athwartships timbers attached to the sternpost which produce a flat stern.

Trapeze. A wire hanging from a racing dinghy's mast, from which a crew member is suspended in order to counteract heeling forces.

Traveller. An athwartships-running track on which slides a car connected to the main sheet blocks; by adjusting the location of the car, the crew can change the mainsail's angle of attack to the wind.

Trim. (1) To pull in (a sheet); (2) the set of a sail; (3) the bow-up or bow-down attitude a boat assumes when she is at rest.

Trimaran. A multihull with three hulls.

Trip. To break loose.

True. Relative to true north, as against magnetic.

True wind. The wind's direction and strength felt by a stationary object.

Tune. To adjust the standing rigging until the mast is straight.

Twist. The amount that the leech sags off relative to the imaginary straight line between the clew and head.

Two-block. Fully hoisted or fully extended.

U

Under bare poles. With no sails set.

Underbody. The part of the hull that is underwater.

Undercanvassed. With not enough sail set.

Under power. With the engine on.

Under way. Moving.

Unreeve. To remove a line from a block or cringle.

Unrig. To remove or disassemble gear after it is used.

Upwind. Toward the direction from which the wind blows.

V

Vang. (1) A boom vang; (2) to pull down on the boom with a boom vang.

Variable. Unsteady.

Variation. The local difference in degrees between true and magnetic north.

Veer. A clockwise shift in the wind direction.

Vent. A ventilator.

Vessel. Any boat or ship.

VHF/FM. A very high frequency radiotelephone.

Voyage. A long passage.

W

Wake. The water turbulence left behind by a moving boat.

Watch. A part of the crew on deck or below according to a schedule; it is under the charge of the 'watch leader' or 'mate of the watch'.

Way. Speed.

Weather. (1) General atmospheric conditions; (2) wind; (3) upwind; (4) to survive a storm.

Weather helm. A boat's tendency to head up, into the wind, unless checked by the tiller or wheel.

Wetted surface. The area of the underbody and appendages.

Whisker pole. A spar similar to a spinnaker pole used to hold out the jib when sailing goosewinged.

Winch. A geared drum turned by a handle used to pull halyards, sheets, and other lines under strain.

Windage. Wind resistance.

Windlass. A special type of winch for pulling the anchor.

Windward. Upwind.

Wire rope. Stainless steel or galvanized wire used in shrouds, stays, halyards, sheets, and other gear.

Working sails. The mainsail and jib.

Y

Yacht. A pleasure boat.

Yacht designer. A naval architect specializing in the design of yachts.

Yaw. To sail a wildly erratic course.

Yawl. A two-masted boat whose after mast, the mizzenmast, is shorter than the forward mast, the mainmast, and is located aft of the rudder post.

YC Yacht club.

The Thirty Key Terms and their Derivations

Although the sailor's language is rich and complicated, the odds are that you cannot get through a typical day spent on the water in the average cruising boat using only thirty terms. All of them are defined in the main glossary, but because they are so important (and have such interesting histories) here we will give them more space. Their etymologies may provide entertainment and may help your memory latch onto their meanings.

Ends, Sides, and Directions

Bow. Pronounced like *now*, this is the front part of a boat, where she begins to narrow toward the extreme tip (the stem). The word is thought to be derived from the Old English word *bog*, pronounced *bough* or *bow* and meaning both 'shoulder' and 'bough of a tree'. In a way the bow of a boat can be thought of either as her shoulder or as a boughlike extension.

Forward. Pronounced *f'ward*, this is the direction toward the bow and comes from the Old English adjective *foreweard*, meaning 'in the front part.'

Stern. Meaning the back part of the boat, it may be derived from the Old Norse and Icelandic *stjorn*, 'steering,' and the Old English *steoran*, 'to steer,' since the old-fashioned steering oar was usually in the back of the boat.

Aft. Derived from the Old English *aeftan*, meaning 'behind,' this word denotes directions towards the stern.

Starboard. In Old English, *bord* meant 'side.' Therefore, the side over which the steering oar—*steor*, 'helm'—was hung was the 'steerside' or *steorbard*, which was usually the right-hand side facing the toward the bow.

Port. In Old English, the left-hand side of the boat was called the *baecbord* or 'the back side' because the helmsman turned his back to it as he faced the steering oar on the right-hand side. That word was later replaced by *ladde-borde*, which was derived from *lade*, 'load.' To protect her valuable starboard-side steering oar from damage, the boat was always tied up for loading and unloading cargo with her left-hand side against the wharf or shore. *Laddeborde* was eventually spelled *larboard* but pronounced *labbord*, which created problems because it sounded too much like *starboard*. The British Admiralty finally replaced *larboard* with the more distinguishable *port* (which, because it also means 'harbour,' equally indicates the side facing land).

Windward. In this term and the next, *ward*—from the Old English suffix -*weard*, 'relative position'-locates an area relative to the wind. Since *wind* has meant 'air in motion' in many European languages for more than a thousand years, *windward* is toward the direction from which the wind is blowing. (Interestingly, of all compass directions only the one for the wind indicates the source rather than the destination. A north wind blows from the north toward the south. Yet a north current flows from the south toward the north, and if you take a north bearing on an object, you are to the south of it). In some areas, *weather* (or 'toward the source of the weather,' presumably the wind's direction) is used in place of *windward*.

Leeward. *Leeward* means 'away from the wind's direction.' When a boat is to leeward of an object she is protected from the wind, so it is not surprising that 'lee' may come from words like the Old Swedish *hlea* and the Old Norse *hly,* which mean 'shelter.' While *lee* sounds like *me,* the normal pronunciation of *leeward* is *looward.*

Parts of the Boat

Hull. The most important of the many parts of the boat, or pieces that make up the whole, is the hull, or shell. It consists of the bottom or underbody, which is the part underwater, and the topsides, which are the sides above the water. The word is derived from the Old English *hulu,* 'husk,' and is a distant cousin of the Old German *hulla,* 'covering, cloak,' and *hulsa,* 'bean and pea shell.' (To continue the container metaphor, mariners have traditionally called boats 'vessels.')

Deck. The lid on the vessel, the top of the hull, is the *deck,* from the Middle Dutch *dec,* 'cover, roof, or cloak.'

Keel. This word comes down to us from the Old Norse *kjol,* the main timber running the full length of the hull's bottom—in human terms, her backbone (which is what this timber is often called). Today, when most boats are built of plastic or metal, the *keel* is the wing-shaped appendage hanging down from the hull to provide both lateral resistance so the boat does not slide sideways and a counterweight so she does not capsize.

Mast. This is the aluminium or wooden pole standing up from the deck and holding up the sails. In Old English, *maest* was either a tree trunk or a tree-grown fruit fed to pigs; it is not hard to tell which meaning our *mast* is derived from.

Boom. Spreading the sail on a horizontal plane is another pole called the *boom,* adapted from the Dutch *boom,* 'pole, tree,' and a close cousin to the English word *beam.* Masts and booms (and a special kind of boom called the spinnaker pole) fit into the generic category of *spar,* a word related to *spear* and similar words in many other European tongues.

Helm. The Old English *helma,* 'rudder,' and the German *helm,* 'handle,' give this one away. By definition the helm is the whole steering system. It includes the rudder (Old English *rother,* 'paddle') and either the tiller (*teiler,* 'wooden beam' in Old French) or the steering wheel that controls the angle the rudder makes to the water. However, most sailors use *helm* to mean just the tiller or wheel. *Windward* (or *weather*) *helm* describes the tiller being held to windward so the boat stays on course; *leeward* (or *lee*) *helm* applies if it must be held to leeward.

Sail. The sail is the shaped cloth that catches and derives forward force from the wind. The name may or may not come from an ancient Indo-European root *segh-,* 'to hold.' More recently, the Scandinavian *segel* means what *sail* does today. A *mainsail* (pronounced *mainsul*) is the biggest sail, or at least it was until about 1965 when genoa jibs overtook them in area. A *foresail* or *headsail* is a sail set forward or on the head (or bow)—what we now call a *jib.*

Jib. Describing the sail set forward of the mast, this word has one of the most curious derivations of all sailing terms, even though it is found only in English. Apparently, it was applied to the highest and forwardmost of the many headsails set on a sailing ship because that sail hung as high as a criminal executed on a *gibbet.* Less gruesome is the history of the term *genoa jib.* The first big overlapping jib that could be trimmed efficiently for close-hauled sailing was set in a race off Genoa, Italy, in 1927 by a Swedish yachtsman named Sven Salen. Why it was not called the *Salen jib* and therefore added to the list of Scandinavian terms in the English sailing vocabulary is not known.

Spinnaker. The newest of all the terms in common usage, this is the name of the light balloon-like sail held out forward of the mast by a boom called the spinnaker pole when the wind comes over the side or stern. Although sails looking like it are seen in paintings and engravings of ships going back to the sixteenth century, this particular sail apparently first appeared in the 1860s on English racing yachts, one of which was named *Sphinx. Sphinx's spanker* might have led quickly to *spinnaker* (except that a spanker was a sail set near the stern, not forward over the bow). According to another tradition, the sail was first called a *spin-maker* because it made boats spin, or go especially fast. Both versions make good stories, if not entirely reliable ones.

Halyard. A halyard is a fibre or wire line (part of a rope) used to pull a sail up and hold it there. The word comes from the Middle English *hallyer,* 'hauler,' and the Old English *gyrd,* 'stick.' In the days of tall ships the line hauled up the *yard,* a boomlike pole that spread the squaresail.

Sheet. Although this word has been used to describe the sail itself, today it is the term for the line that adjusts the sail's shape and angle to the wind. The sheet is attached to the sail at or near its aft corner, the *clew* (derivation unknown). In Old English, the clew was called the *sceata* and the line attached to it the *sceatline.* *Sheetline* eventually was simplified to *sheet.*

Shackle. Lines, blocks, and sails are secured to each other and the deck, mast, and boom with metal, removable rings called shackles, whose name originated with the Old English *sceacul,* 'fetter.' Like many nautical nouns, it is also used as a verb: 'Shackle the halyard to the jib.'

Block. A pulley through which a sheet or halyard is led, the word apparently comes from the Middle German *bloch,* 'an enclosed place.' A block's shell encases and strengthens the turning part, the sheave. Some blocks are permanently fixed on the deck, mast, or boom, while others can be relocated using shackles.

Winch. On most boats longer than about 20 feet, the pull on sails is too hard for an unassisted sailor, so sheets and halyards are wrapped clockwise around a metal drum that is turned with a handle to trim the lines. The drum (and any gears inside) is called a *winch,* from the Old English *wince,* 'reel, crank,' The handle is called a *winch handle.* Lines are *winched* in when they are trimmed on a winch.

Cleat. A metal, plastic, or wooden object on or in which a line is secured so that you do not have to pull against its strain, a cleat is a modern version of an Old Low Germanic *klot,* a wooden wedge in which lines were stopped. Like *trim* and *shackle,* the word can also be used as a verb.

Manoeuvres and General Terms

Head up. The bow was often called the *head* of the boat (in fact, a marine lavatory was first called a head because it was located on the bow), and *up* suggests climbing higher up the hill down which the wind is pouring. So this command means 'alter course to windward.'

Bear away. This is the opposite of *head up. Bear* here means 'apply force'; to alter course away from the wind, a helmsman must often apply considerable force to the tiller or wheel. Synonymous commands include *bear off* and *head off.*

Tack. This means (1) fomerly, the windward fastening of the sail to the deck or a spar, and nowadays, the forward lower corner of a sail (or a spinnaker's windward corner)—this definition may come from the Old French *tache*, 'nail'; (2) the relative angle between the course and the wind so that when the starboard side is the windward side, the boat is on the starboard tack and when the port side is to windward, she is on the port tack—this meaning originates in the first definition, since the side on which squaresails were tacked was the windward side; (3) to change course by heading up until the bow is directly in the wind, then bearing off with the wind on the other side, thereby *changing tacks*. Today, tacking in this last sense is often called *coming about*.

Gybe. Gybing entails changing tacks by bearing off until the stern is directly in the wind, then heading up with the wind on the other side. The word comes from the Dutch *gijben*, 'to shift,' and in America it is spelled jibe. Either way, it rhymes with imbibe.

Trim. This word has four meanings: (1) A boat is *in trim* when she is floating just as she should and *out of trim* if she is not; (2) The *trim of the sail* is the sail's angle to the wind and general shape. When the angle is narrow and the sail is relatively flat, the trim is flat; when broad and round, the trim is full. (3) To *trim sails* means to optimize the sail's shape and angle for the prevailing conditions. Finally, (4) to *trim sheets* is to pull in on the sheets, flattening the sails and narrowing the angle to the wind. All this overlapping derives from the all-purpose usefulness of the Old English *trymman*, 'to strengthen or set in order.' In fact, the adjective *untrum* meant 'infirm,' so a poorly trimmed sail or boat is, in a way, a sick one.

Ease. To *ease sheets* is the opposite of to trim sheets, for by letting out the sheets you make the sails more round and widen the angle between them and the wind. You can also lower the strain on any loaded line by easing it. The word is probably derived from the Old French *aaisier*, 'to provide comfort' (originally, 'to provide elbowroom').

Course. This is the direct heading to the destination, indicated usually by compass degrees (the *compass course*) but also by landmarks or buoys. You are *on course* when steering in the right direction. The word originates in the Latin *cursum*, 'a running.' Over the intervening millenia it has been applied to several types of running, among them the hunting of hares with greyhounds, the charge of two combatants in a mediaeval jousting tournament, a place where horses are raced, the flow of time, and the lower staysails run out on a squarerigger's yards.

Index